DRUM LISTENS TO HEART

INVENTORY PRESS   *.+ The Wattis Institute

THE PERCUSSIVE

ANTHONY HUBERMAN

4

GLOSSARY

THE PERCUSSIVE

THE PERCUSSIVE

THE PERCUSSIVE

THE PERCUSSIVE   ANTHONY
                                  HUBERMAN
THE PERCUSSIVE

THE PERCUSSIVE

THE PERCUSSIVE

THE PERCUSSIVE   ANTHONY
                                  HUBERMAN
THE PERCUSSIVE

THE PERCUSSIVE

THE PERCUSSIVE

THE PERCUSSIVE   ANTHONY
                                  HUBERMAN
THE PERCUSSIVE

THE PERCUSSIVE

THE PERCUSSIVE   ANTHONY
                                  HUBERMAN
THE PERCUSSIVE

THE PERCUSSIVE

THE PERCUSSIVE

THE PERCUSSIVE   ANTHONY

INTRODUCTION

Let's begin with the drum, but move away from it, bit by bit, until all that is left is the feeling of its presence in the room.

Because percussion reaches far beyond the drum. There is music and rhythm, sure, but in a more general sense, the percussive relates to a wide range of aesthetic, expressive, and political forms.

To percuss means to strike or to hit, but it also means to move, or to groove. It means to interrupt or to break. To worship and to heal. To gather and to accompany. To control but also to protest and demand freedom from forms of control. To beat at the speed of the heart.

Artists and writers have long used music and a musical vocabulary to talk about art. The artist David Hammons says that he's "trying to make abstract art out of my experience, just like Thelonious Monk." A painting is described in terms of its rhythm, and an exhibition is said to hit different notes or to have a *tempo*, a *cadence*, a *beat*. Sitting down to write this essay, I began by considering the right *tone* or *key* to use. My goal is not to tell a truth or win an argument but to create a mood, a temperature, maybe even some kind of *music* with which a viewer can visit an exhibition.

What happens when we use the drum to talk about art and politics? What is an artwork, or a community, that is described as "percussive"? Are there percussive sculptures or percussive gestures? An artwork is said to *represent*, to *address*, or perhaps sometimes to *mean* something, but can it also *percuss*? Can it exist in the world as a vibratory force, outside of language, that shakes the body and makes it dance with the mind? Can it do what a drummer does when they play the trap set, with sticks moving over and under each other, finding a groove within endlessly overlapping beats? Can it point to a place that is not about harmony but still about community?

BA DUM TSS

There's a great Miles Davis line that goes something like this: "I do not play jazz." No, he plays something that invents its own vocabulary—a vocabulary that is shared only by those who don't need to know what to call it or how to contain it within language in order to understand what it is.

Meanings tend to congeal and fasten themselves around words, like mud on a shoe. In art, we have words like *abstract*, *representational*, *conceptual*, *expressionist*, *minimal*, *activist*, *political*, *socially engaged*, and so on, and while they each mean something, they also sometimes prevent an artwork from

being what it wants to be—something harder to contain. The simple act of framing an artwork within a different type of vocabulary can loosen it from the grip of a predetermined meaning, even for a moment, so that glimpses of something else appear.

For example, the art historian Kobena Mercer, in his book on abstraction, borrows a term from the poet Nathaniel Mackey and suggests *discrepant*: "from a root meaning of 'to rattle, to creak,' I relate discrepant engagement to the name the Dogon of West Africa gave their weaving block … they call it 'the creaking of the word.'"[1] A discrepant engagement is one that acknowledges noise, creaks, breaks, and rattles. Ralph Ellison's invisible man is discrepant, never quite on the beat but slipped into the breaks, looking around, unrecognizable to others.[2] A discrepant abstraction, Mercer explains, carves out a space where abstraction is not just about spirituality, purity, opacity, or even alienation but something closer to *infection*, where the abstract slides into the cracks of an

1   Nathaniel Mackey, quoted in Kobena Mercer, "Introduction," in *Discrepant Abstraction*, ed. Kobena Mercer (London and Cambridge, MA: Institute of International Visual Arts and The MIT Press, 2006), 10.

2   Ralph Ellison, quoted in Fred Moten, *In the Break: The Aesthetics of the Black Radical Tradition* (Minneapolis: University of Minnesota Press, 2003), 65.

image or an object, making it a bit more brittle or twitchy, as if it has a spring in its step.

Another example comes from the writer and poet Fred Moten—a master in the art of using music to not talk about music—who takes the word *ensemble* and pushes it the way a horn player twists the bend of a note. His ensemble is not a group of people but a condition, a state of generative and collective becoming, of being without a center. His ensemble is not a point of intersection but a force that cuts across and refuses to close. It refers not to a specific situation but to the totality of an ecosystem—to everything that is generated by a situation, everything that emerges from it, everything that is entangled within it, even everything that works to oppose or contradict it. His ensemble is a political model where diverging perspectives don't agree, disagree, or even work toward a consensus but where they gather, coexist, contradict, listen to each other, make something with each other, and mutually adapt to a context as it evolves.

Pushing the word further still, until it becomes a verb, would allow for the possibility of *ensembling*. Building on Moten, *to ensemble* would not mean "to complete" or "to harmonize" but something messier and unrulier— something harder to contain—like "to augment" or "to intensify," via an act of improvisational rupture. *To ensemble*

is to slip into a beat, to cut in and out of a beat, to thicken or color a beat, to contribute to a beat by complicating a beat, and to feel others as they beat their beats.

In that sense, an artwork that ensembles is an artwork that could be called *percussive*—and while musical metaphors are often used in the context of a politics of liberation or emancipation, perhaps the specificity of percussion or the percussive could outline something more precise about what the abstract has to do with the political.

QUMA QUIMBAMBA

Drumming and percussion have appeared in cultural traditions around the world for thousands of years. They're incredibly basic and foundational to the human story. In fact, the act of striking was an art our earliest ancestors were particularly skilled at—not only because they needed to be in order to kill, eat, or protect themselves, but also because they found percussion in their own bodies. It's reasonable to imagine that music itself began with early humans mimicking and externalizing their own heartbeat, tapping it out with their hands or feet—and if birdsongs inspired the discovery of melody, the heartbeat surely established an understanding of rhythm. But even if every body has a similar pulse, rhythm is far from uniform: there are

countless ways bodies might express that pulse, countless reasons a body might choose to do so, and countless structures that govern how it does.

Even defining the drum as a specific type of musical instrument proves difficult, because what *isn't* a drum? Almost anything could be, whether it's an object specifically crafted to make percussive sounds, such as a snare drum, a bass drum, a tom-tom, a cymbal, a gong, a marimba, a maraca, or something more improvised, even just lying around, like a glass bottle, a tin can, a kitchen pot, a cowbell—not to mention any wooden floor or the hand, thigh, head, or chest of one's own body. Paleolithic excavations have revealed gourd rattles, stone or bone scrapers, and stamping pits—what historian James Blades termed *idiophones*, or instruments made of naturally resonant materials from which sound can be produced—placing percussive tools within the very earliest stages of humankind.[3]

During the classical antiquity of ancient Greece, the gift of making music came from the Muses, the daughters of Zeus, and the drum was the means to summon them and the instrument through which they spoke. More precisely, the frame drum was "the point of contact between the worlds of the unmanifest and the

---

3   James Blades, *Percussion Instruments and Their History* (London: Faber and Faber, 1984 [1970]), 36.

manifest, of the living and the dead, of the divine and the human."[4] Women, gifted with the ability to give birth, were considered holy and were the first "technicians of the sacred,"[5] performing many of the religious functions. As a result, the drummers were often women—up until Christianity imposed a radical new order, with consequences that remain in place in much of the world today. Replacing the goddesses was a single male god, served by a celibate all-male priesthood. Women found themselves reframed as a negative influence and were sometimes banned from playing music and even from singing and dancing. The drum—along with its female drummers—became a symbol of pagan worship, a dangerous abstract and seductive force that takes hold of the body and makes people hard to contain. Replacing it came the voices of the church choir and the written words of scripture.[6] By the sixth century, the pope had even outlawed the tambourine.

The spiritual force of percussion is woven throughout non-Western cultures as well: in India, the physical and human world is nothing but a manifestation of different frequencies of a root vibration—"the heartbeat behind all heartbeats"[7]— and the god Shiva enables all life by dancing to the rhythm of the drum. In her account of Haitian voodoo, *Divine Horsemen* (1953), the filmmaker Maya Deren describes the drum as what the shaman uses in order to enter the trance that allows the loa spirit to possess him, "mount" him like a horse, and share the wisdom of the ancestors. But what is sacred is the drum, not the drummer, who is nothing but the mechanism the drum needs to generate its beat, and the character of a drummer's drumming has nothing to do with skill but with the nature of the ritual. The drum is the magnetic core and engenders all the crucial transitions: it carries the loa into the body of the shaman, and then it also provides a beacon that helps the shaman find his way back.[8] To use Mackey and Mercer's term, the drum is *discrepant*: when a shaman is hosting a loa, both subjects exist in the same physical body at the same time, one riding the other like a horse, inserting itself into the cracks, making it rattle and creak.

In Africa, trance-based and shamanist cultures continue to thrive to this day,[9] but in Europe (and in its many colonies around the globe), the drum went from being a means for spiritual transformation (often led by women) to a means of summoning warriors to battle (always led by men).

TICK TICK TICK

The idea that a drum could be an instrument of war is perhaps rooted in what historian William H. McNeill calls "keeping together in time." Our earliest ancestors noticed that gathering people into social groups would increase everyone's collective chance of survival. One way to do that was to coordinate and synchronize the muscular and bodily movements of many people so that large physical tasks could be accomplished with greater ease and efficiency. Applying a Darwinian logic of evolutionary

4   Layne Redmond, *When the Drummers Were Women: A Spiritual History of Women* (New York: Three Rivers Press, 1997), 135.

5   Ibid., 1.

6   Ibid., 150.

7   Ibid., 70.

8   Maya Deren, *Divine Horsemen: The Living Gods of Haiti* (New York: McPherson & Company, 1970 [1953]). This book mysteriously arrived in my mailbox one day. It was only later that I figured out it was a gift from the artist Trisha Donnelly, and I thank her for it.

9   Daniel F. McCall suggests that Africa maintained a strong connection to the drum because the worship of goddesses in Neolithic times stretched from Europe all the way to sub-Saharan Africa, but once the Sahara became a desert, West Africa found itself cut off, which not only protected it from Christianity's takeover, but also allowed it to maintain stronger links to the ancestral goddesses and their drums (Daniel F. McCall, referred to in Mickey Hart, *Drumming at the Edge of Magic* [San Francisco: HarperCollins, 1990], 206).

selection, McNeill argues that those who developed methods for keeping together in time were able to generate a stronger sense of group cohesion and, therefore, became the genetic pool that survived. As a result, the benefits of synchronized collective movement baked themselves into the human body—work became far less tedious when done together, rhythmically, and the overall resilience of a community was connected to the "emotional solidarities aroused by keeping together in time."[10]

It's easy to recognize the way this plays itself out in the context of not just farming or construction, but on the battlefield: the drum becomes the tool that both coordinates and energizes soldiers, providing not only a common point of reference, but also the emotional thrust that comes from the *feeling* of being connected to others. Percussive rhythm generates an affective web of solidarity— one to which our bodies are inherently predisposed—and it can galvanize, motivate, and propel individuals to do more than they could do alone.

In physics, there is something called the Law of Entrainment: when two similarly tuned vibrations are in close proximity to each other, they will synchronize and link up—they will *entrain*. It was first discovered in 1665, when a Dutch physicist set a room full of pendulum clocks in motion at different moments, only to find, upon his return a short while later, that they had all fallen into sync. Human bodies, made up of vibrating electromagnetic signals, will also naturally entrain, with the rhythms of one internal organ linking up with that of another—and healers have learned how to tune vibrations to specific frequencies and create "sound baths" that entrain parts of the body in ways that activate its natural restorative functions. But the effect works externally as well, and the percussive rhythms or vibrations of tens of thousands of bodies who are in physical proximity to each other will naturally entrain—an exhilarating feeling familiar not only to a foot soldier in a large army but also to anyone at a rave or techno party.

And yet, like all things, entrainment has its flip side. Its percussive force doesn't just coordinate people but standardizes, polices, authorizes, and enforces a certain behavior. It demands consensus and obedience. It drills habits into bodies, *drumming them in*, proving that "it's not people that process rhythms but rhythms that process people."[11]

In this way, the percussive can be a means of controlling and determining the way bodies move—police batons or even bombs are percussive instruments. In the context of military drills in China in the fourth century BCE, for example, those who missed a beat were immediately executed, and the exercises were repeated over and over again, with larger and larger groups, until not a single error occurred.[12] Anyone who slips out of the groove of keeping together in time threatens the stability of the group and must be eliminated. To use a contemporary example, borrowed from a quip an artist made to me during a studio visit, "Mitch McConnell is the drummer. He keeps and sets the pace."[13]

Everything depends on who is doing the drumming and who is being drummed. One rhythm can demand consistency and obedience and suppress any forms of difference, while another can just as easily encourage improvisation and multiplicity and exert a powerful demand for freedom—"groove is the iron fist *and* the velvet glove."[14]

---

10   William H. McNeill, *Keeping Together in Time: Dance and Drill and Human History* (Cambridge, MA: Harvard University Press, 1995), 27.

11   Veit Erlmann, quoted in Daniel Muzyczuk, "It is Not People That Process Rhythms, but Rhythms That Process People," in *The Museum of Rhythm*, eds. Natasha Ginwala and Daniel Muzyczuk (Łódź: Museum Sztuki; Berlin: Sternberg Press, 2017), 60.

12   McNeill, 110.

13   Eli Keszler, in conversation with the author, 2020.

14   Peter Erskine, "In the Pocket: How a Drum Set Player Grooves," in *The Cambridge Companion to Percussion*, ed. Russell Hartenberger (Cambridge, UK: Cambridge University Press, 2016), 192. Emphasis added.

BA BA BUH-BA

They say that drummers keep time and set the tempo. That they establish the rhythm and provide the beat. But *rhythm* often gets confused with *meter*, and they are not the same thing. Meter is a unit of measurement, occurring over time, while rhythm is physical and directional. In the words of Gilles Deleuze and Félix Guattari, "Meter is dogmatic, but rhythm is critical."[15] Meter *is*, while rhythm *does*. A military march, for example, has a percussive meter, but there is nothing rhythmic about it, even as many bodies are keeping together in time. Like meter, rhythm requires repetition, but the pattern of its beats doesn't need to be regular in order for them to be meaningful, unlike the ticking hands of a clock. This is what leads Trinh T. Minh-ha to say that "rhythm is the feeling of freedom … free to play with a recurrent beat, to miss it, or to fill in the gap with one's own beat; free to follow; to leave off or to meander along a trajectory."[16]

Perhaps rhythm is a knot that gives time a different shape. "Rhythm makes time turn off," an artist once told me. "It's about being inside something, being present, getting rid of distance."[17] It is equally concrete *and* abstract. It has no visible shape or mass, and yet it affects and impacts the body, or perhaps it even *enlists* the body. "Being beats,"[18] meaning that rhythm is the dialectical syncopation between being and thinking—"the body in a state of music."[19] While a pattern implies something visual or infrastructural, a rhythm contributes a sense of temperament, attitude, or mood. It doesn't just capture the way things are organized but gets at the way it feels for things to be organized the way they are. Music, via rhythm, is a "quantified time opening onto a qualitative sense of time losing rigidity, gaining plasticity. Counting four but feeling three."[20]

If rhythm enlists the body, it can also dominate and take hold of bodies—

literally, as in a trance or a military drill, but also metaphorically, as in an ideology or a belief system that is *drummed into you*. In his book *How to Live Together* (1977), the philosopher Roland Barthes recognized the relationship between rhythm and power: "the first thing that power imposes is a rhythm (to everything: a rhythm of life, of time, of thought, of speech)."[21] Building on that, the Marxist sociologist Henri Lefebvre focused on the rhythms imposed by capitalism and developed a critique of capitalism by attempting to understand the effects its rhythms have on the body. His book *Rhythmanalysis: Space, Time, and Everyday Life* (1992) was divided into biological, psychological, and social rhythms: "everywhere where there is interaction between a place, a time, and an expenditure of energy," he wrote, "there is rhythm."[22] His central aim was to expose capitalism as a rhythm—as a beat that gives bodies no options other than to inhabit the oppressive groove of capital and profit. In much the same way as a military drum does, capitalism standardizes and optimizes, ruthlessly extinguishing

15   Gilles Deleuze and Félix Guattari, *A Thousand Plateaus: Capitalism and Schizophrenia*, trans. Brian Massumi (Minneapolis: University of Minnesota Press, 1987 [1980]), 313.

16   Trinh T. Minh-ha, "Rhythm at Play," in *I Will Draw a Map of What You Never See: Endeavours in Rhythmanalysis*, eds. Elena Agudio, Anna Jäger, Saskia Köbschall, and Bonaventure Soh Bejeng Ndikung (Berlin: SAVVY Contemporary and Archive Books, 2019), 40.

17   Michael E. Smith, in conversation with the author, 2021.

18   Jean-Luc Nancy, quoted in John Mowitt, *Percussion: Drumming, Beating, Striking* (Durham, NC: Duke University Press, 2002), 184.

19   Roland Barthes, quoted in Mowitt, *Percussion*, 150.

20   Jan Verwoert, "Log Out from the Canon: Exhibit Outtakes," *Portable Gray* 4, no. 1 (Spring 2021): 24, https://doi.org/10.1086/715555.

21   Roland Barthes, *How to Live Together: Novelistic Simulations of Some Everyday Spaces*, trans. Kate Briggs (New York: Columbia University Press, 2012 [1977]), 35.

22   Henri Lefebvre, *Rhythmanalysis: Space, Time, and Everyday Life*, trans. Stuart Elden and Gerald Moore (London/New York: Bloomsbury Academic, 2013 [1992]), 25.

anything or anyone that misses a beat. Borrowing an equestrian term, Lefebvre likens rhythm to a form of "dressage," or a way to "break in" a body, domesticate it, and expunge all irregularities from it.[23]

While Lefebvre framed rhythm as a form of oppression—of something being *drummed in*—Barthes also recognized it as a form of agency and a way to reconcile the duality between the individual and the collective—of *marching with others, but to the beat of one's own drum*. He points to the history of Christianity: as it became a state religion across Europe and northern Africa in the third and fourth centuries, most Catholic monks lived in communal settings. And yet, a subset of monks in the Syrian and Egyptian desert, whom Barthes calls *idiorrhythmic* monks, preferred to live in their own cells—according to their own rhythms—while still faithfully fulfilling their religious duties. They recognized the ways larger social norms tend to "metrify" and petrify human subjectivity and sought to safeguard their own space while still living in a monastery setting. In other words, they illustrate the possibility that personal rhythms don't have to contradict or threaten larger social or religious orders but can inflect or brush up against a collective, create a pulse between an individual body and social

forms, and establish a model for being alone *and* being a part.[24] The demand for idiorrhythmy, Barthes argues, is always made in opposition to power, but in favor of a collectivity that shares common beliefs. Rhythm can therefore satisfy the need for both regularity and difference. In the timeless words of the poet Amiri Baraka, it is "the changing same."[25]

Because the problem for all monolithic rhythms—religions, capitalism, colonialism—is that the human body is nothing if not *irregular*. A healthy heart is one that is arrhythmic, always beating slightly irregularly, and human subjectivity is inherently polyrhythmic. Can't society be made to move more like the heart does?

TIT TOT TAT

Taking her cue from Lefebvre, the curator Natasha Ginwala organized *The Museum of Rhythm* as part of the 2012 Taipei Biennial. Playing the role of a rhythmanalyst, an "observer of rhythm irregularities who can analyze the impact

of capitalism on bodies,"[26] she looked for "a counter-point to the abstract calculations that mechanize post-industrial life, giving back agency to human measure"[27] and for ways to reassert the natural arrhythmia of human bodies and their ability to participate in the body politic on their own terms. If, as she writes, the "untrained body—or the trained yet defiant body—is cast as dysfunctional, forced into modernity's scenes of aberration,"[28] she imagines there are ways to empower and mobilize that defiance and develop a language of protest through offbeats and discontinuous rhythms. And since the human condition has always been a polyrhythmic experience of coexisting differences, Ginwala uses rhythm as a way to imagine a museum where history itself, or a range of historical moments and voices, is given pitches, frequencies, and tempos. She argues that when history is conceived as a rhythm, it can be reorganized: instead of a linear progression of winners and losers, it can become a polyrhythm of overlapping and colliding parallel stories that coexist with delays, repetitions, reversals, accidents, and other rhythmic characteristics. Perhaps even the complexities of colonial and

24   Brandon LaBelle, "Togethering, of
the Open Body," in *The Middle Matter:
Sound as Interstice*, eds. Caroline
Profanter, Henry Andersen, Julia
Eckhardt (Brussels: Umland Editions,
2019), 71.

25   Amiri Baraka, *Black Music* (New York:
Da Capo Press, 1967), 180.

23   Ibid., 49. It is perhaps not a coincidence that the French term for
"practice" is *entrainment*.

26   Natasha Ginwala, "The Museum of
Rhythm: A Constellation of Anomaly,"
in *The Museum of Rhythm*, 23.

27   Ibid., 22.

28   Ibid., 27.

postcolonial consciousness, both past and present, could be mobilized and disrupted by way of rhythmic coherences and incoherences.

Sure enough, the percussive force of rhythm can be one of liberation, emancipation, and healing—sometimes even a necessity for survival. It is central to protest movements and helps urban activists unite and cohere, and in a more metaphorical sense, it helps them collectively refuse to march to the beat of empire's drum by interrupting its beat, breaking free of it, and replacing it with one of their own. Without needing words or images, the percussive can threaten forms of authority and voice a powerful demand for freedom. In a moment when historical narratives are being renegotiated to bring forth voices that have been subjected to colonial erasure and systemic racism, it provides a form of expression, communication, celebration, and protest that marginalized voices have long used to be heard and be seen.

Operating outside of language, logic, or narrative, percussion is well-suited for replacing *meaning* with *feeling*, or for asserting feeling as a type of meaning. During the industrial revolution, as the Western world was getting noisier, percussion emerged as a jolt able to make an audience *feel*—something like what color was to the Fauvist painters a century earlier.[29] "Music," Timothy Rice notes, "does something else for humankind besides creating meaning, something just as important."[30] Sound doesn't speak in words; it speaks in vibrations, and in that sense, it is less a concept that needs decoding than a vibration that triggers other vibrations, which then create forms of pleasure, pain, or combinations of both. It is qualitative in nature, not quantitative, and is measured in intensities, bumps, and waves. Being invisible, it is often described as "abstract," and yet it makes a very concrete impact on any object, surface, body, or space it encounters. Trinh notes that in the context of African American culture, for example, art (and music) is not about legibility or resemblance, or even intelligibility, but about locating a "breath" that runs through a lived experience—the way sap runs through a tree. Rhythm, she continues, is what nonverbally determines the quality of a relationship.[31]

Can percussion be a way to express the unmeasurable? Can it perform an act of assembly without mediation? Can it represent without representation? Organize without politics? Govern without sovereignty?[32] Drums aren't there to *make sense* but to break up the senses. They are incomplete. They cut language open. They *ensemble* communication and community.

DJIGA DJIGA DJIGA DJIGA

When enslaved Africans brought their drums to the New World, they were outlawed.[33] Enslavers perceived the drum to be a subversive tool, capable of not only inciting insurrection but also of communicating in code. And, in the words of Baraka once more, when

29 Steven Schick, *The Percussionist's Art: Same Bed, Different Dreams* (Rochester, NY: University of Rochester Press, 2006), 14–15.

30 Timothy Rice, *Ethnomusicology: A Very Short Introduction* (New York: Oxford University Press, 2014), 59.

31 Trinh, "Rhythm at Play," in *I Will Draw a Map of What You Never See,* 35, 39.

32 Le Mardi Gras Listening Collective, "Music and Economic Planning," *The South Atlantic Quarterly* 119, no. 1 (January 2020): 138, https://doi.org/10.1215/00382876-8007701.

33 The one urban center where enslaved people were allowed to gather and drum was New Orleans, in what became known as Congo Square—until that, too, was outlawed in 1875. This placed rhythm within the bloodstream of New Orleans, soon leading to blues, jazz, and rock and roll, each one invented by African Americans. It was also in New Orleans that Edward "Dee Dee" Chandler, a little-known drummer, is seen in an 1896 photograph with what is the first known proof of a new invention—the foot pedal. For the first time, one person could do the job that previously took three people to do, and many rhythms could take place within one body.

they ban your
oom boom ba boom
you in deep deep trouble[34]

The painter Jack Whitten, in allegorizing how music became so central to Black American life, said that "when my white slave masters discovered that my drum was a subversive instrument, they took it from me…. The only instrument available was my body, so I used my skin: I clapped my hands, slapped my thighs, and stomped my feet in dynamic rhythms."[35] Because even if something as wordless and abstract as a drumbeat can be seen as a threat deserving to be outlawed, percussion can't be stopped or silenced.

Part of what was powerful about the enslaved person's drum was not only its use as a cipher of coded messages but its use as an abstract portal to a lost ancestry, to the spirits of previous generations, and as the glue that made members of a community feel connected to a common heritage. Within the beat of the drum, groups of enslaved people, much like the African shamans in the communities they were taken from, could access the strength of the generations that came before them—creating an army of ghosts that surely provided moral and emotional power and the resilience that comes from "emotional solidarities aroused by keeping together in time," as McNeill put it.

And percussion runs throughout that ancestry, like the sap within a tree. Each of the countless tribes across the vast African continent use different drums and beat them in different ways for different reasons—the *djembe* used by the Bambara people in Mali, the *dundun* used by the Yoruba people in Nigeria, the *atsimevu* used by the Ewe people in Ghana, the *bougarabou* used by the Jola people in Senegal, *fontomfrom* used by the Bono people on the Ivory Coast, to name only a very few. Some tribes in West Africa have perfected the so-called talking drum, allowing them to communicate messages across vast distances, but this is only one of many potential functions or purposes of the drum.[36] In a general sense, "rhythm is to the African what harmony is to the European,"[37] and

Western culture, in fact, is the only one that marginalizes the drum—outlawing it as recently as the nineteenth century, when British colonial authorities banned the drums in Trinidad because they believed their presence turned carnival celebrations into anti-police riots. Until less than a century ago, percussion in Western classical music served to provide only the punctuation, color, and rhythmic drive to support the melodies and harmonies that drove the composition.[38] Percussionists were to play only in a way that made *others* sound better. It was only in 1931, with Edgard Varèse's *Ionisation*, that a work of Western classical composition was written exclusively for percussion—a chaotic assembly of sirens, drums, rattles, bells, and so on.[39] Meanwhile, in African, Indian, Indonesian, Japanese, Native American, and South American contexts, percussion has been at the center of artistic life for centuries.[40]

34 Amiri Baraka, "Wise I," in *Wise, Why's, Y's: The Griot's Song* (Chicago: Third World Press, 1995). I thank Fred Moten for this reference, which he used in a lecture he gave in Berkeley in 2020, during which he cautioned all of us to learn to protect our oom boom ba boom.

35 Jack Whitten, quoted in Barry Schwabsky, "Post-White? On 'Blues for Smoke,'" *The Nation*, April 30, 2013, https://www.thenation.com/article/archive/post-white-blues-smoke/.

36 Kofi Agawu, *The African Imagination in Music* (New York: Oxford University Press, 2016), 128.

37 A.M. Jones, quoted in John Miller Chernoff, *African Rhythm and African Sensibility* (Chicago: University of Chicago Press, 1979), 40.

38 Adam Sliwinski, "Lost and Found: Percussion Chamber Music and the Modern Age," in *The Cambridge Companion to Percussion*, 97.

39 The Cuban composer Amadeo Roldán's *Ritmicas V + VI*, also exclusively for percussion, was written one year earlier, in 1930.

40 Sliwinski, "Lost and Found," in *The Cambridge Companion to Percussion*, 103.

Many Indigenous African languages have no word for music—and yet none lack one for dance, and none have only a single word for rhythm.[41] The scholar Kofi Agawu describes three distinct roles for African musics: work (songs sung during work, chores, or even as used by street vendors), ritual (to celebrate birth, marriage, and death), and entertainment. Each one demands participation and collectivity, and together they form "a will to communal truth."[42] The beats of the drum aren't there to be an expression of identity or individuality, in the sense of being the work of an individual "artist," but to access a way to live and be with others that can contribute to the survival of all. They operate as call-and-response, reinforcing the reciprocity of communal living.[43] They are an accompaniment, "a music-to-find-the-beat-by,"[44] and they help people work together in making sense of the world around them.

In that way, percussion lays the foundation for an ethic—a way of being. It follows the principle of "I am because we are,"[45] or, to use an Igbo proverb often evoked by the late curator Okwui Enwezor, "*ife kwulu, ife akwuso ya*"—where something stands, there is something else standing next to it.[46] Drummers in communities across the African continent almost always play with others, so not only is every beat accompanied by someone *else's* beat, but something *else* is also always going on when the drums are played—there is music but never just music. There is dance and often song, but there is also the presence of ancestors, who watch over the moral life of the community and provide it with a sense of continuity. Percussion lubricates the integrated experience of an entire social situation, what Christopher Small famously termed "musicking," referring not only to music, but to an entangled social web of activities: making music, listening to music, convening around music. What gives a beat a sense is its taking place, its musicking, "its assembly of the community to which it belongs."[47] Percussion *musicks* the drum: the drummer is the one who makes the beat, the drum is the beat itself, and the drummed is the community that is being assembled. In the West, the focus tends to be on the skill of the drummer, which is admired by the collective, but an alternative perspective would be to recognize that the drum is not a demonstration of individual skill but a nonverbal expression of community.

The Rwandan philosopher Isaïe Nzeyimana describes life, in musical terms, as a process of mutual generosity: it is a rhythmic bond of giving-receiving-giving. The word he uses to describe that rhythm is *injyana*, where *kujya* means "to go, to walk, to move, to put into motion;" and *–na* means "with."[48] Rhythm is not just about movement, but about movement alongside others. To move is to move with. To live is to live with. Rhythm, he argues, "is a concept that goes with movement, a movement of a 'together.' This has enormous implications. Social, political, economic implications. To develop oneself is to develop with others. And in social terms, to live in a society is to live with the other, it is to coordinate the gestures. Politics, it is done with the other."[49] Rhythm always begets other rhythms, empowering an endlessly mutating cycle of relations, and

41   Agawu, *The African Imagination in Music*, 30, 192.

42   Ibid., 15.

43   Ibid., 169.

44   Chernoff, *African Rhythm and African Sensibility*, 50.

45   Agawu, *The African Imagination in Music*, 249.

46   Okwui Enwezor, in Massimiliano Gioni, "Songs of Mourning, Songs of Resistance," in *Grief and Grievance: Art and Mourning in America*, eds. Okwui Enwezor, Naomi Beckwith, Massimiliano Gioni, Glenn Ligon, and Mark Nash (London: Phaidon Press; New York: New Museum, 2020), 188.

47   Mowitt, *Percussion*, 74.

48   Isaïe Nzeyimana, quoted in Christian Nyampeta, "One's Own Rhythm: Footnotes on 'Comment Vivre Ensemble,'" in *I Will Draw a Map of What You Never See*, 103.

49   Isaïe Nzeyimana, quoted by Christian Nyampeta, performance lecture at FET Düsseldorf, March 25, 2017.

always makes space for the invention and reinvention of new subjects and new realities. As James A. Snead says, a beat can go from being something an individual creates, with a goal in mind—the white beat—to being something many people tune into, that's always already there—the Black one.[50]

The very structure of polyrhythm embodies the idea that contradiction and disagreement can paradoxically form the basis of a productive, and even joyful, relationship. Unlike what is known as a canon, where the same musical pattern is played against itself, a polyrhythm is when different patterns interlock, over and under each other, next to each other, at the same time. Steve Reich's *Drumming* (1970–71) is a canon, whereas West African drumming is polyrhythm. Polyrhythm is an art that demands extraordinary precision and practice, or what Agawu calls "a disciplined plurality."[51] As a mindset, it's already embedded into many African cultures, since "African music is polyphonal, their religions are polytheistic, their calendars polycyclic, their plastic arts polyangular, and … their social organizations polycentric…."

Marriage is customarily polygamous."[52] Most importantly, polyrhythms are *idiorrhythmic* in nature, since each beat remains autonomous while also forming part of the collective. They are the changing same.

Informed by Nzeyimana and from these African sensibilities more broadly, a contemporary percussive aesthetics and politics could be one that always expects dialogue, always anticipates movement, always stays open to influence, and always makes room for another beat. It could establish polyrhythms where beats don't *entrain*, they *ensemble*—and therefore stand against a regime of competition and domination.

Because that's what drums do. They accompany. They happen next to. Echoing the distinction Trinh T. Minh-ha makes when referring to the impossibility of representing another culture, the drums don't speak about, they don't speak for, but they speak nearby.

OOM BOOM BABOOM

Capitalist rhythm, settler rhythm, white rhythm, algo-rhythm—whichever it is, the question is not to stay with the rhythm but to stay with the trouble.[53] If sociopolitical

forces once tried to strive toward sameness, toward consensus, toward a utopia of a harmonious colorblind society, we have learned that what needs to be more forcefully recognized and celebrated is how different we all are from each other. Returning to Fred Moten, it's to live in the break and the undercommons. To *ensemble*, to *percuss*. Nzeyimana's *injyana* and Moten's undercommons provide useful tools to imagine a percussive form of making and being, one that hopes to "detect the multiple and the diverse, to perceive the potential and the not-yet-expressed, to unravel the confused and the unspoken."[54] Like with the Haitian loa, percussion provides a means of transition, of finding a way in while also finding a way out, in an endless rhythm of being and unbeing at the same time. "No sooner do we grasp one rhythm," John Miller Chernoff notes, "that we lose track of it and hear another."[55] It establishes a reciprocity whereby anyone is also always someone else, beating alongside another beat, allowing one rhythm to occupy, undo, redo, and intensify another one nearby. The promise of the drum, again following Moten, is that it provides

50   James A. Snead, "Repetition as a Figure of Black Culture," in *Black Literature and Literary Theory*, ed. Henry Louis Gates, Jr. (York, UK: Methuen, 1984).

51   Agawu, *The African Imagination in Music*, 179.

52   John Collins, quoted in Agawu, *The African Imagination in Music*, 182.

53   Elena Agudio, Anna Jäger, and Saskia Köbschall, "When We Get Out of Rhythm, We Get in Trouble," in *I Will Draw a Map of What You Never See*, 27.

54   Séverine Kodjo-Grandvaux, quoted in Nyampeta, "One's Own Rhythm," in *I Will Draw a Map of What You Never See*, 106.

55   Chernoff, *African Rhythm and African Sensibility*, 46.

a means to remain *incomplete*, where any one beat is always subject to the ensemble. It is not about putting individuals in relation but about a sociality not based on the individual at all and rooted, instead, in being an attachment, being a part, being incomplete.[56]

Getting to the percussive means breaking the beat. The break is the moment of recalibrating the rhythm, and Moten has used it to describe a charged space of potentiality: it is "a kind of lyricism of the surplus … the sound of love … an erotics of the cut, submerged in the broken."[57] The break is that space of transition, of flight, where one beat is on its way to another. It's a space where visibility and invisibility—or recognizability and unrecognizability—don't cancel each other out but color each other, the way a *baah* inflects a *buhhh*. The break values repetition and interruption rather than progress. The break is the interval—and if Western music demands that one play the "right" note, non-Western cultures listen for the right interval.[58] Echoing the African or Haitian drummers, it is when one leaves the self and inhabits a collective, so that one can develop "a feel for feeling others feeling you."[59]

Freedom, for anyone, necessarily happens in the cut, in the break, in a state of flight. It is not the search for another rhythm, one that replaces the settler rhythm, but a cut—something without a center, something that doesn't *do* or even *know* harmony, like the drum. It's not a place for winners and losers but a place of *ensemble*, where a leader is the drummer who initiates a movement for others but doesn't determine where it will go—allowing it to "unexpectedly click in, come apart, meet halfway, and so on; in other words, how they do and undo one another in their diversified movements, forming a strong assemblage of No Thing, rather than something or nothing."[60]

In today's reality of extreme social and political divisions, where disagreement instantly triggers hatred, can a percussive approach, a percussive sensibility, be one that scrambles and blurs and makes way for other forms of assembly and relation? One where opacity and abstraction overpower representation as forces of healing? Where the urge to compete gives way to forms of mutual well-being? Where rhythms work to confuse and undermine power dynamics rather than enforce them, keeping everyone on their toes? Where the goal is not necessarily to understand each other but to listen to each other? Not to harmonize, but to percuss? And if *understanding* is a form of taking hold of—*comprendre* (where *prendre* is French for "to take")—then *percussing* might provide a form of assembly that doesn't involve taking but listening, obscuring, interrupting, and rendering incomplete.

There's a great Fred Moten line that goes something like this: when asked to describe the work of Nathaniel Mackey (him again), Moten responded by saying that "'everything' is a counting term. This plus this plus this. 'All' is a mass word. It's not about the coalescence of separable things. It's *all*." Shakespeare is Everything. Mackey is All.[61] Percussion is *all*. It is not poly- but it is generative. It's not measurable but is a direction, a pointing, with each beat already containing parts of the next one. A drum is not an instrument but a possibility. All.

56 Stefano Harney and Fred Moten, *All Incomplete* (New York: Minor Compositions, 2021), 122.

57 Moten, *In the Break*, 26.

58 Trinh T. Minh-ha, "The Voice of Multiplicity," lecture at the Wattis Institute, November 7, 2019.

59 Stefano Harney and Fred Moten, *The Undercommons: Fugitive Planning & Black Study* (New York: Minor Compositions, 2013), 98.

60 Trinh, "Rhythm at Play," in *I Will Draw a Map of What You Never See*, 39.

61 Fred Moten, quoted in Hua Hsu, "Nathaniel Mackey's Long Song," *The New Yorker*, April 12, 2021, 27.

More specific and precise than "rhythm," percussion or the percussive can provide a model for a different kind of aesthetic and sociopolitical architecture, a new literacy, a different way of organizing ourselves. Non-Western (and colonized) cultures have centered the percussive for centuries, but their beats have been ruthlessly oppressed and drowned out. Listening for them might help define a society that is once again attuned to the irregular movements of the heart—a percussive community bound by bodies moving together, the dead alongside the living, the mind dancing with the heart, outside of language. The percussive could replace harmony with rhythm, progress with cycles and mutations, and could allow alignment to coexist with the freedom to break away at any moment. The percussive could provide an emancipatory model where the abstractions of rhythm have political agency and where difference is energized and *ensembled* rather than resolved. The percussive can cut into one beat, insert another one in the break, and trouble the rhythms of a dominant marching order. It can generate an expressive language of beats, pulses, tones, and tempos that binds art and politics to each other in new ways. If one way to think about art is not to ask what it is but to ask what it does, then a percussive artwork is one that doesn't explain but *ensembles*. Whether or not a drum is involved is not the point, because just as Jean-Luc Godard claimed not to make political films but to make films politically, we can learn to make art percussively. To percuss is to vibrate. Sometimes, those vibrations simply tickle us, causing a chuckle or a gasp, and provide access to a liberating space outside of reason, intention, and purpose. Other times, those vibrations are strong enough to shake the world, changing it forever.

If percussion is the score, what's the exhibition?

First and foremost, *Drum Listens to Heart* takes places in a series of galleries, not in the pages of a printed book, and reading descriptions of artworks is like looking at the instruments, not hearing the symphony.

To understand the drum, the late Milford Graves studied the heart by hooking people up to a homemade EKG machine that connected the scientific and the empirical with the spiritual. All bodies are drums, he would say, each one playing at the speed of its own heart, and all drums are bodies, each one made of a skin that vibrates differently.[1]

1 It was when Milford passed away, in 2021, that I finally settled on a title for this exhibition, *Drum Listens to Heart*, a phrase written on one of these sculptures, which gave me a way to dedicate this whole project to him and to the short but incredibly inspiring time we spent together.

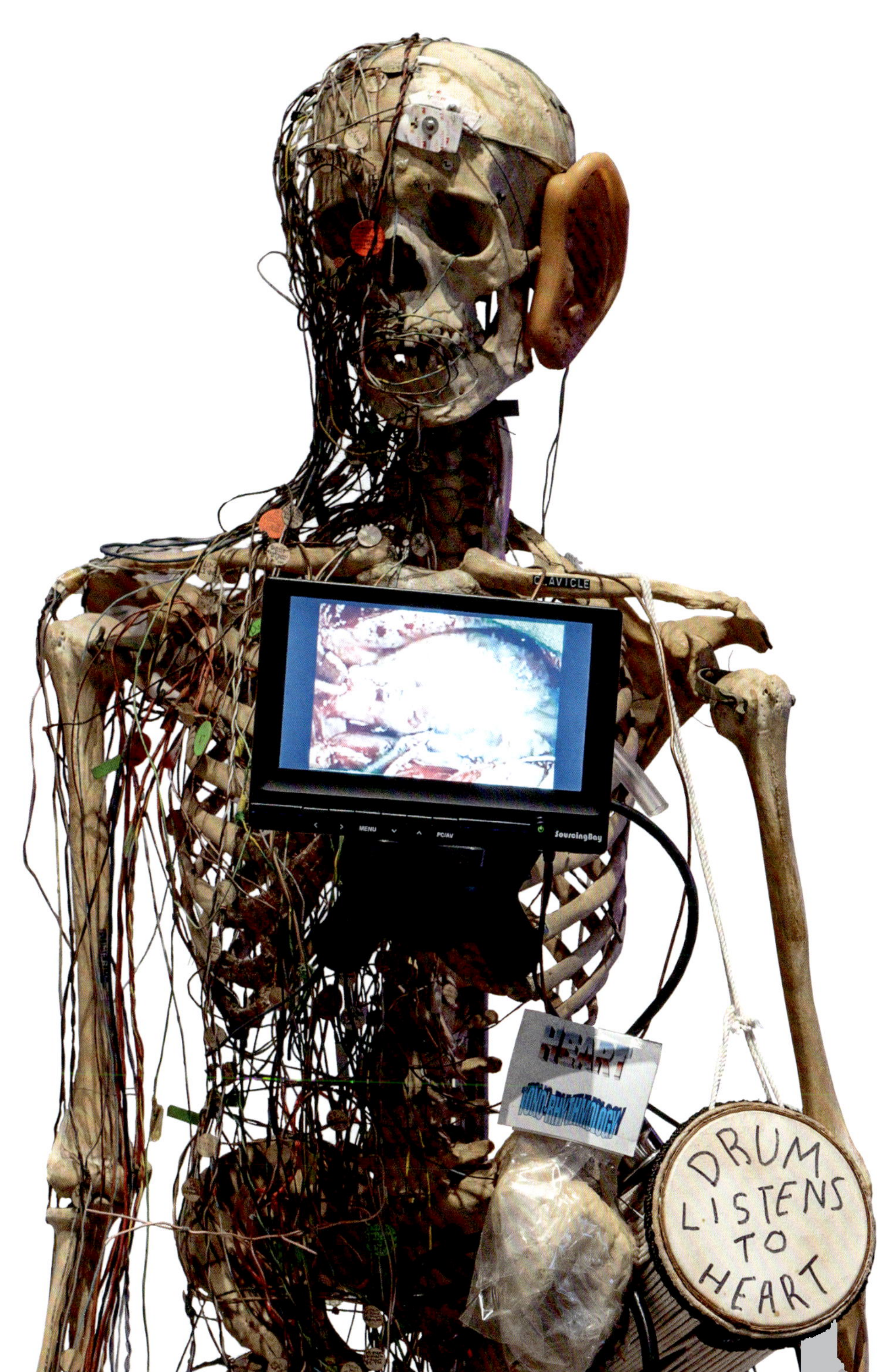
CLAVICLE
MENU
PC/AV
SourcingBay
HEART
DRUM
LISTENS
TO
HEART

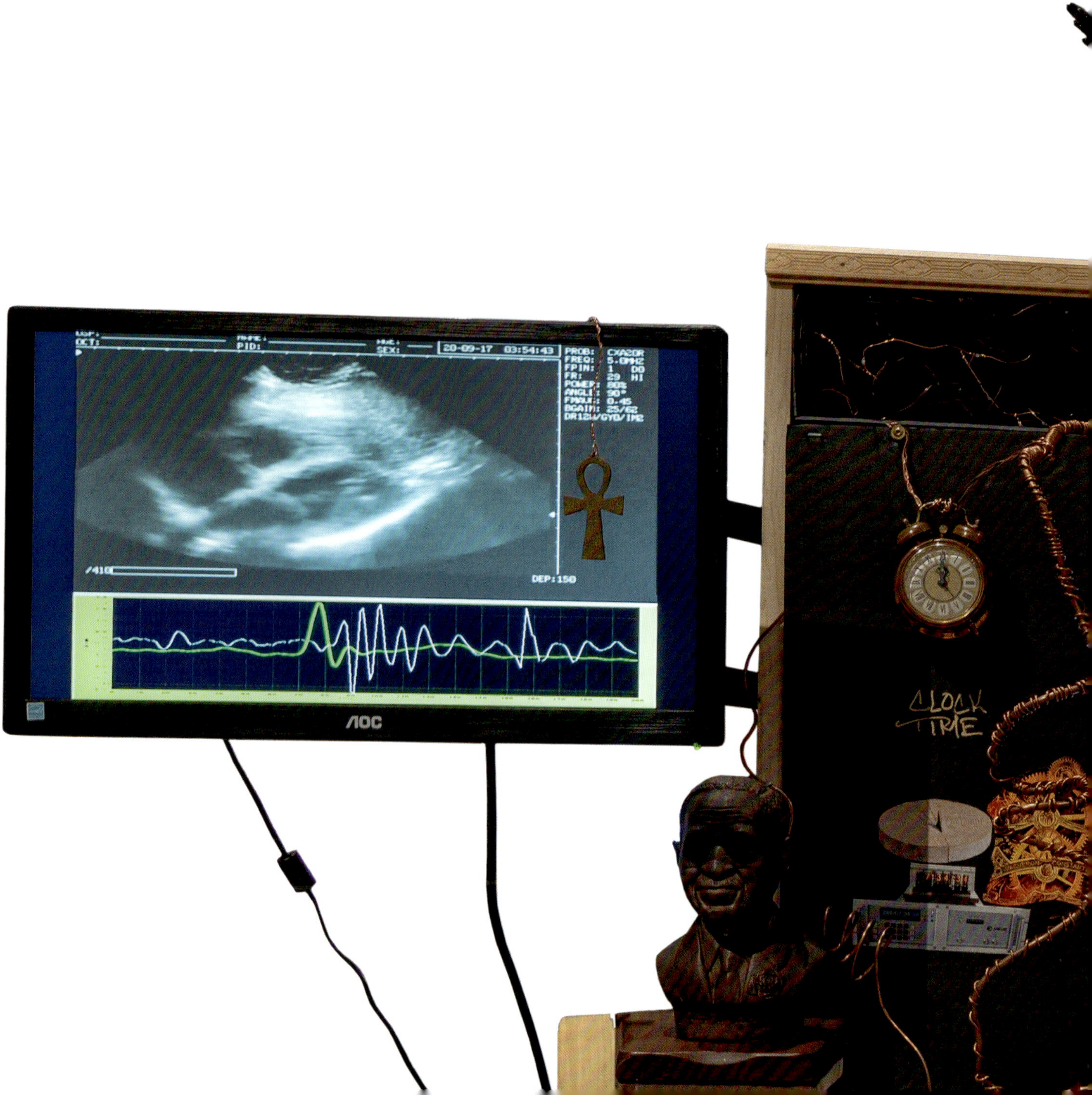

22

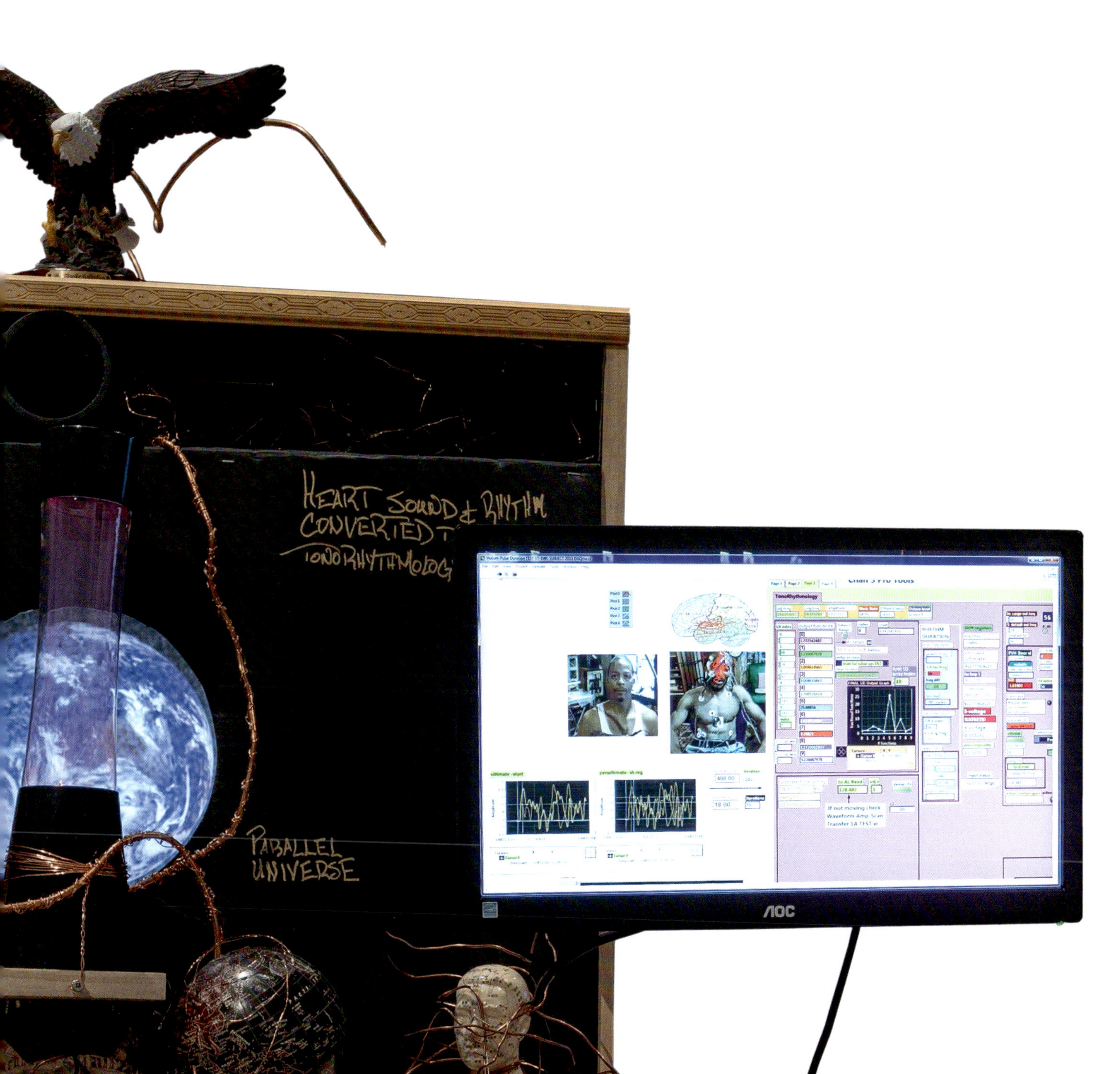

HEART SOUND & RHYTHM
CONVERTED T
TONORHYTHMOLOG

PARALLEL
UNIVERSE

TonoRhythmology

AOC

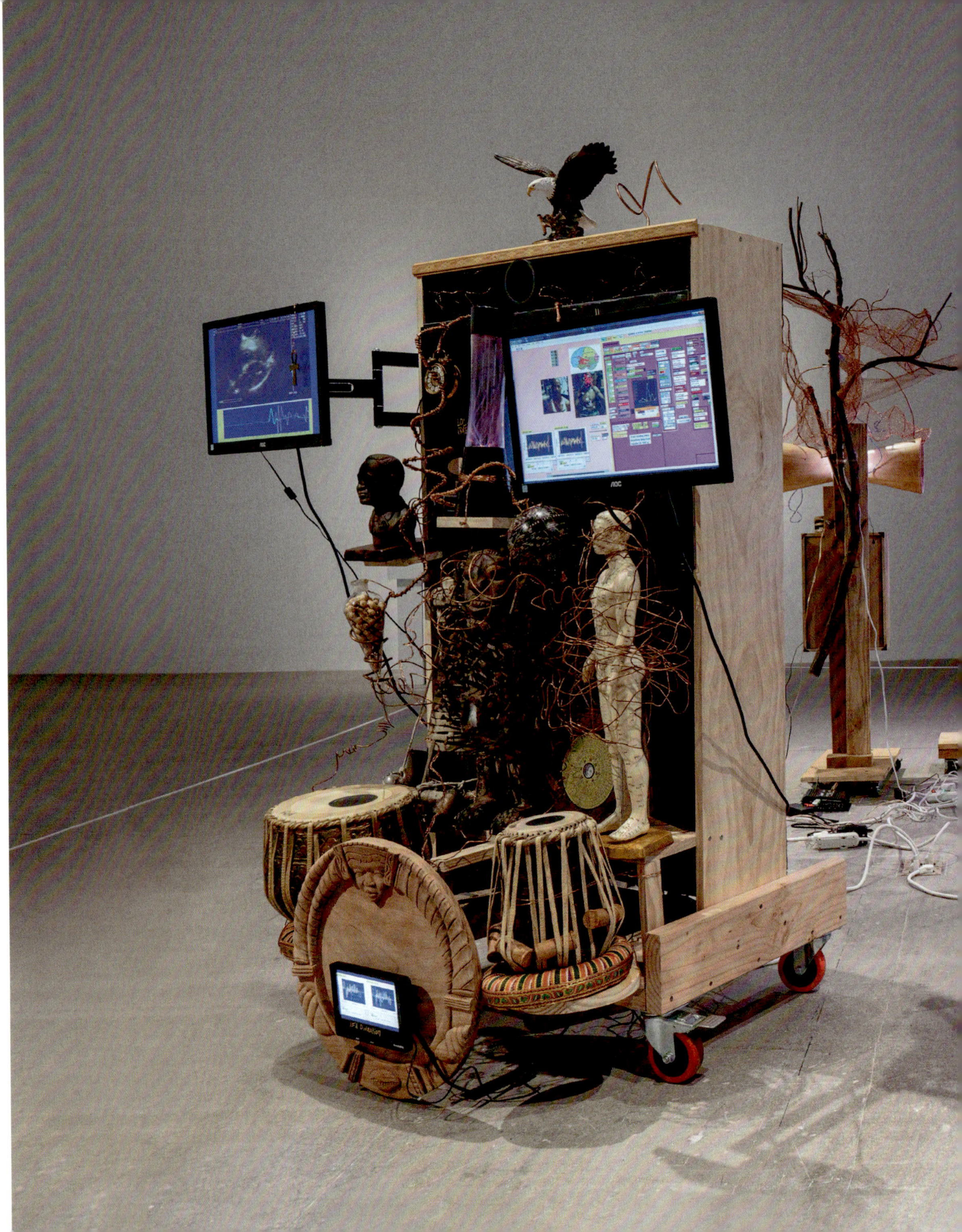

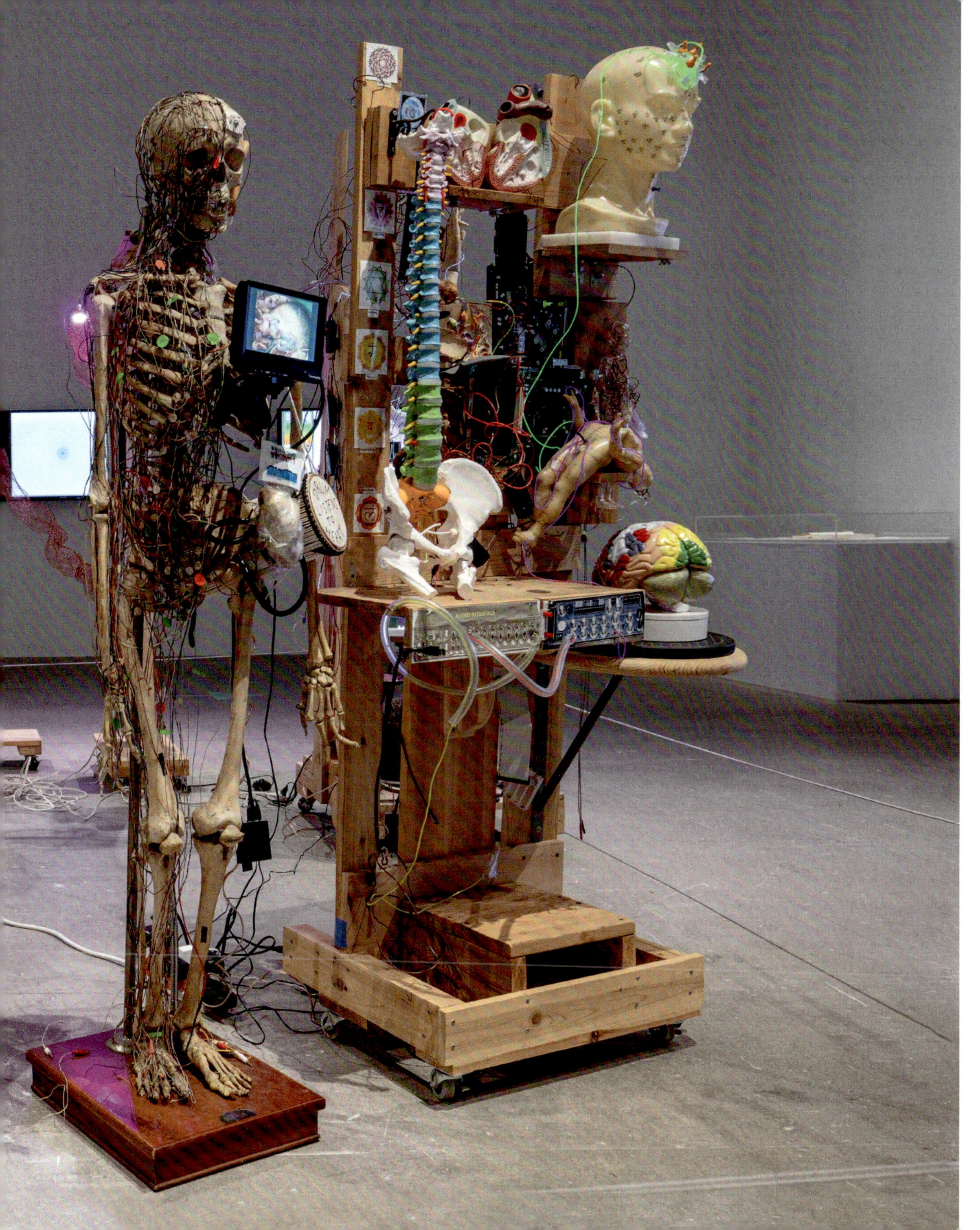

The body also gets
dissected, stripped down to its heart, by Michael E. Smith, who points a laser
beam that moves up and down over the surface of an object, providing an
artificial heartbeat to an inanimate situation, or marking it the way a predator
targets its prey;

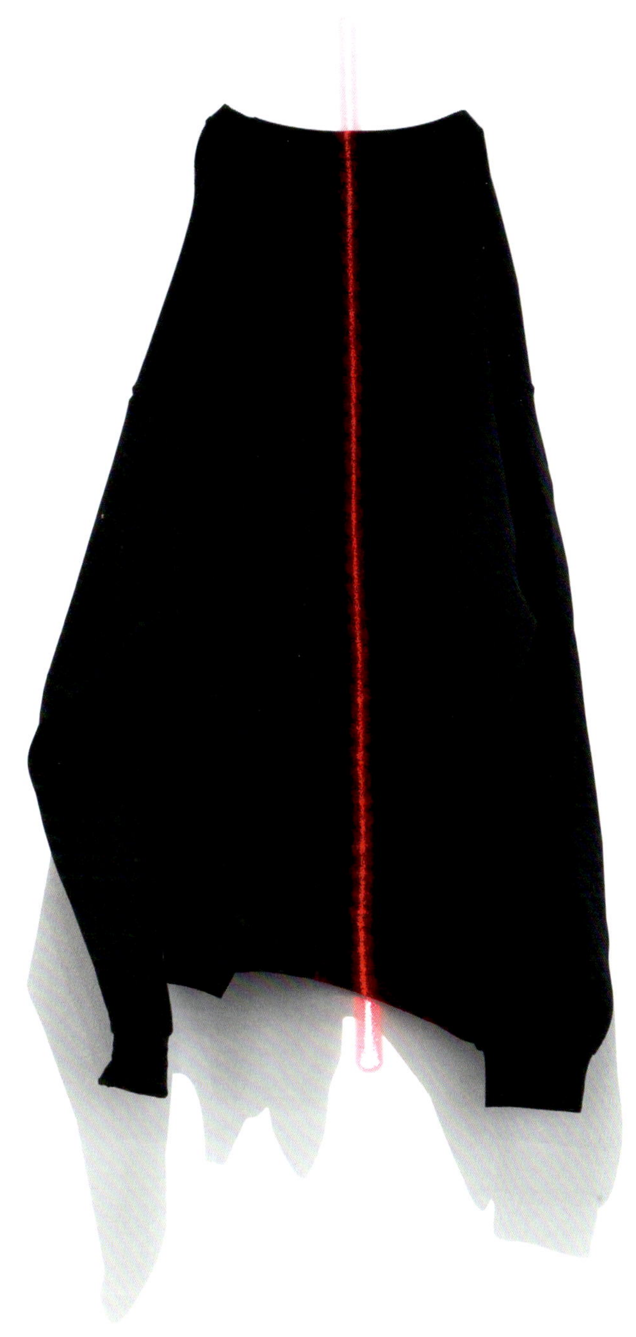

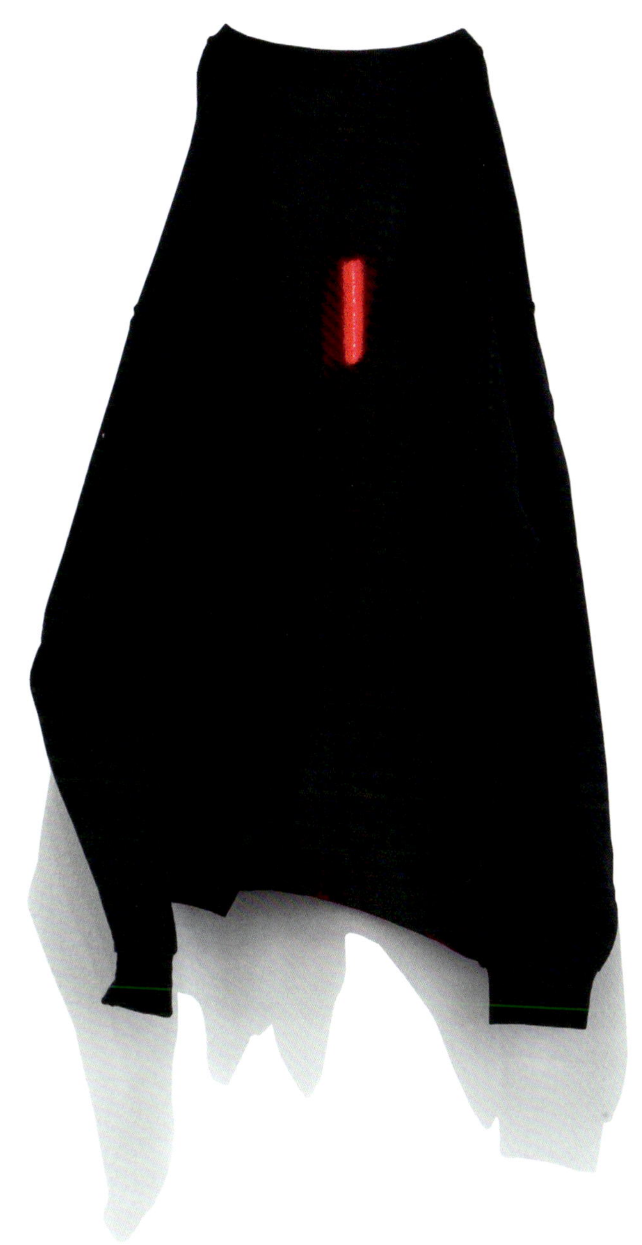

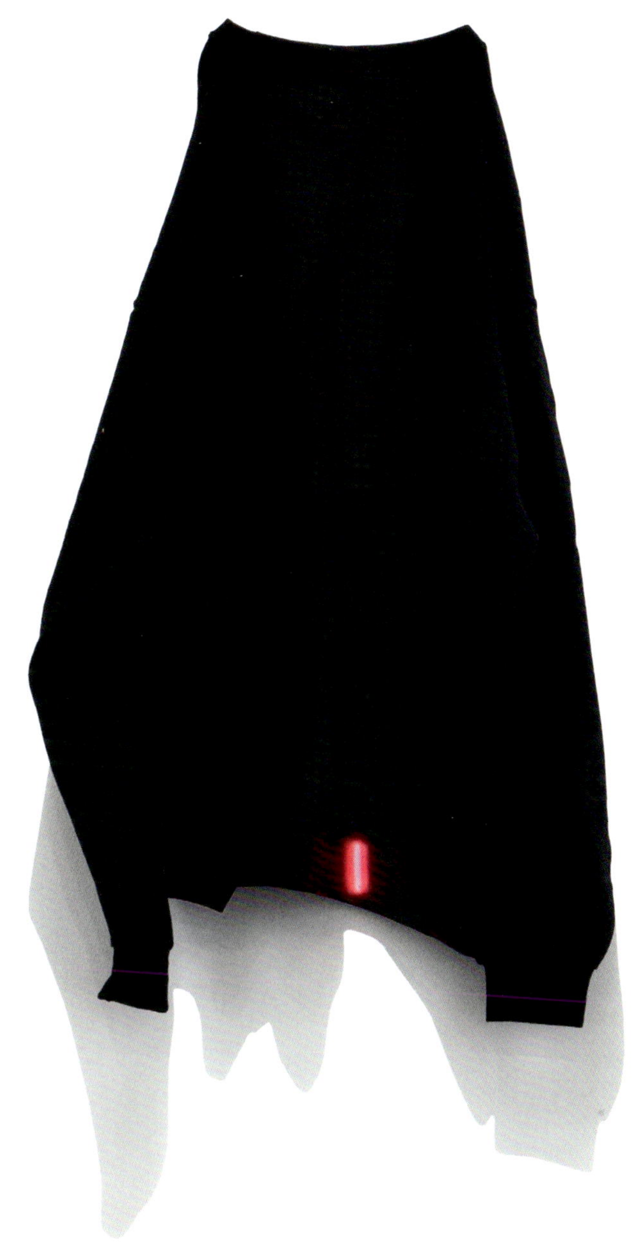

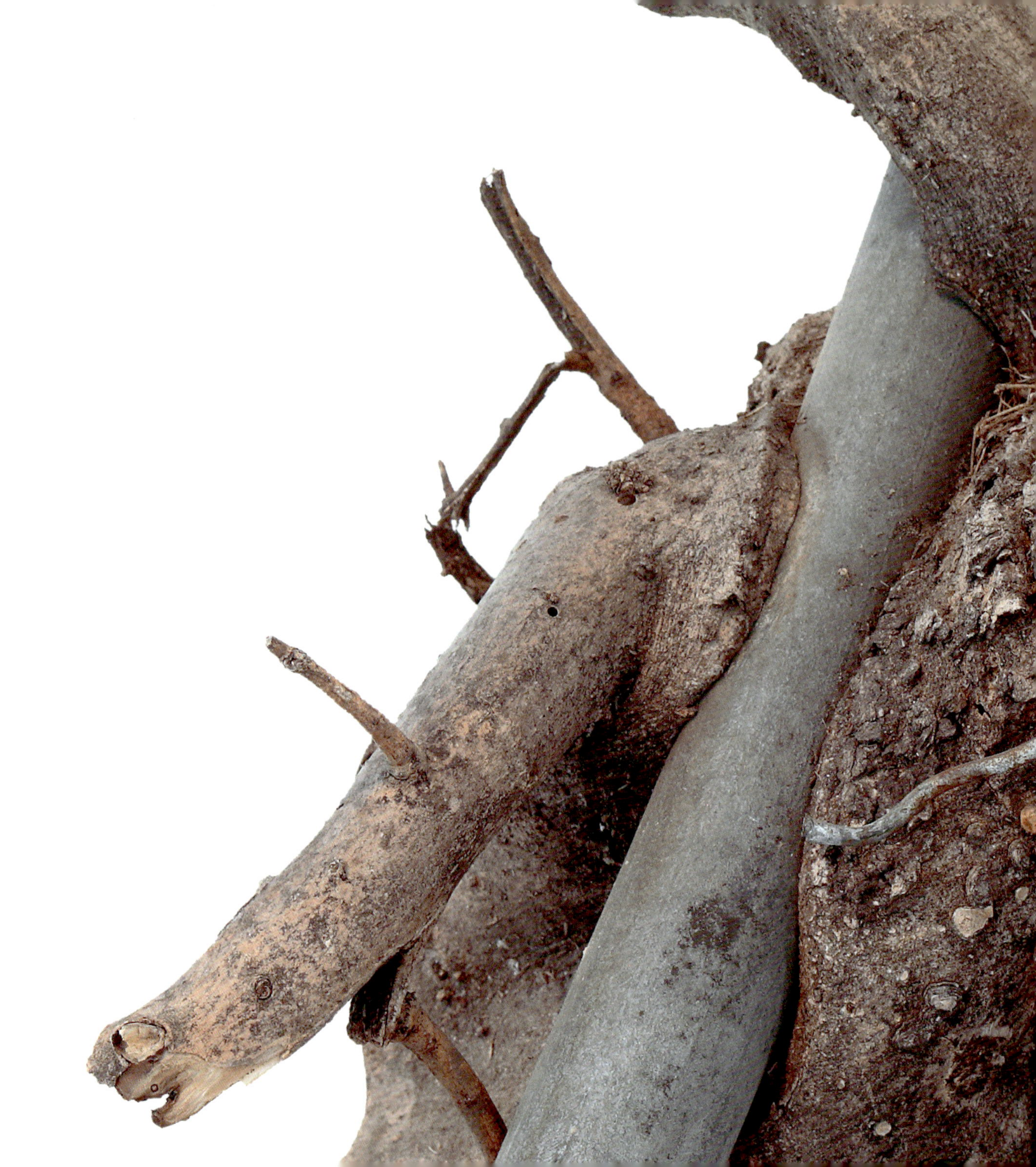

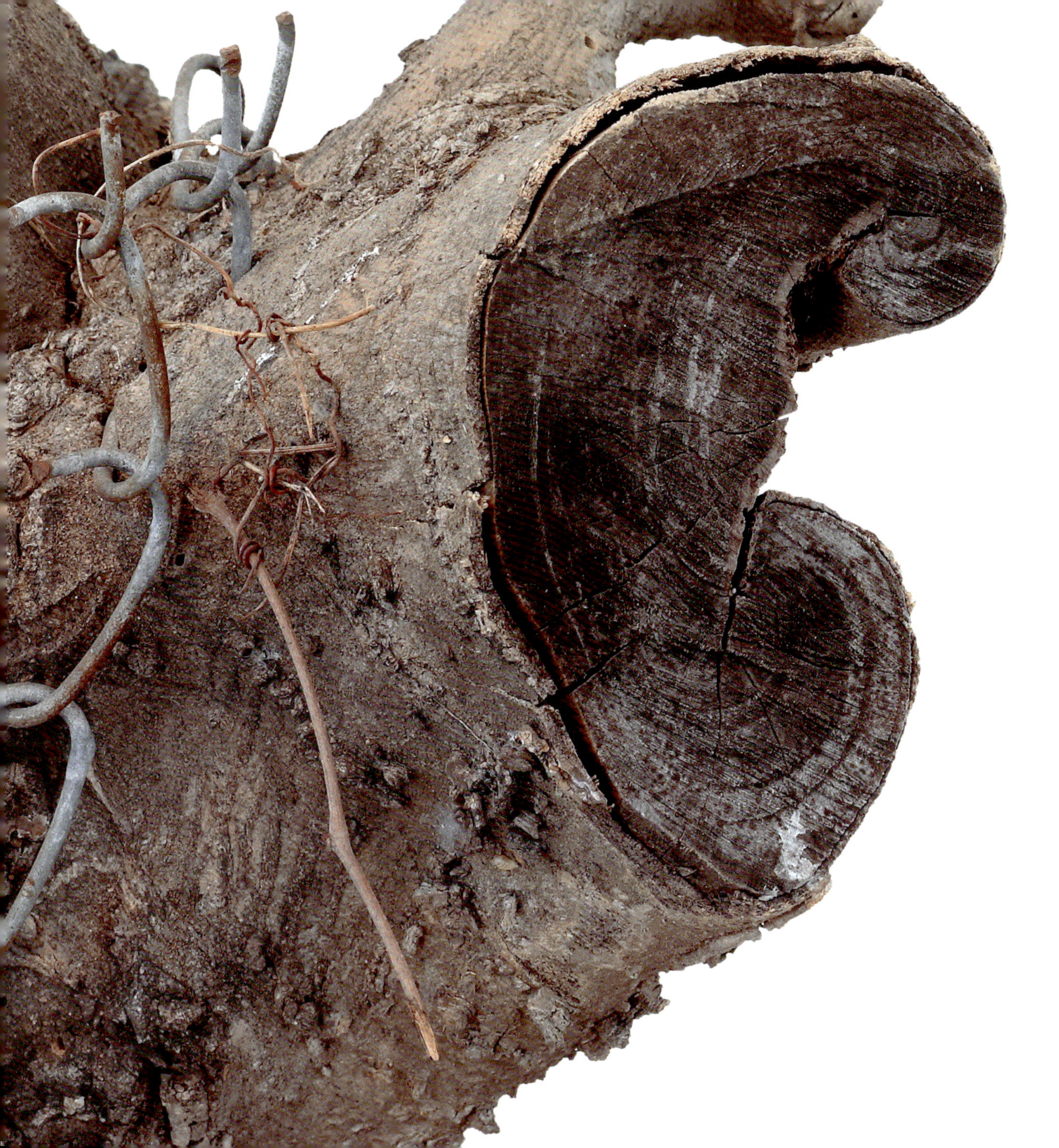

and in Harold Mendez's found sculpture of a metal fence pole,
where all that is left is a wooden heart, laid bare.

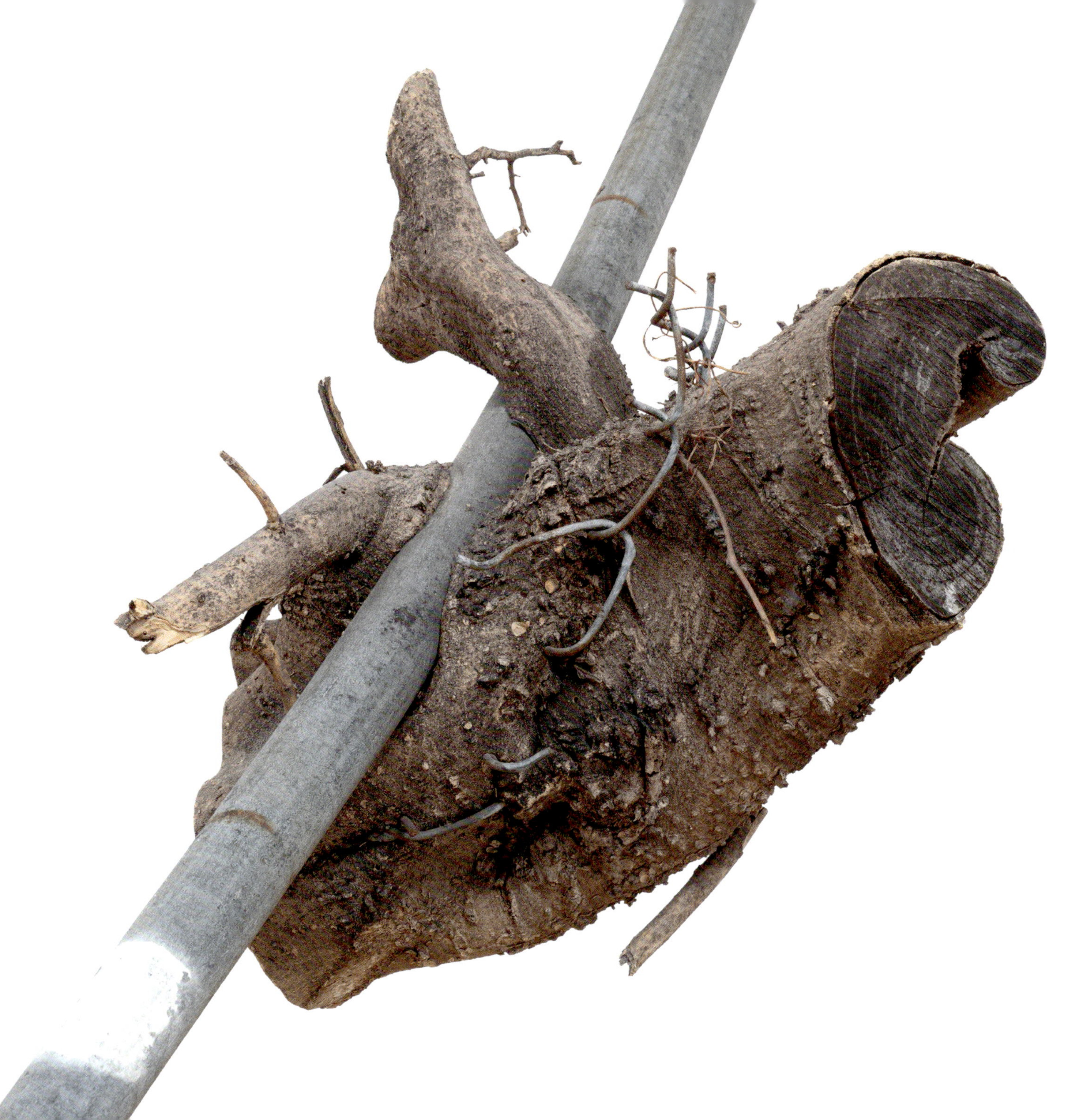

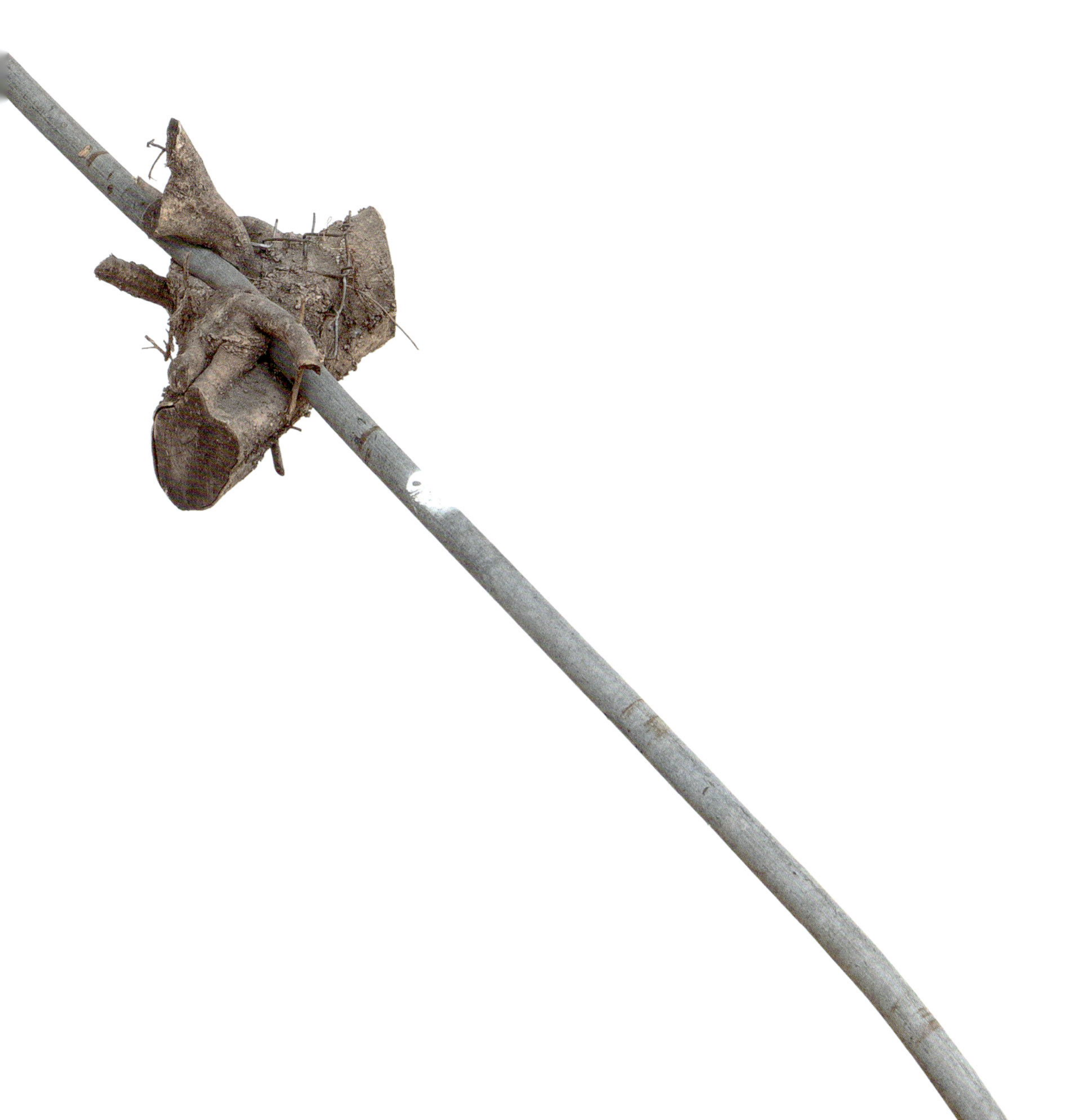

Nearby is a sculpture by Barry Le Va that requires delivering multiple blows to a stack of glass sheets, causing them to shatter;

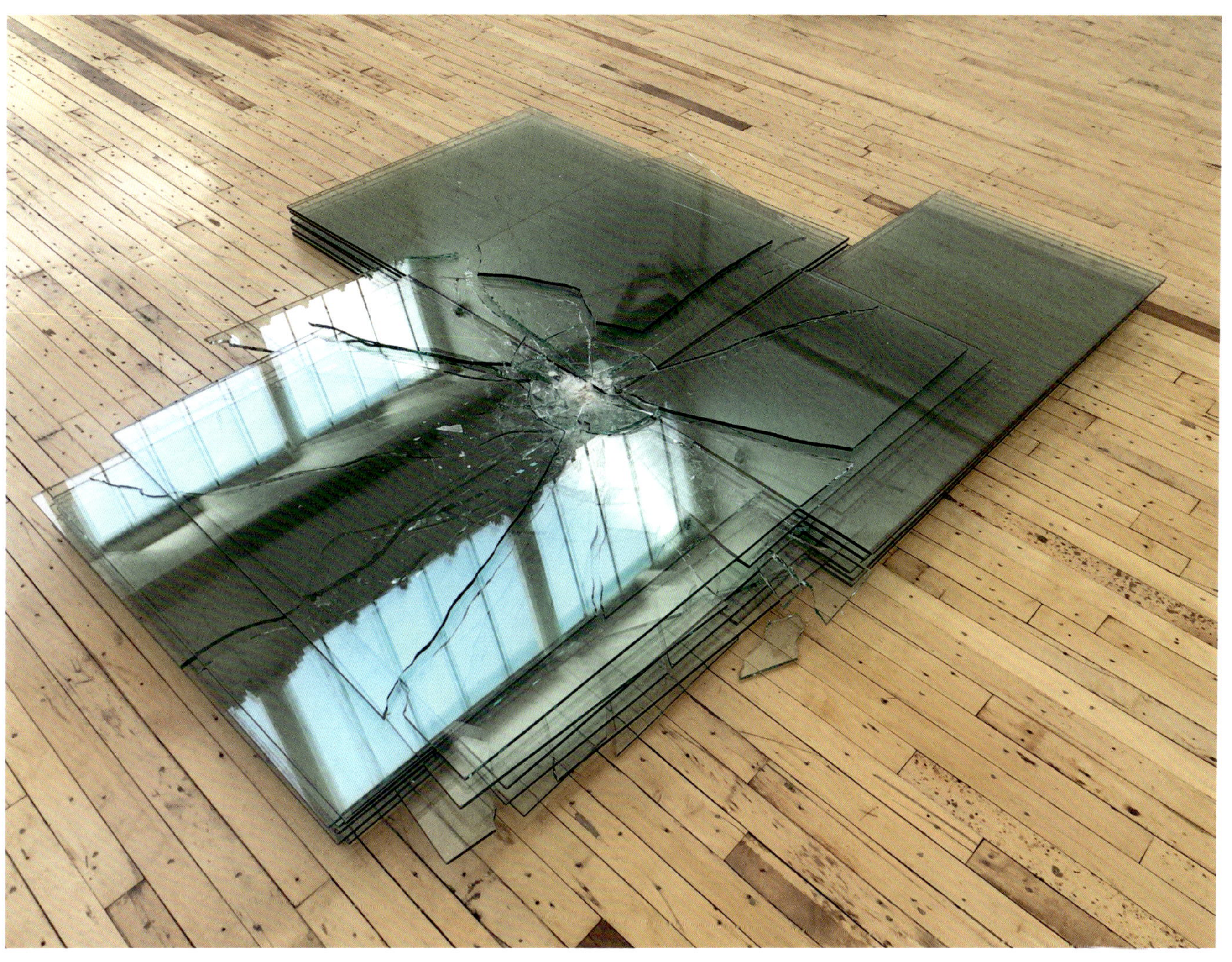

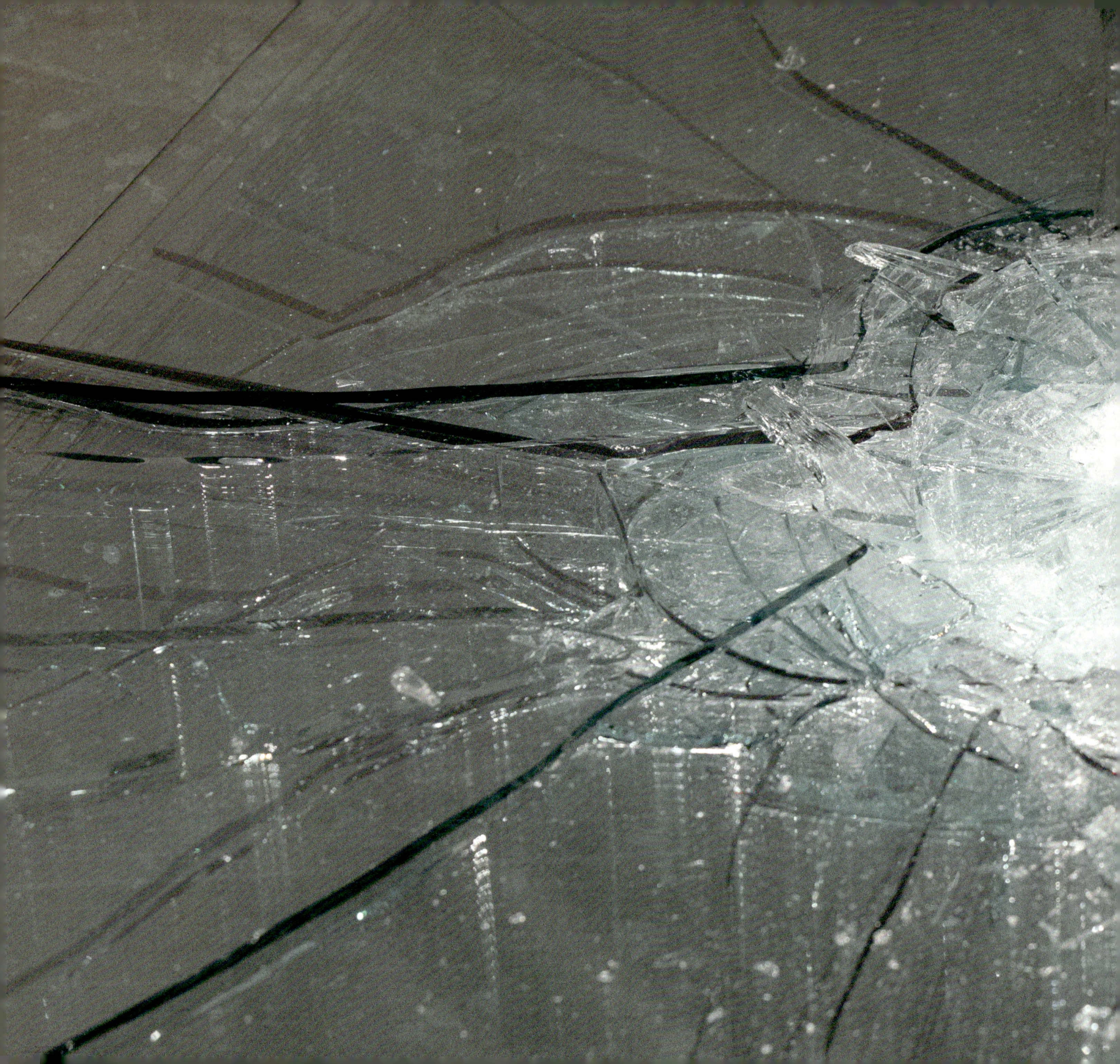

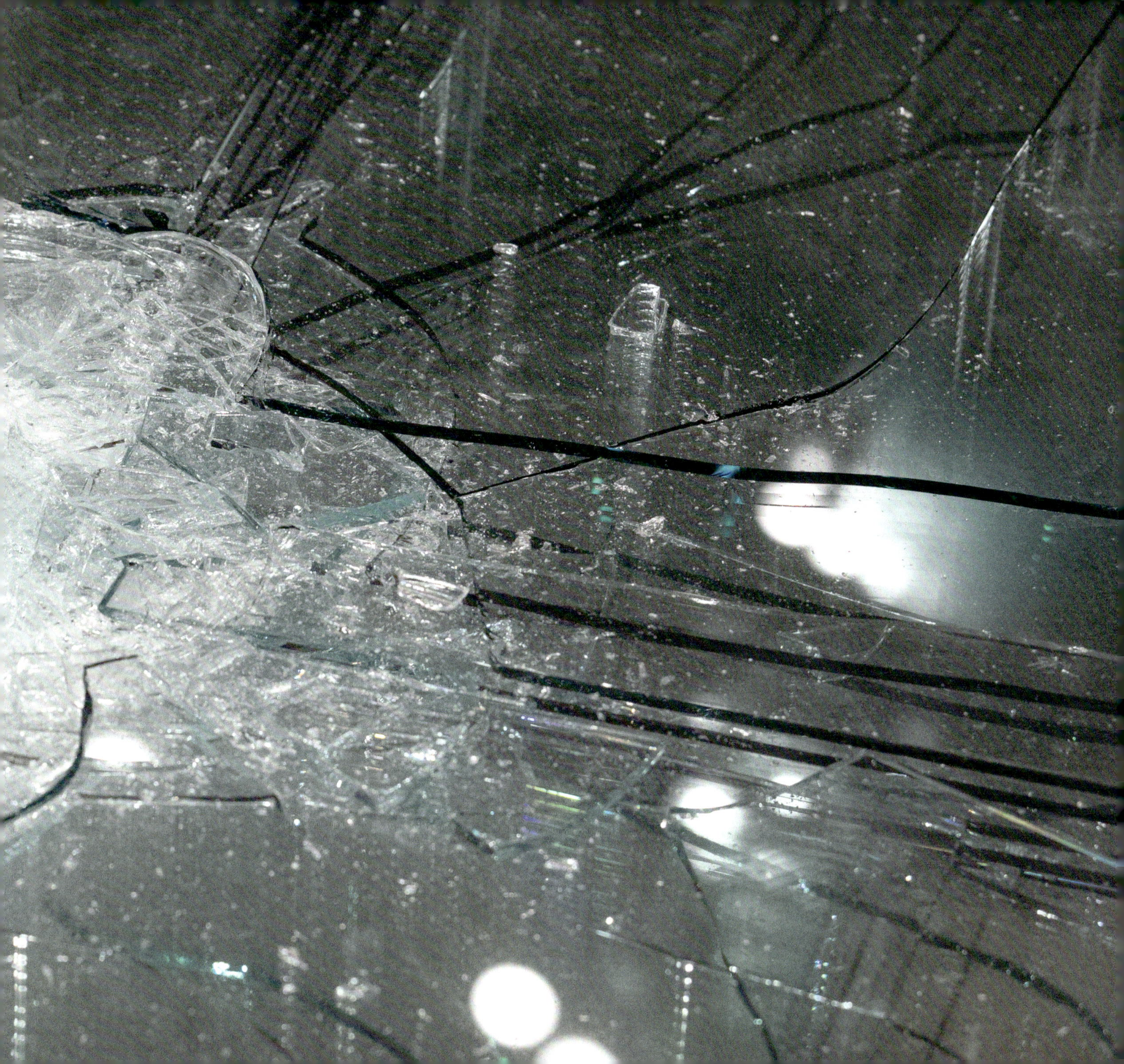

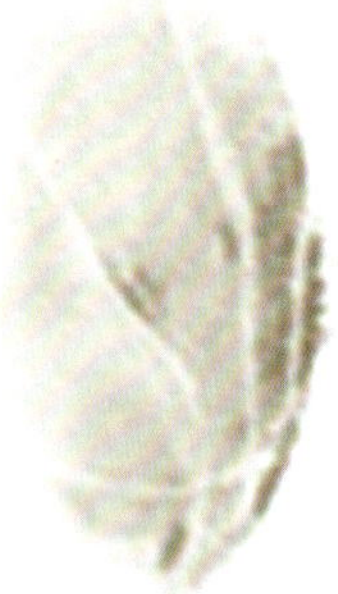

or these marks, by David Hammons, made by bouncing a dirt-covered basketball onto a wall, which transforms a casual (and often racialized) activity into an empowered form of claiming space;

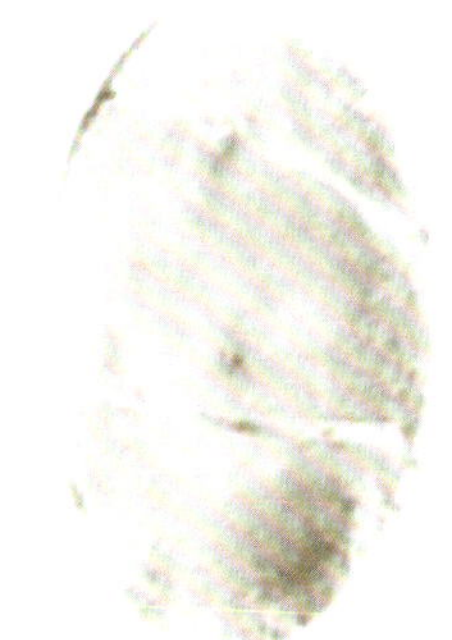

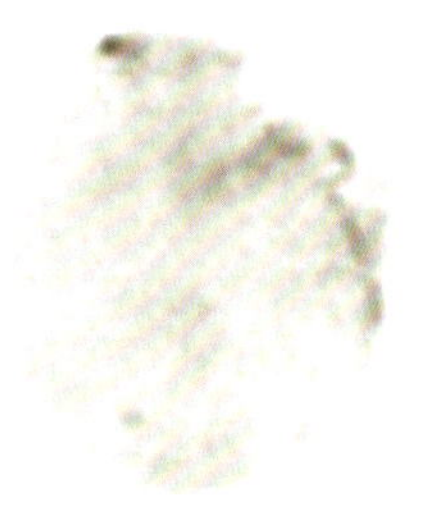

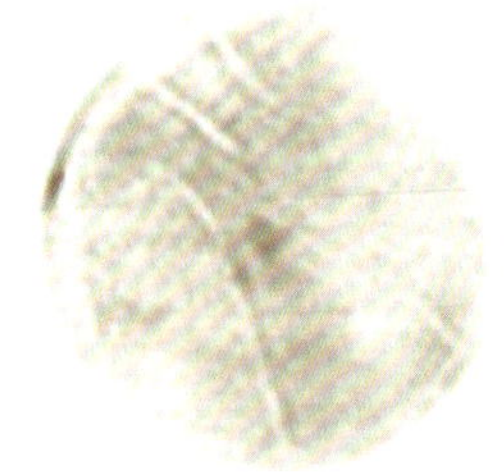

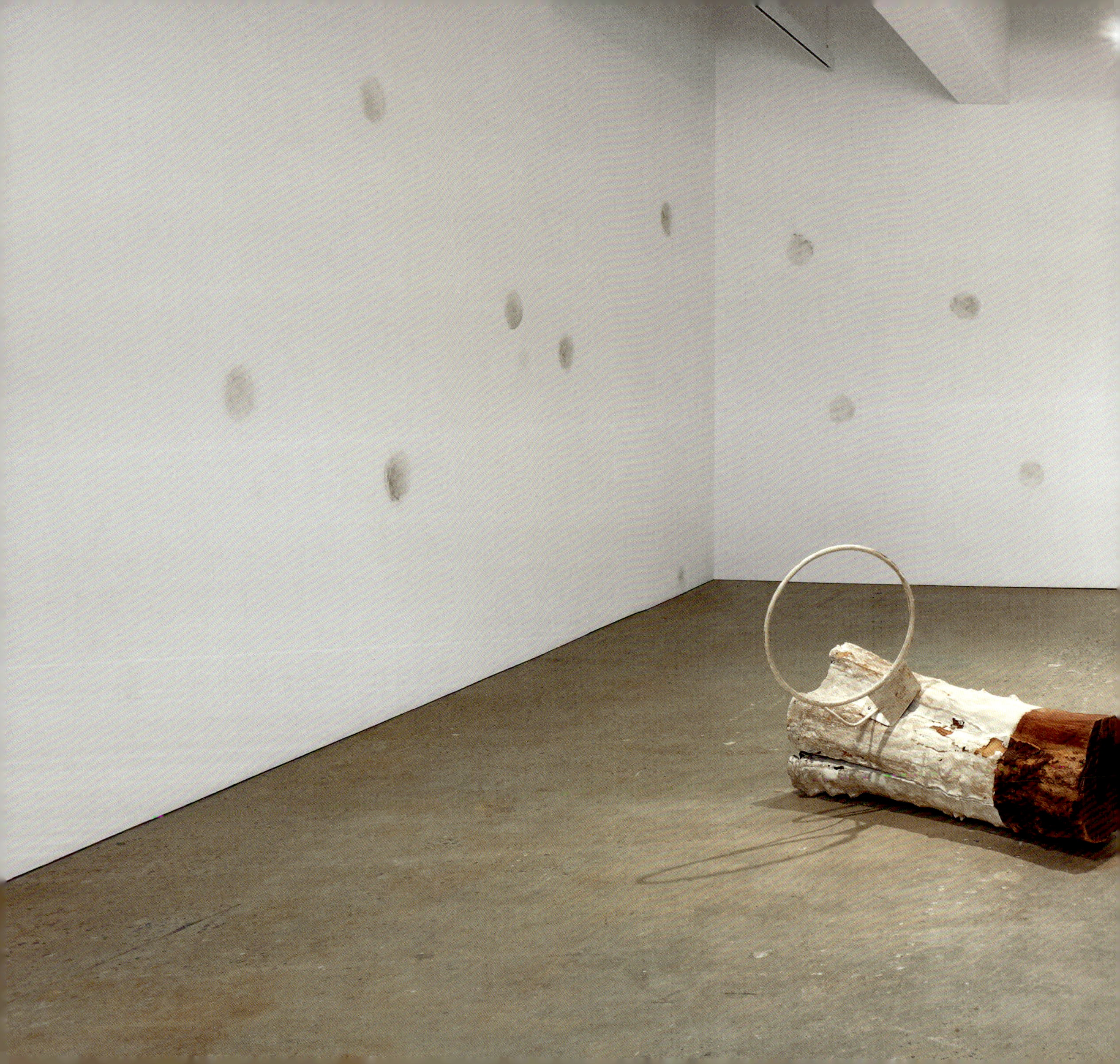

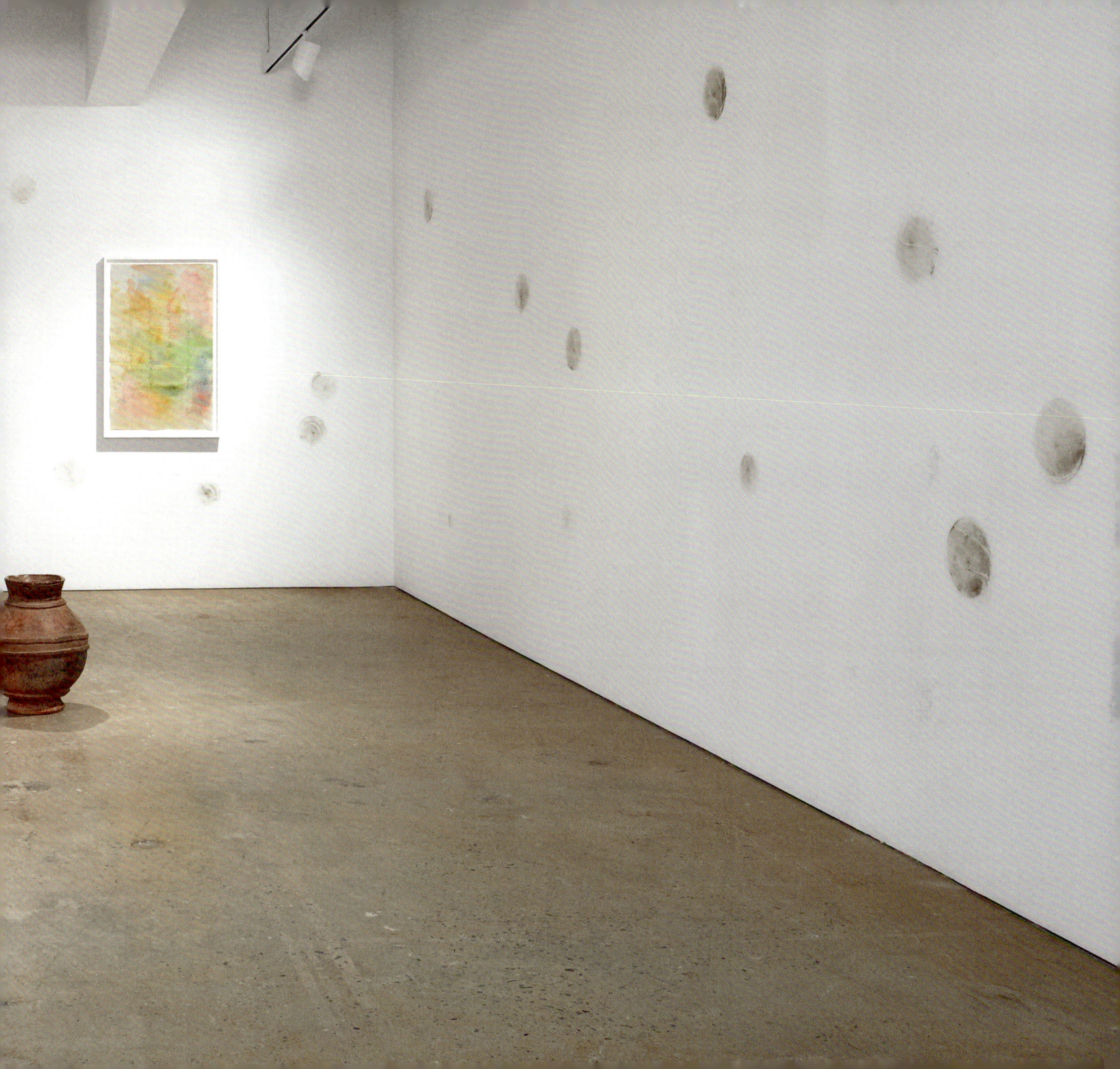

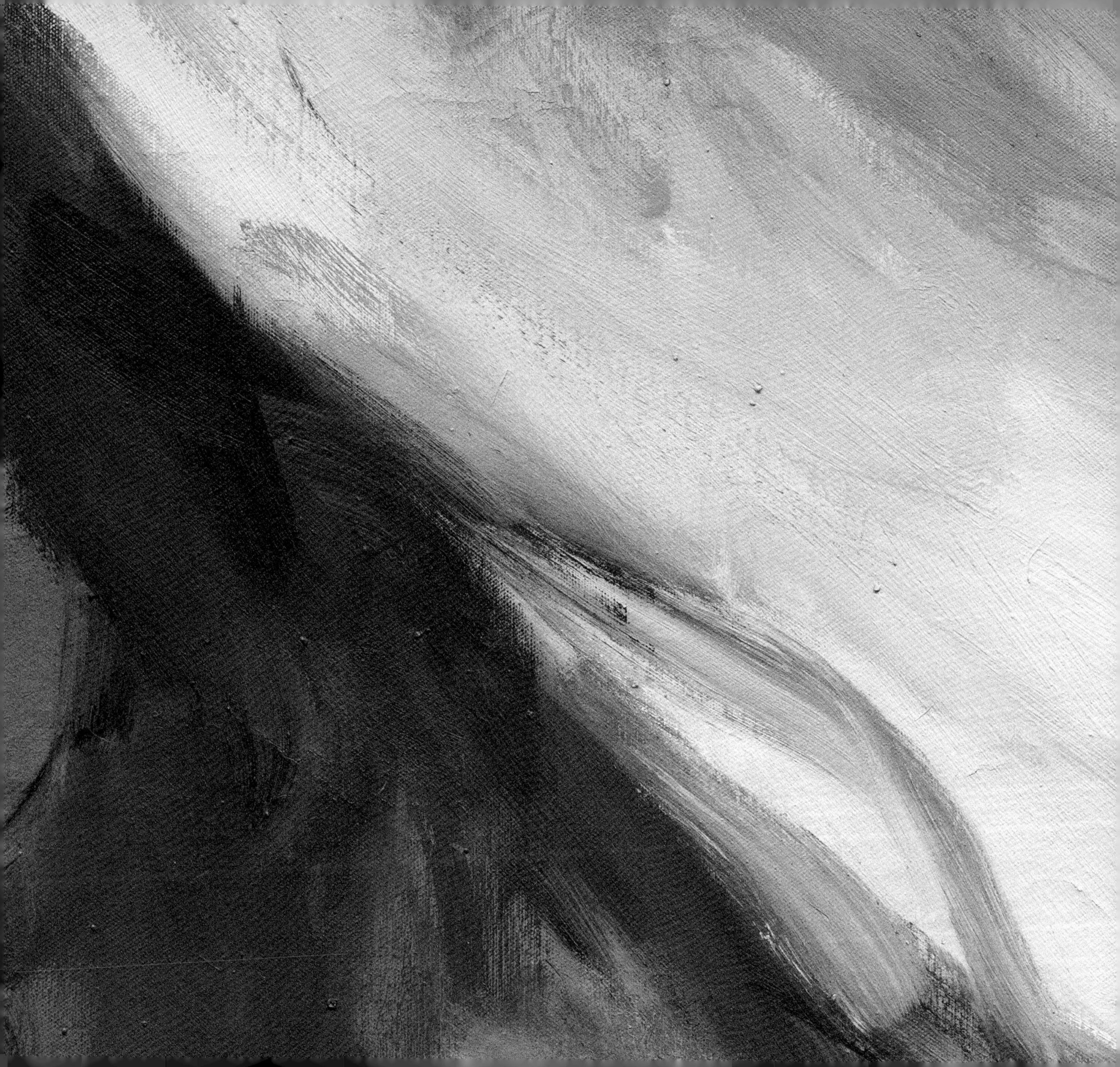

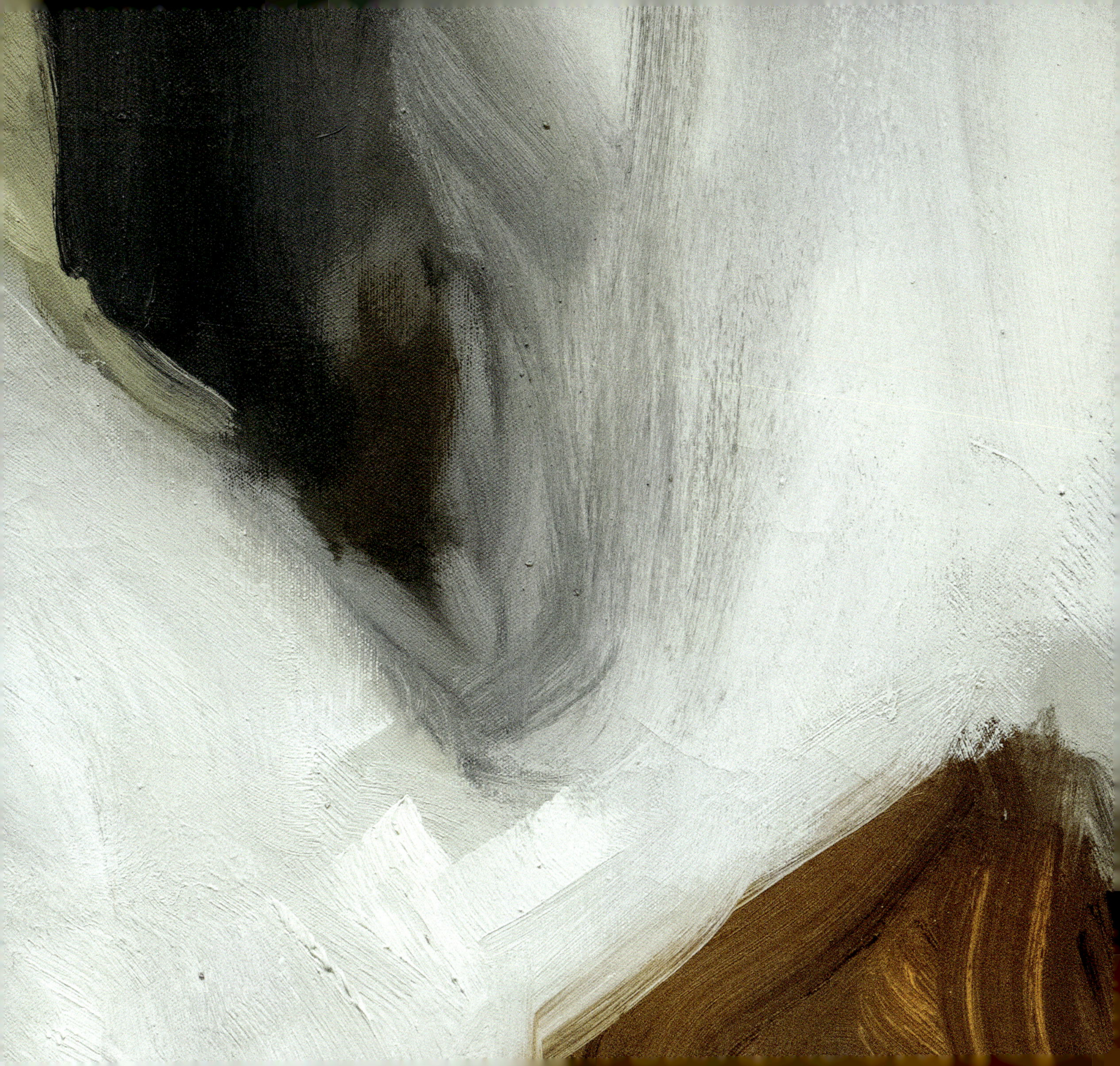

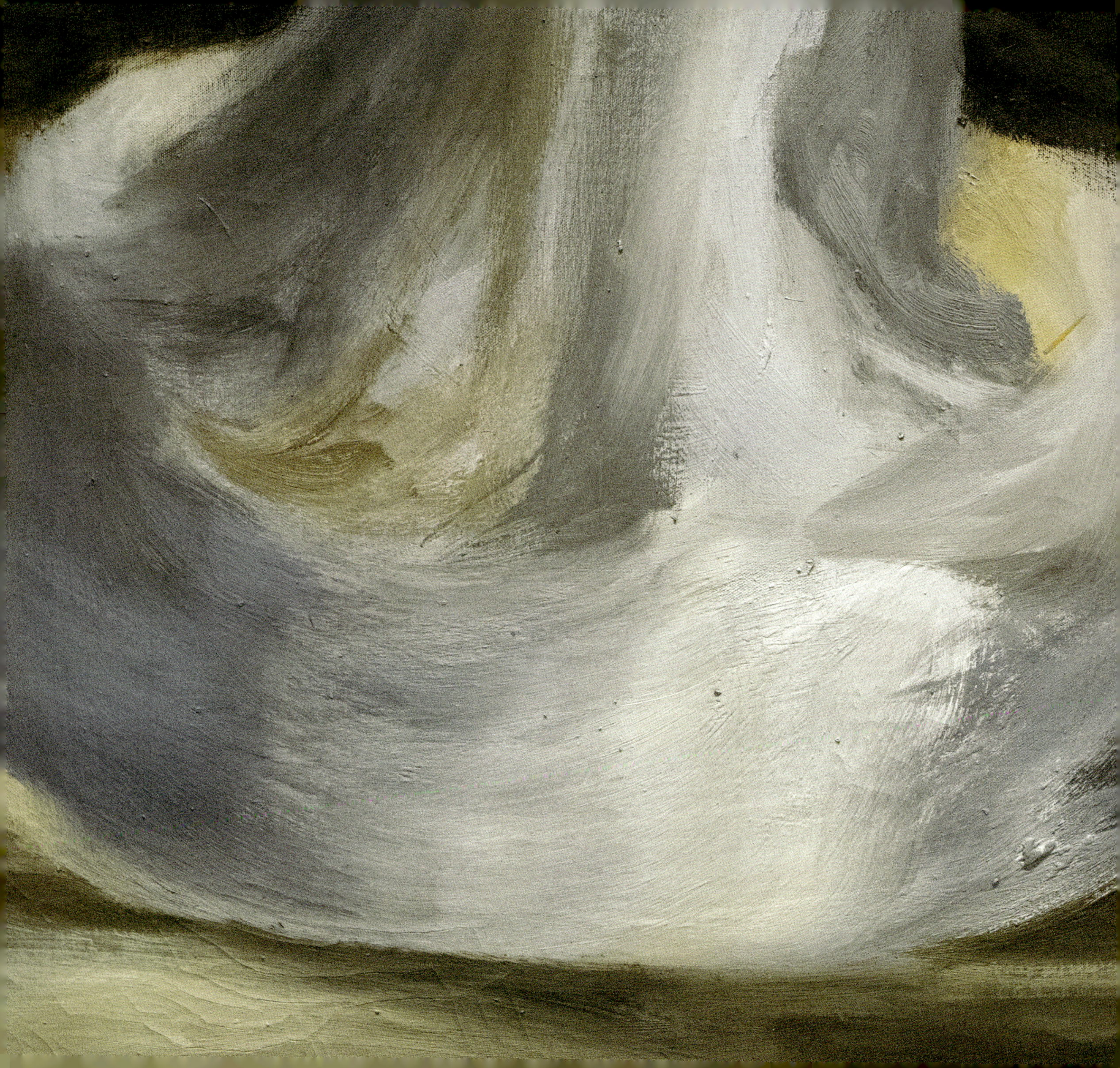

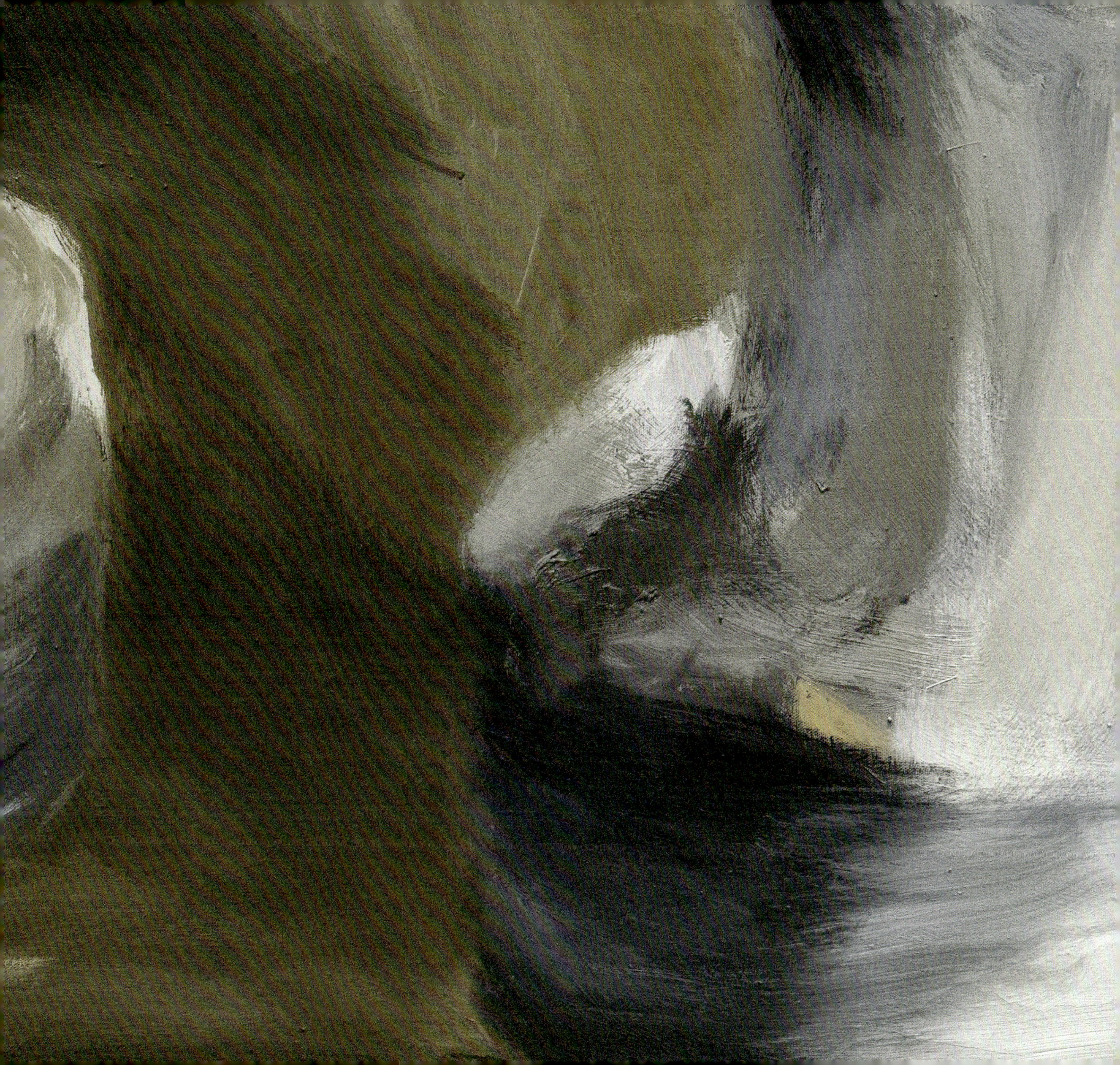

and a "triple hammer"
painting by Lee Lozano, which doesn't just strike but does so polyrhythmically,
with many moments of impact happening at once.

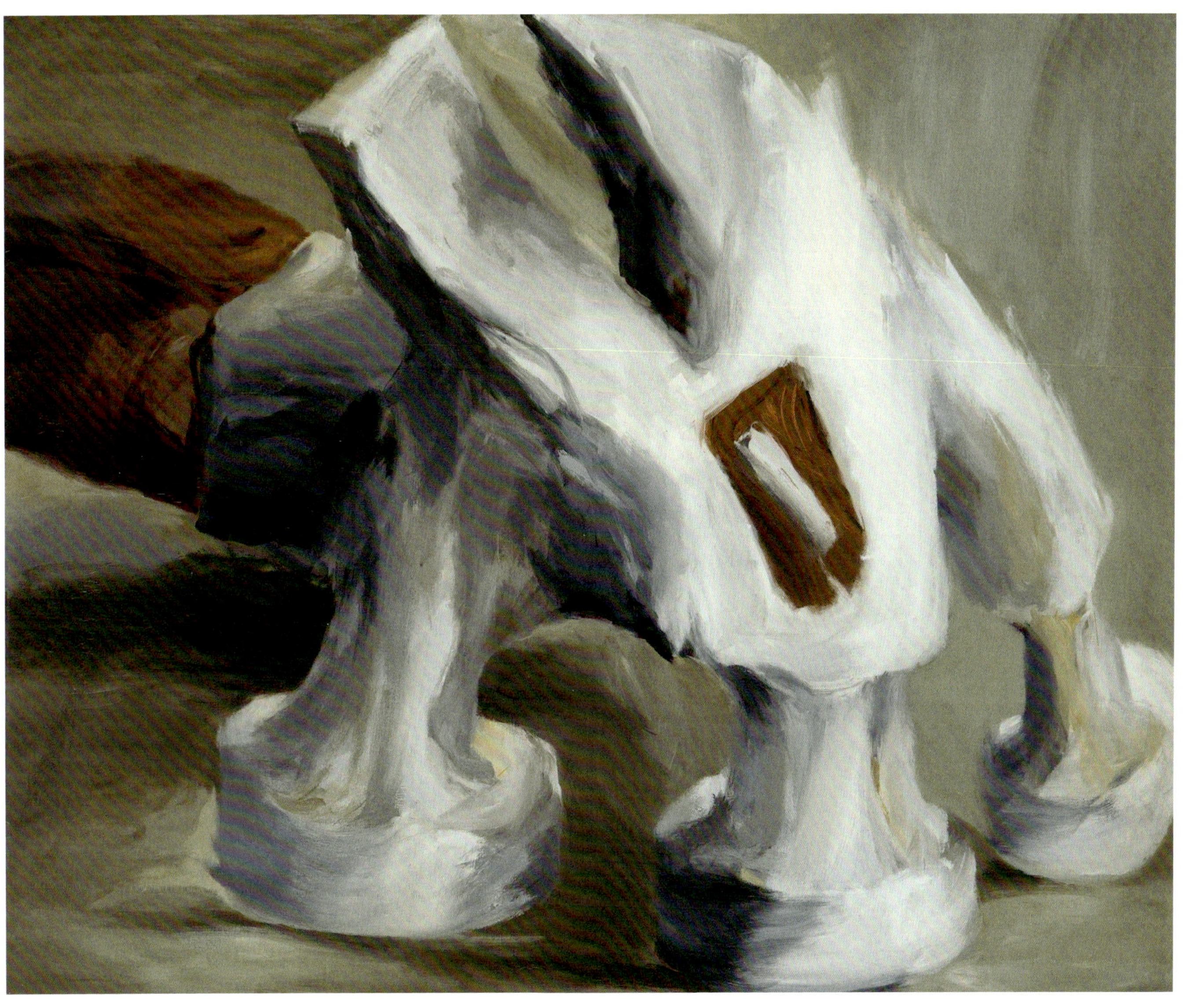

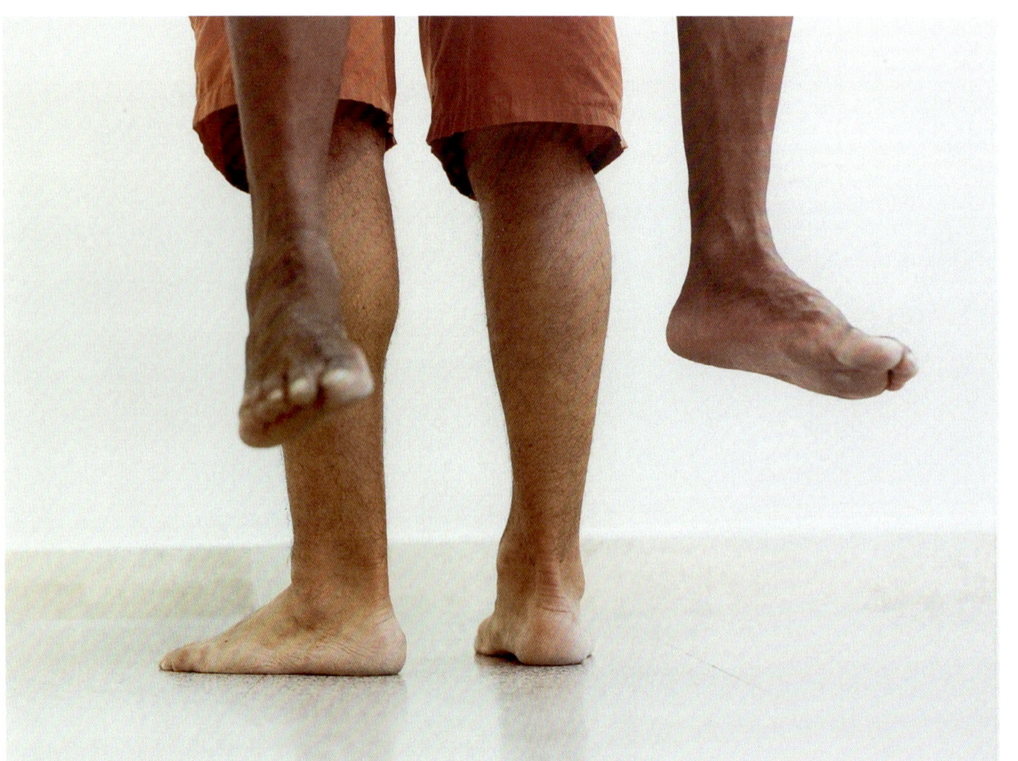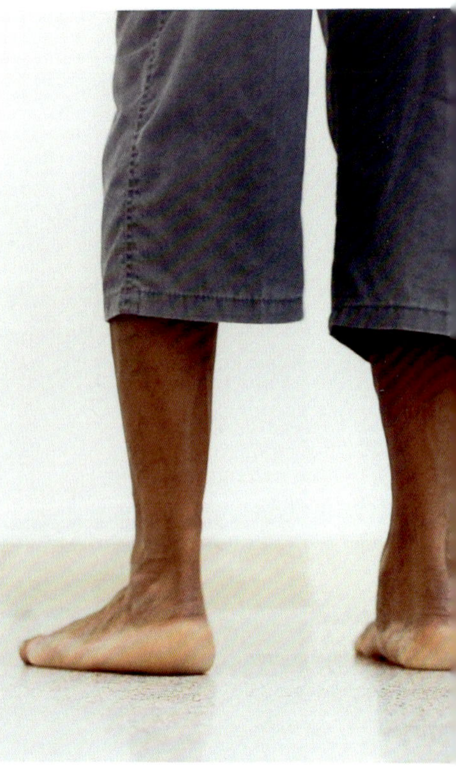

Three photographs by David Zink
Yi depict six pairs of feet, some in a state of suspension and others standing firmly
on the ground. Their magical levitations form a percussive choreography, a pause
before the crash, a break before the beat;

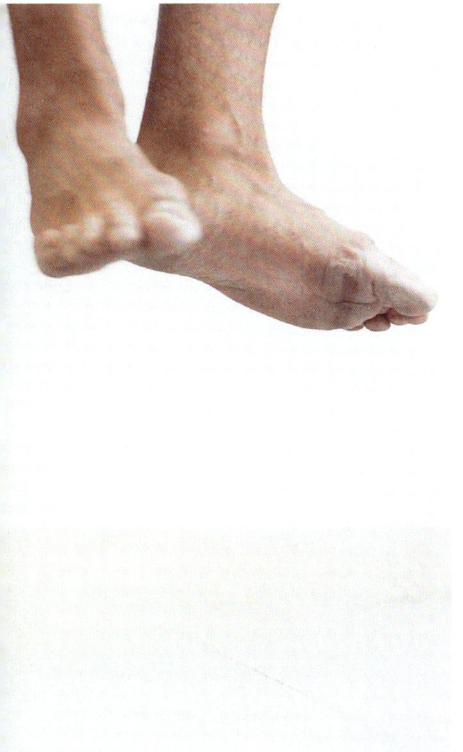

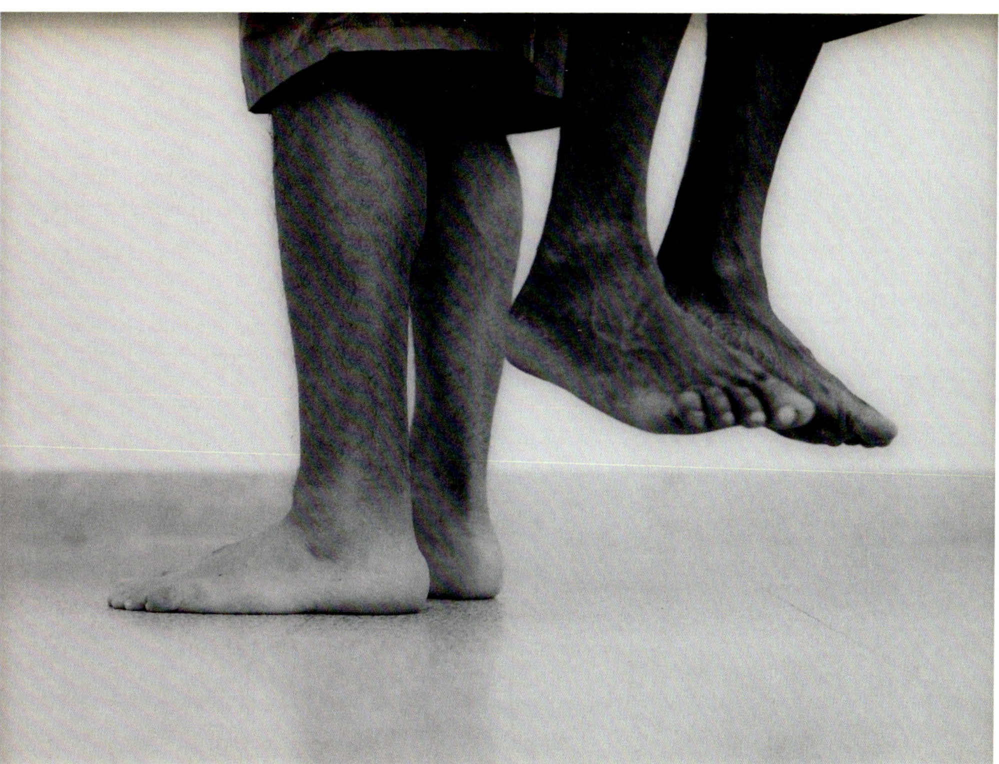

and a text piece by Consuelo Tupper Hernández
consists of an applause dictionary, unraveling some of the countless codes, assumptions,
and emotions behind what has become a near universal percussive gesture.

Applause of collective accomplishment /*n* **1** Executed within a group that has successfully completed a task or gone through a rough situation fairly unharmed. It usually has no other recipient than the people clapping, since its main objective is to reinforce the feeling of satisfaction and self-confidence built among the participants themselves. **2** The accomplishment celebrated by this applause doesn't need to be heroic or tremendously important, but rather relevant to the group's interests and needs. In this sense, and despite having subtle differences in their level of enthusiasm or conviction, these claps portray a moment of agreement and, therefore, create a strong –even if ephemeral– feeling of belonging that may attach new meaning to the situation as a whole.

Applause of collective commitment and complicity /*n* **1** Executed after a political speech, chant or slogan among supporters, usually during socio-political or cultural acts such as protests, assemblies or councils. For being a genuine and highly subjective response closely attached to the public sphere, it tends to be accompanied by both screaming and accelerated heartbeat (both expressing the emotion that comes from feeling understood by strangers). **2** Its relationship to time is rather unusual since it is executed after a certain event but, in fact, it is mainly directed towards the present (as a ratification of the collective struggles that are taking place at that moment) and the future (as an anticipation of the goal that wants to be achieved). Its nature, therefore, is primarily symbolic. **3** It constructs a deep sense of community and motivates its participants to take concrete action, sometimes effectively enough to generate a real transformation in the world beyond its physical boundaries. When this happens, its nature may change from symbolic to concrete, operating as an engine that pushes people's limits and changes non-participant's minds.

Applause of exaggerated slowness /*n* **1** This kind of applause has an interval of approximately two seconds between each clap. It is usually a solitary response to an especially poignant event or situation, although it can also be ironic and run towards something that, according to the criteria of the person performing the applause, deserves disapproval. **2** When not being ironic, this applause is rather unusual not for the strangeness of the circumstances to which it might respond, but because its excessive theatricality makes it be perceived as a parody of itself. On the other hand, when performed ironically, the line between being playful and offensive gets very thin, reason why it tends to work only in the very specific scenarios of either trustworthy friendships or open conflicts.

Applause of required repetition /*n* **1** This applause is usually responsive to a series of brief and repetitive events that occur in a limited period of time, all of which demand (either implicitly or explicitly) an applause at their end. **2** This is a kind of applause that interweaves honest responses with consensual responses, depending on the nature of each particular event and the order in which they have been experienced by the people performing the clapping. During the final repetitions, it is common to feel itching in the palms of the hands and/or fatigue in the wrists. **3** From the recipient's side, the noise of this applause usually starts feeling meaningless after several repetitions, yet a change in its volume or duration may trigger a new set of emotions despite the general weariness.

Applause of simultaneously consensual and genuine response /*n* **1** This is held at a time when applause is by consensus the most appropriate action, usually at the end of a public event, an artistic performance or a speech. **2** Although this applause mainly responds to a social convention, it coincides with the will of the people performing the clapping since they mostly consider what they just witnessed as something worthy of appreciation. **3** The volume of each clap is very important here, since it is the most effective tool for people to depict different levels of admiration towards the recipient (especially when screams might feel uncomfortable or not likely to be well received). This way, and even though the general sound tends to be homogeneous, each person involved

A film by Rose Lowder
turns a landscape of flowers swaying in the wind into a jittery vibration, as if the invisible
yet omnipresent pulsations of the earth had been unlocked and made visibly electric.
Try flipping through the next few pages very quickly, to get a sense of what I mean.

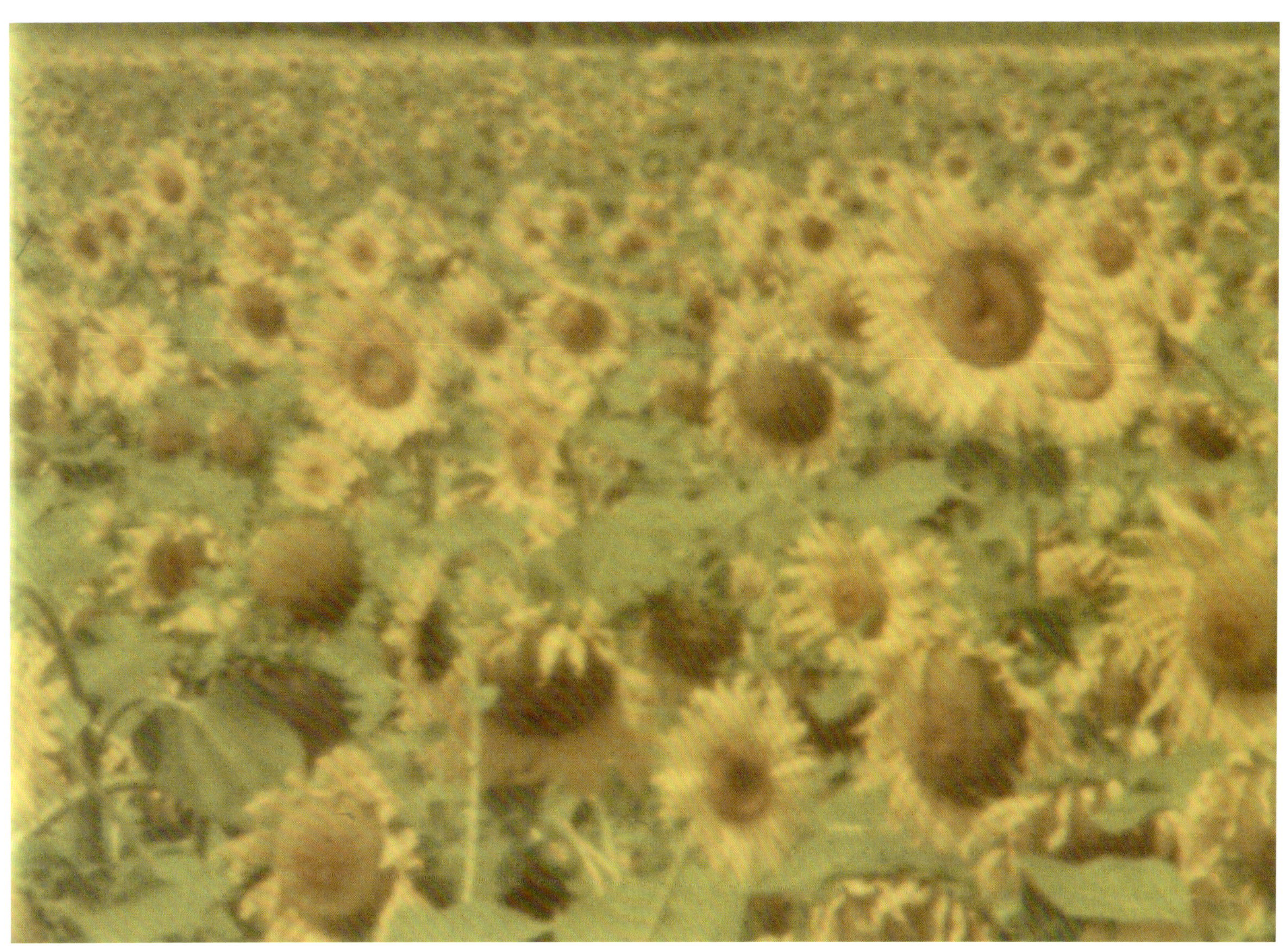

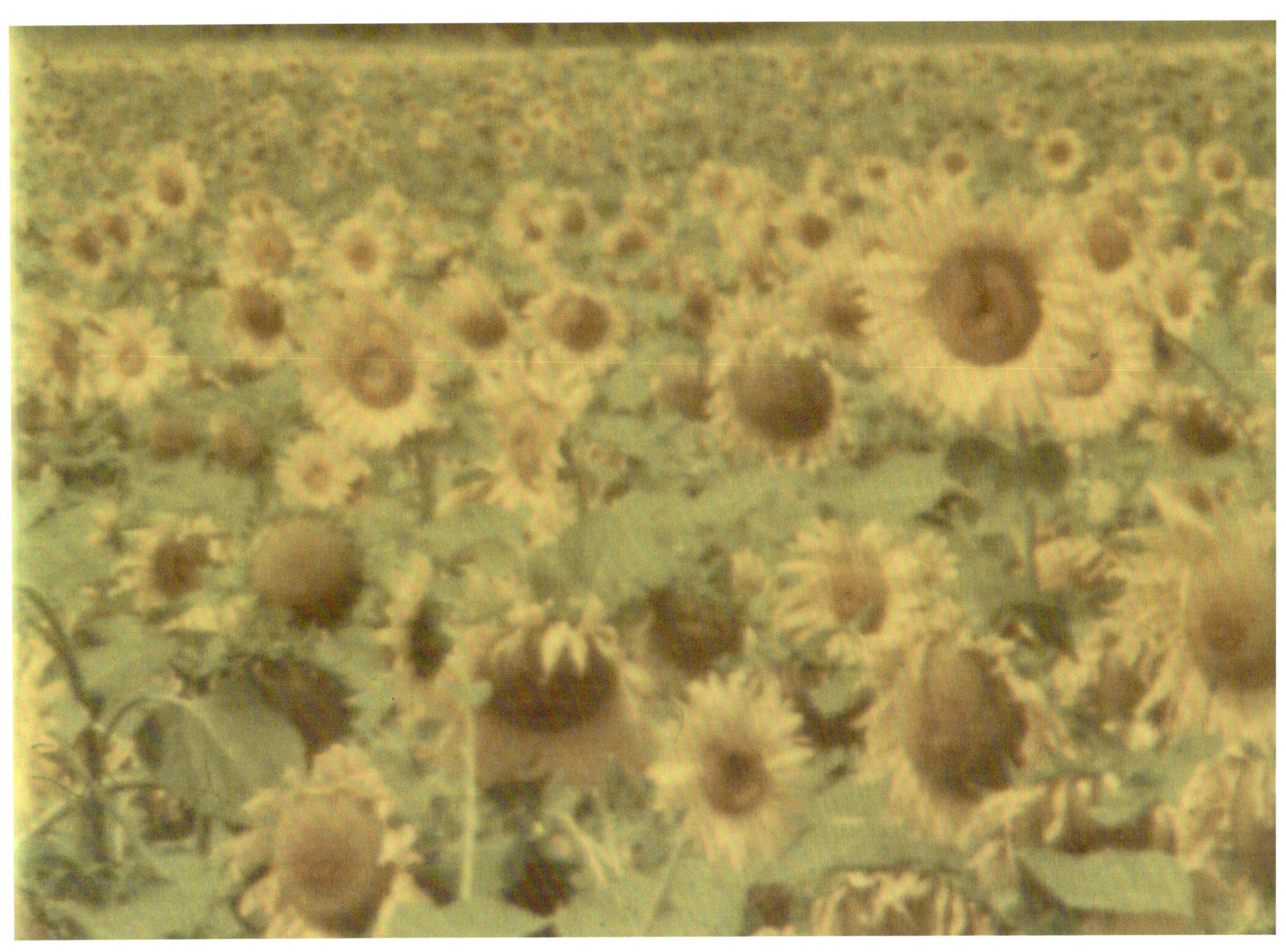

And even if none of these works make any sound or involve a drum in any way, each of
them is percussive.

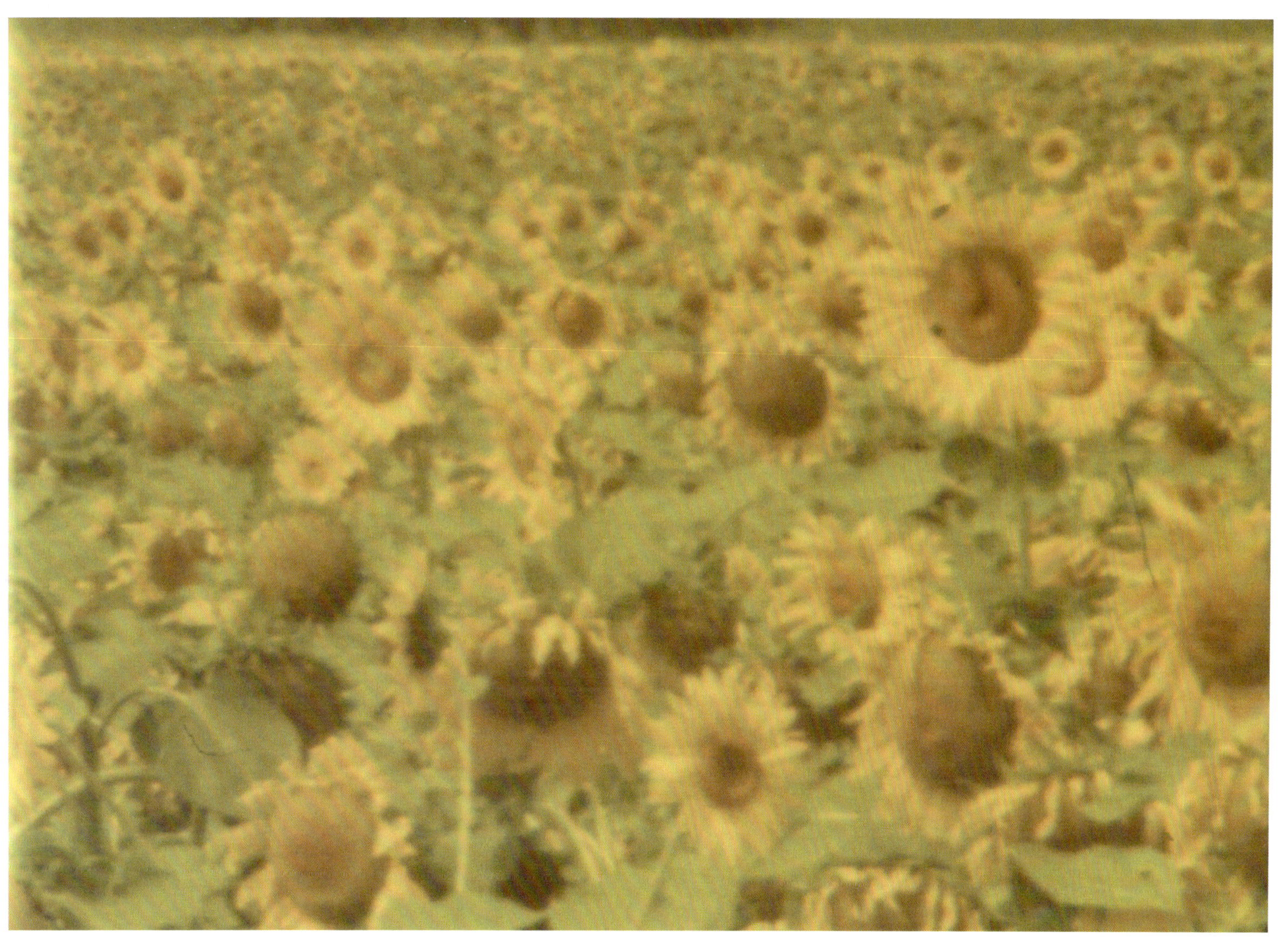

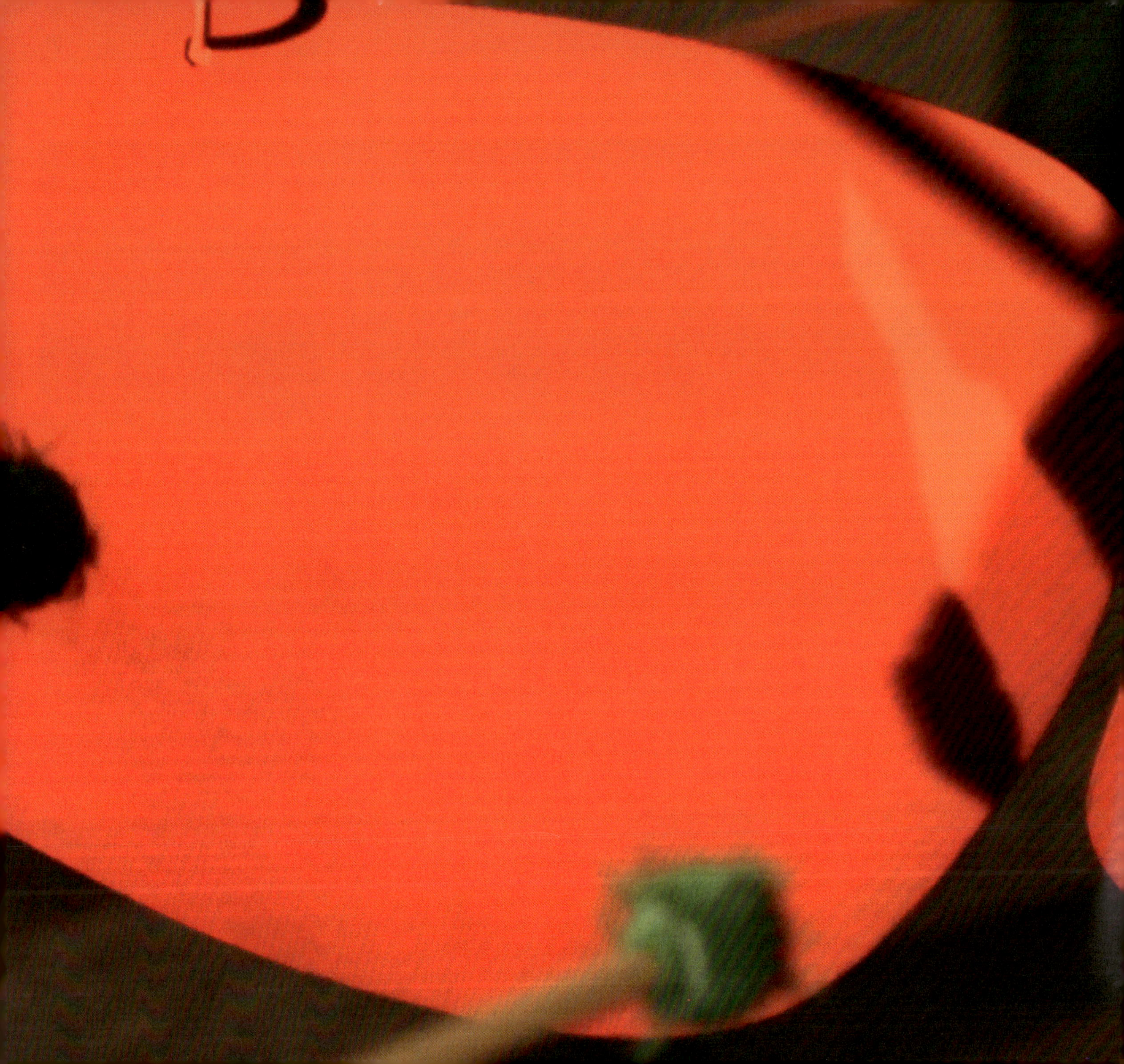

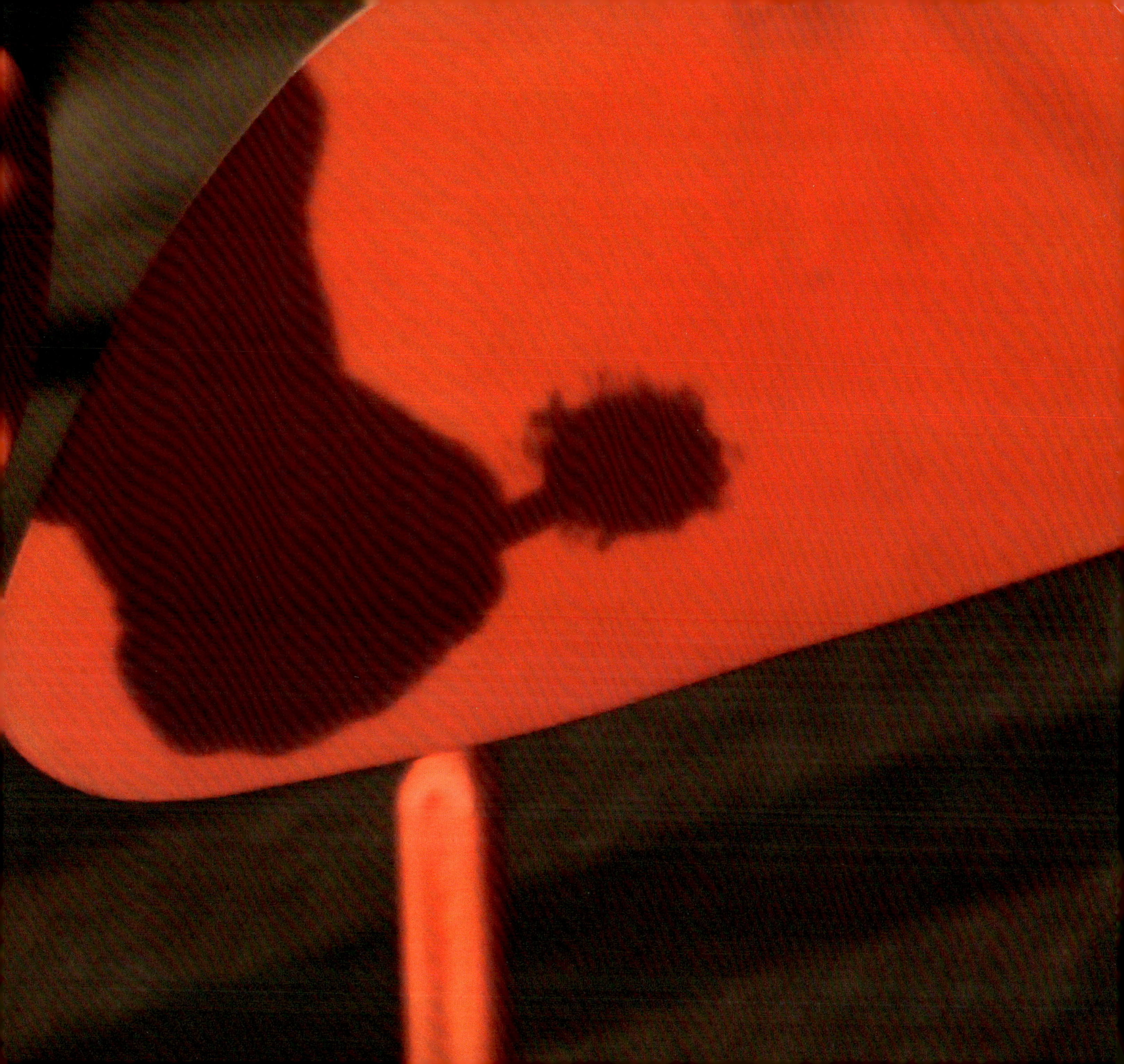

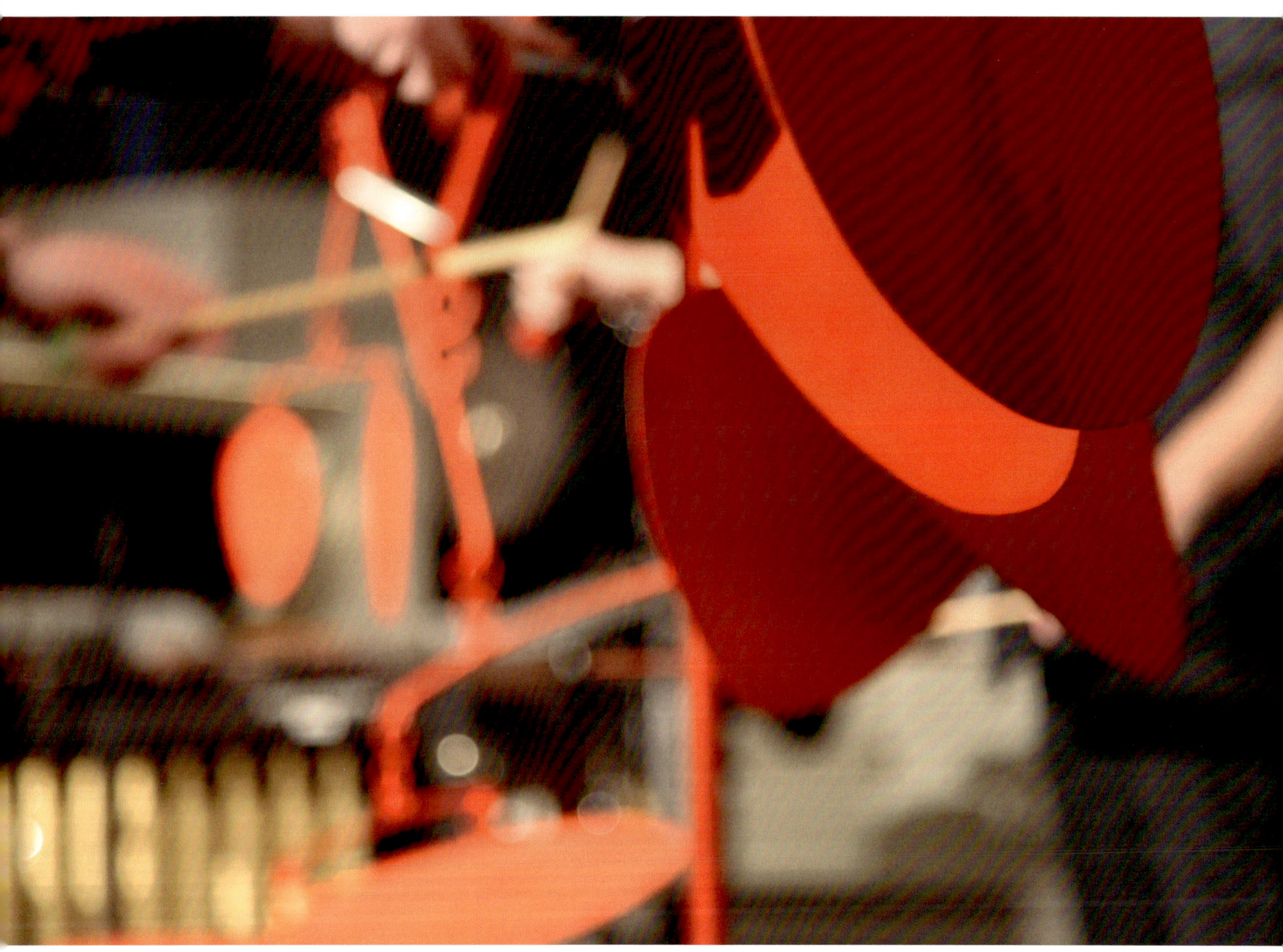

More direct links to music appear in Lucy Raven's stop-motion animation of a percussion ensemble that uses an Alexander Calder mobile as its instrument to play a graphic score by Earle Brown,

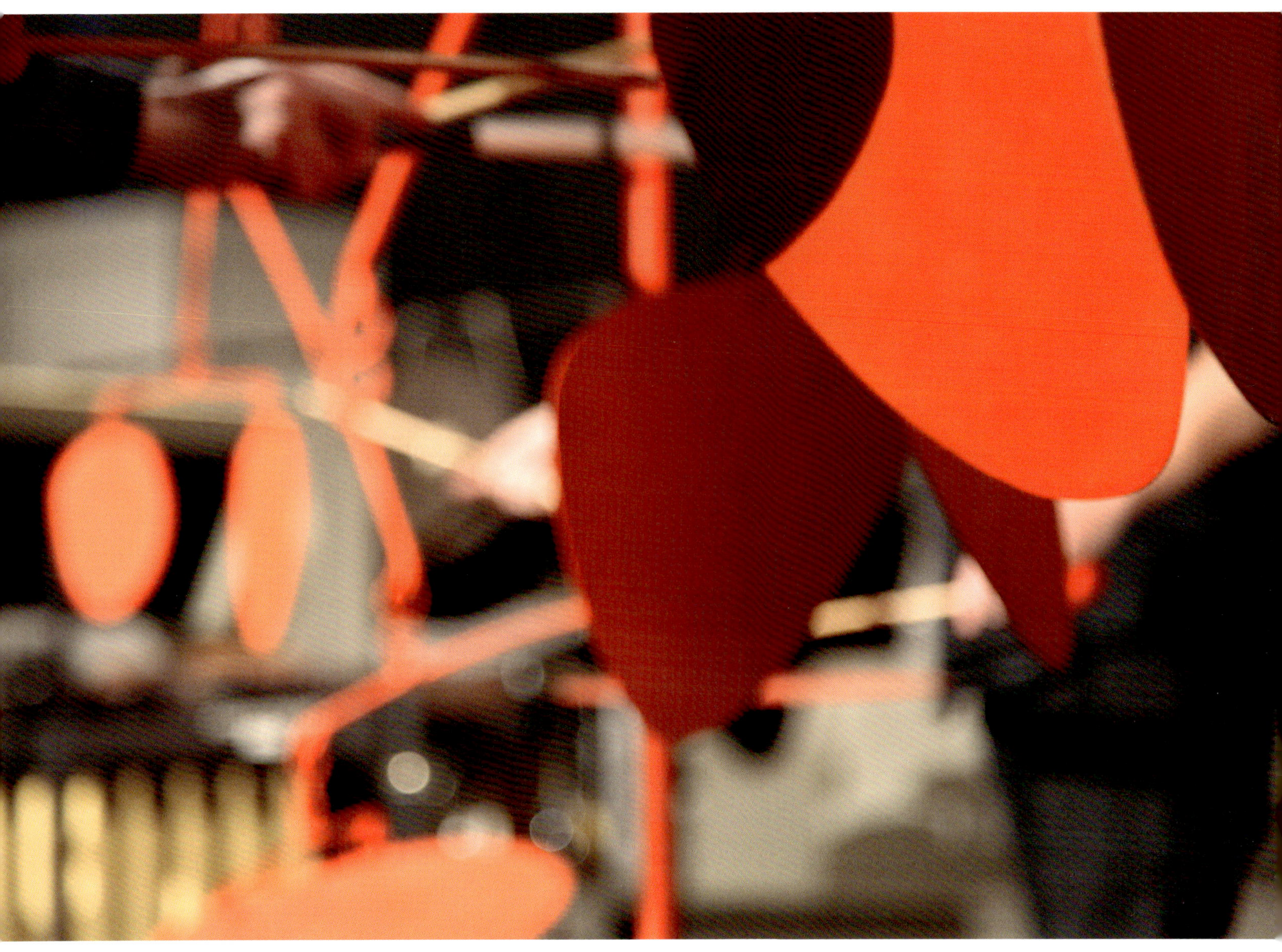

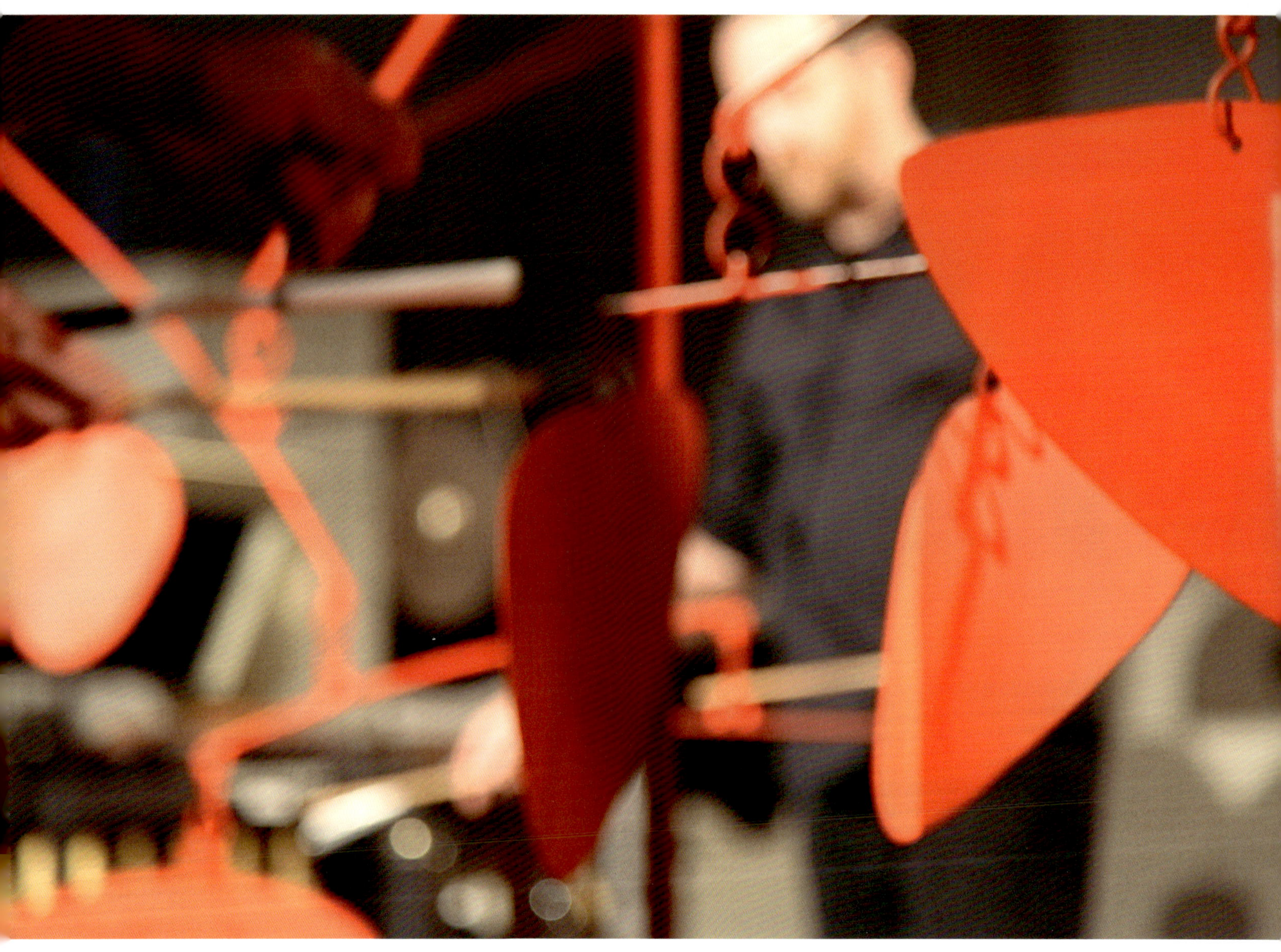

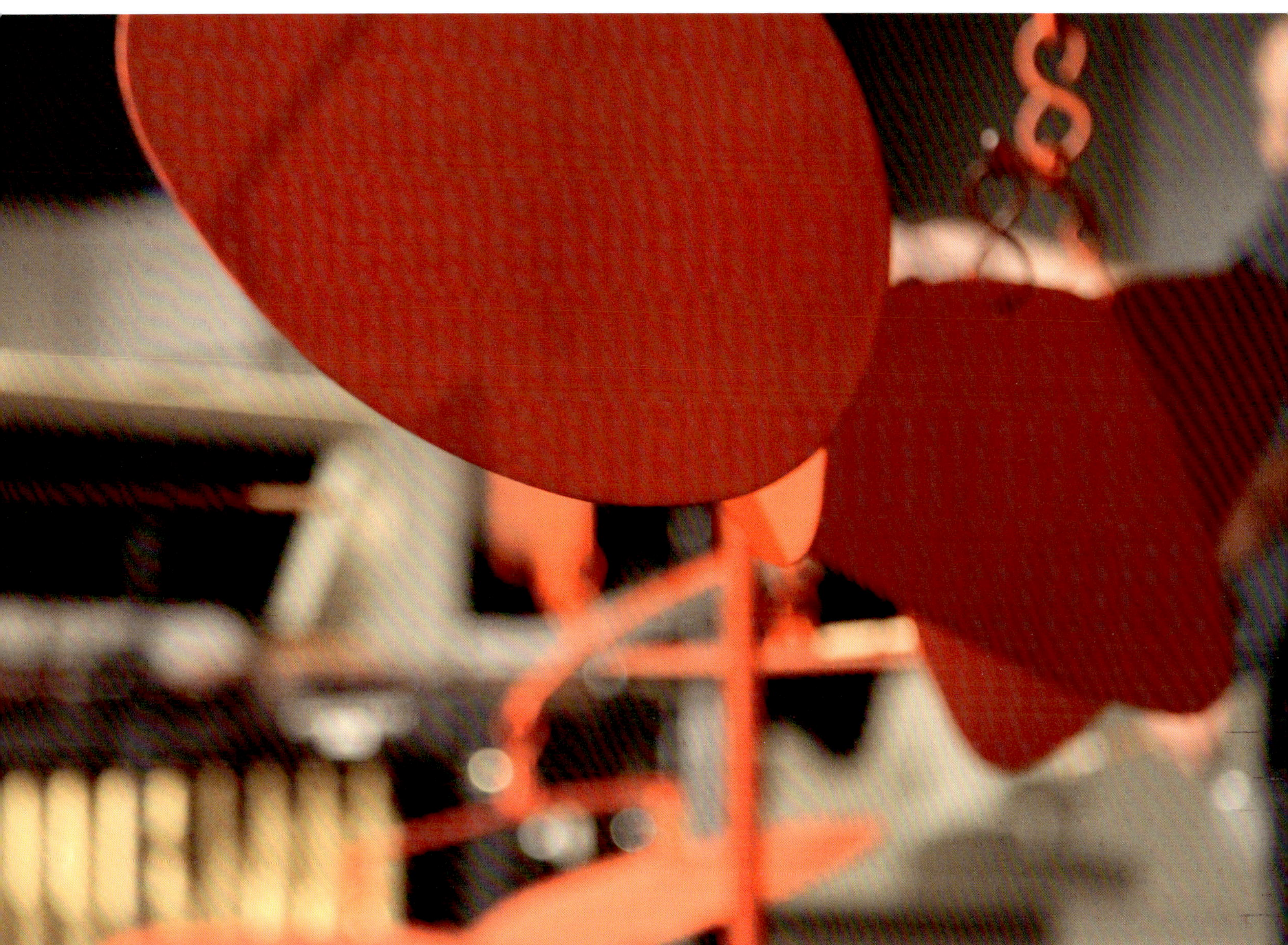

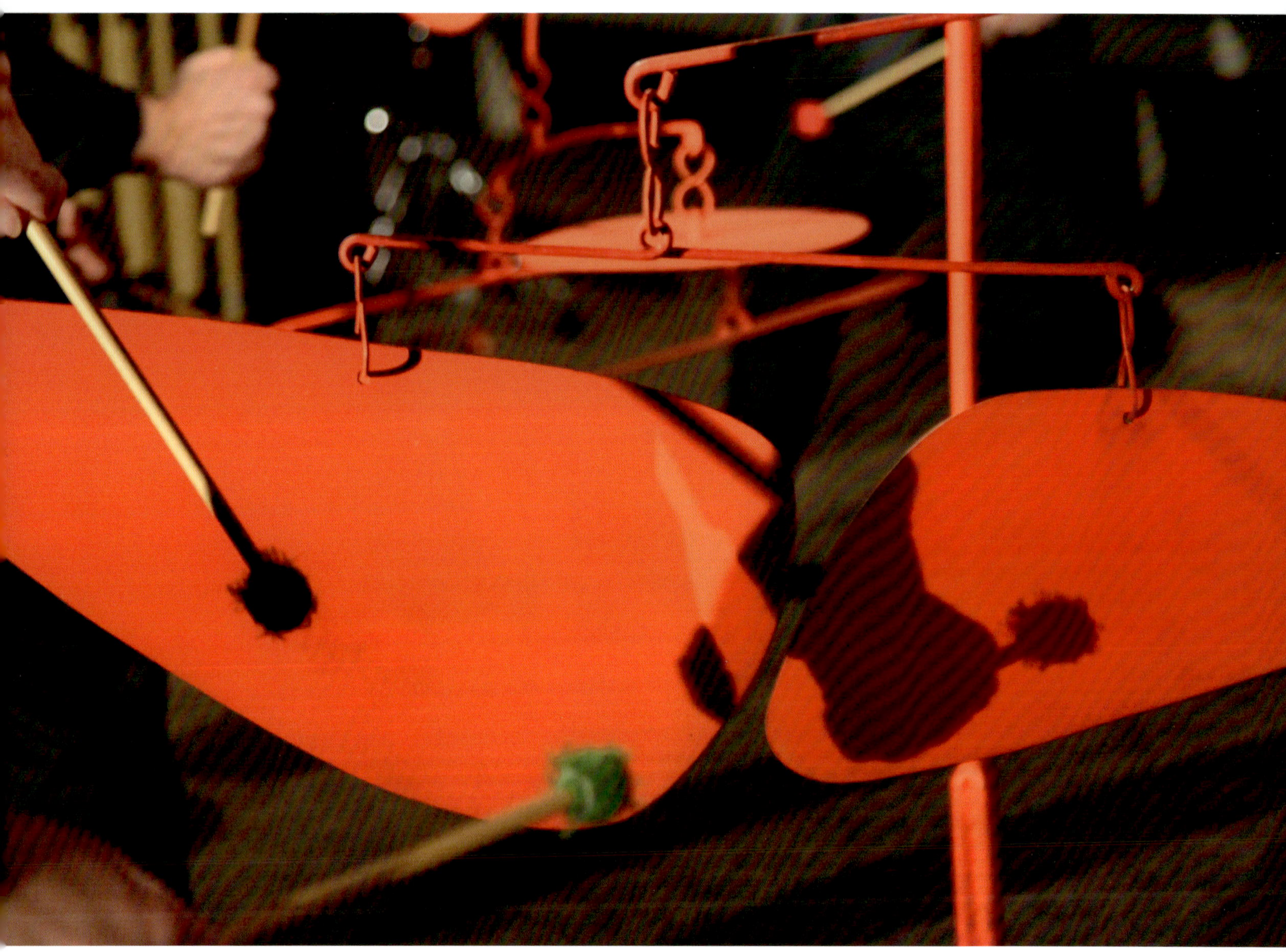

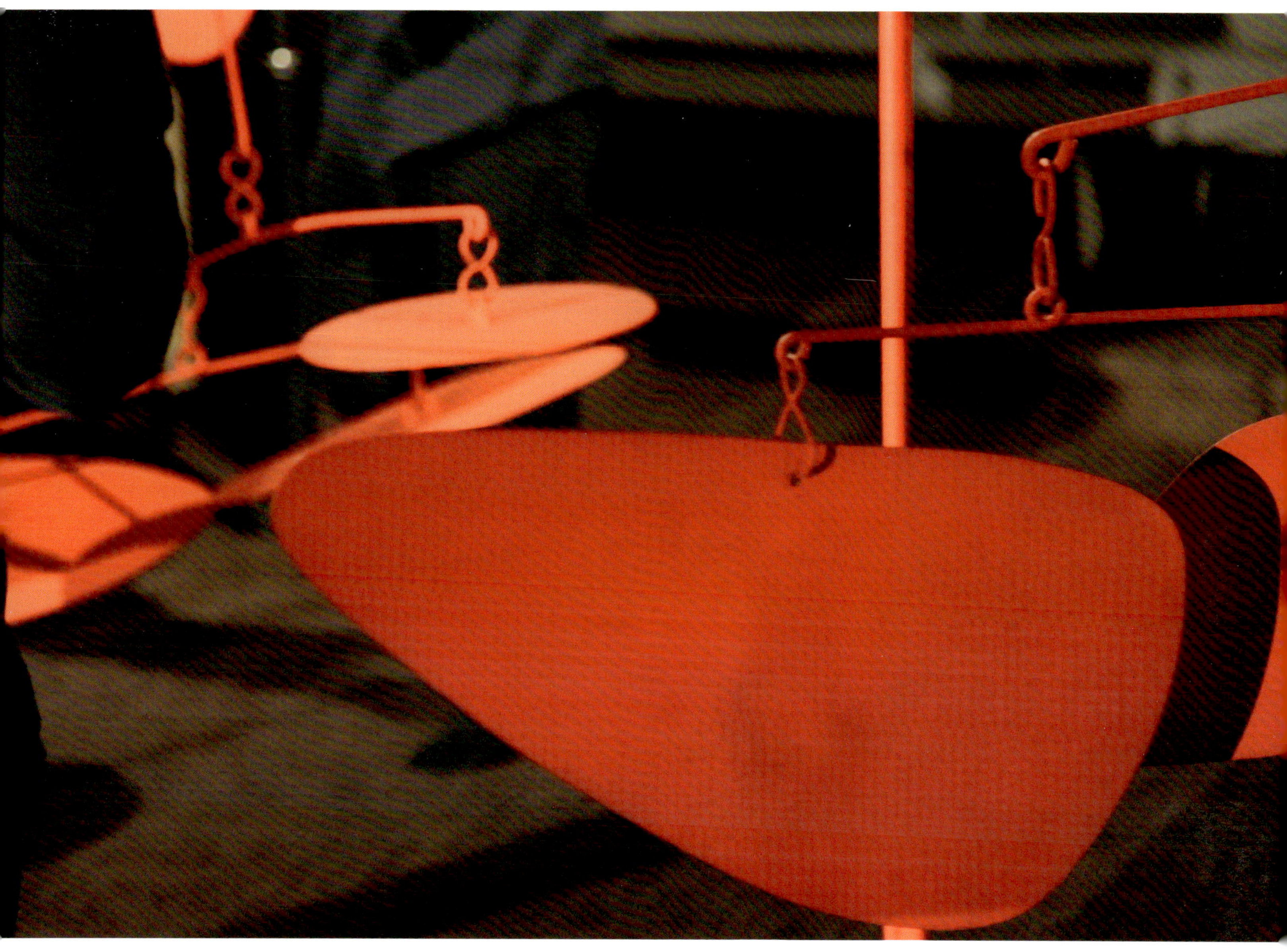

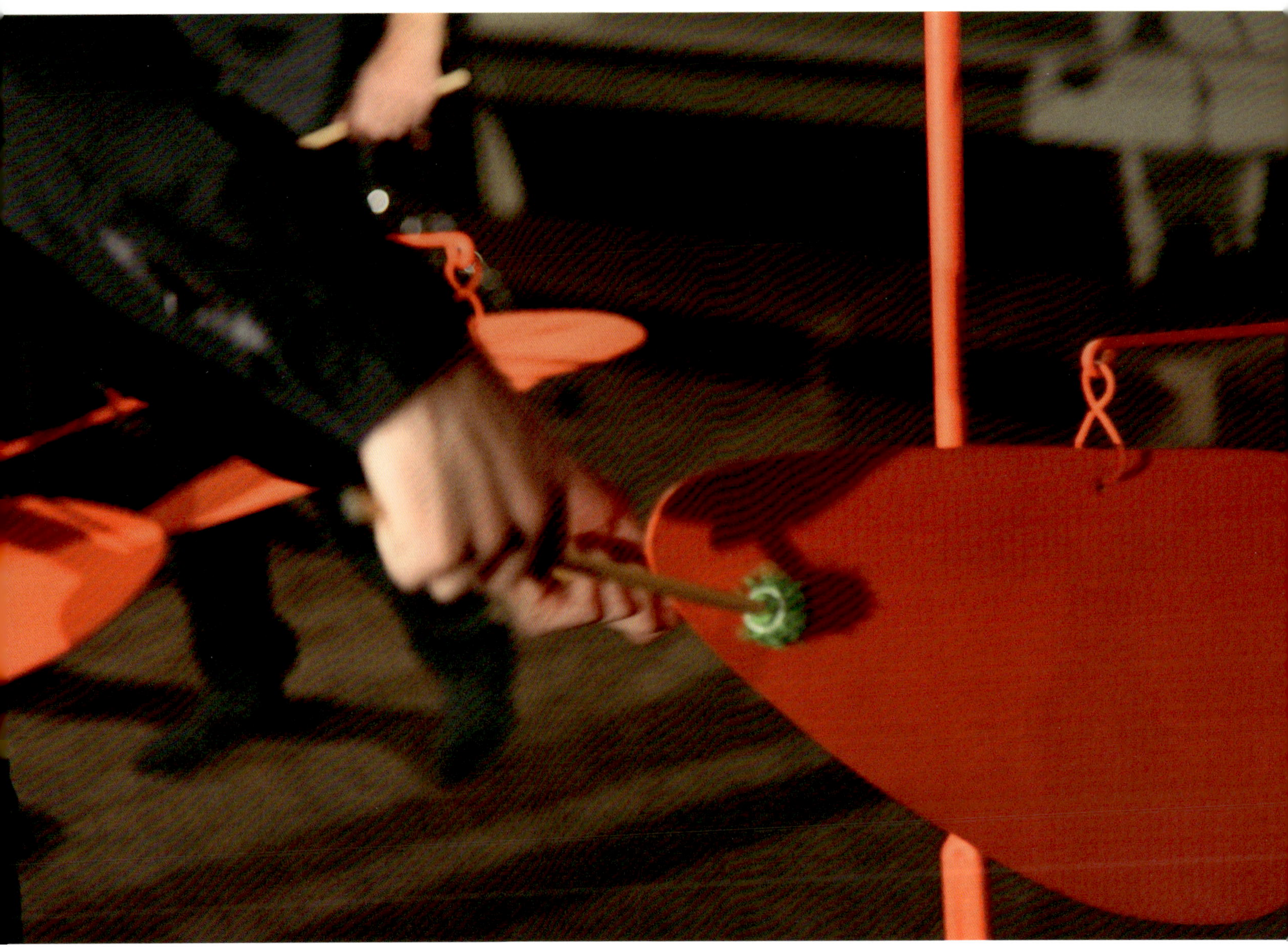

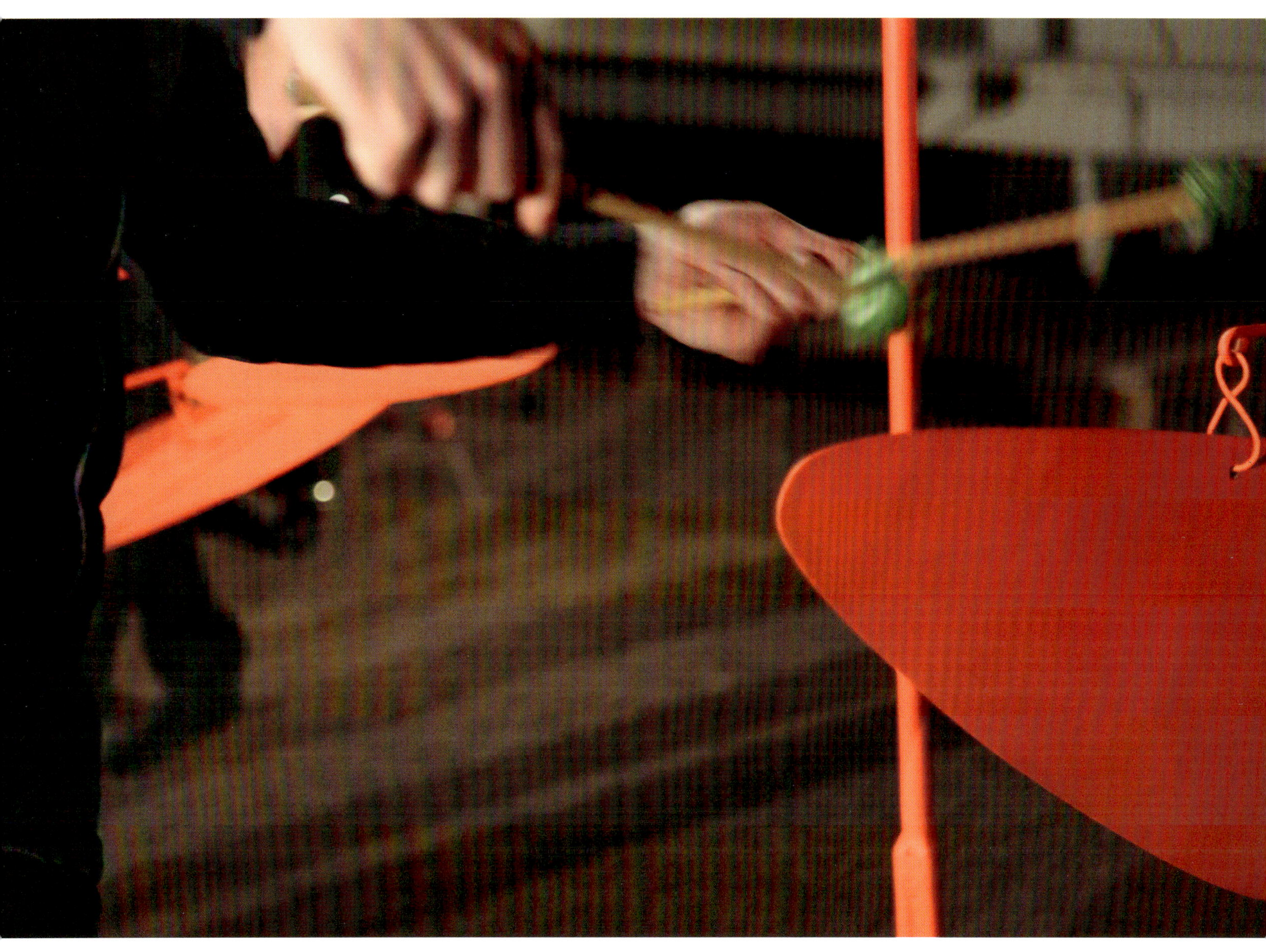

in the video *Gone are the Days of Shelter and Martyr*, where Theaster Gates, along with his ensemble the Black Monks, roams around a debris-filled church, lifting heavy doors found on the ground amid the rubble, flipping them over and over in a series of crashing slams,

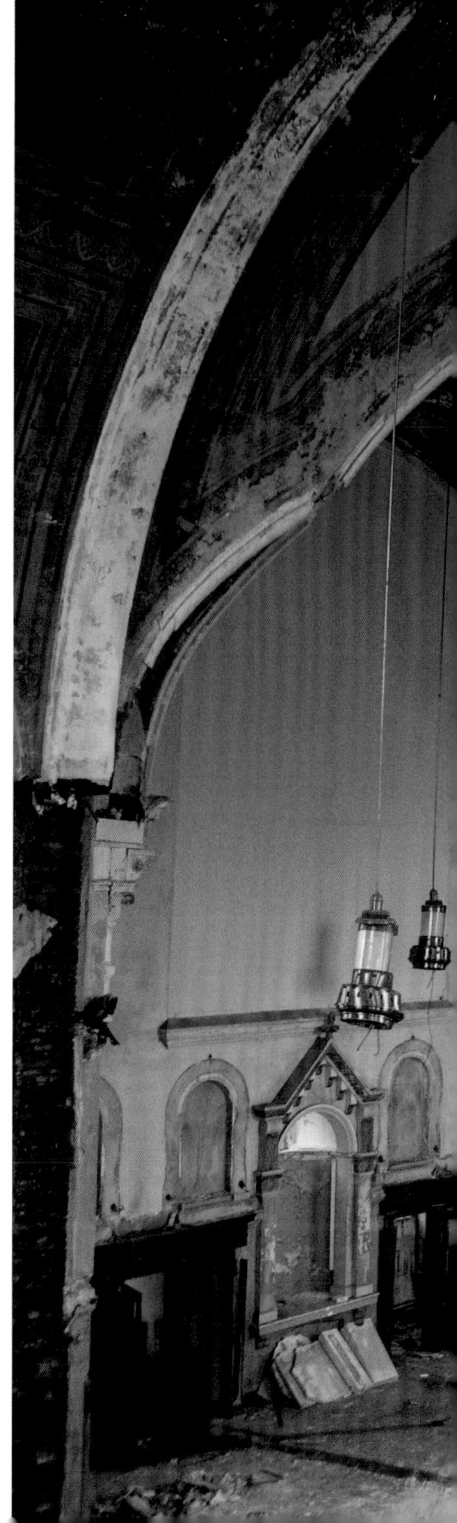

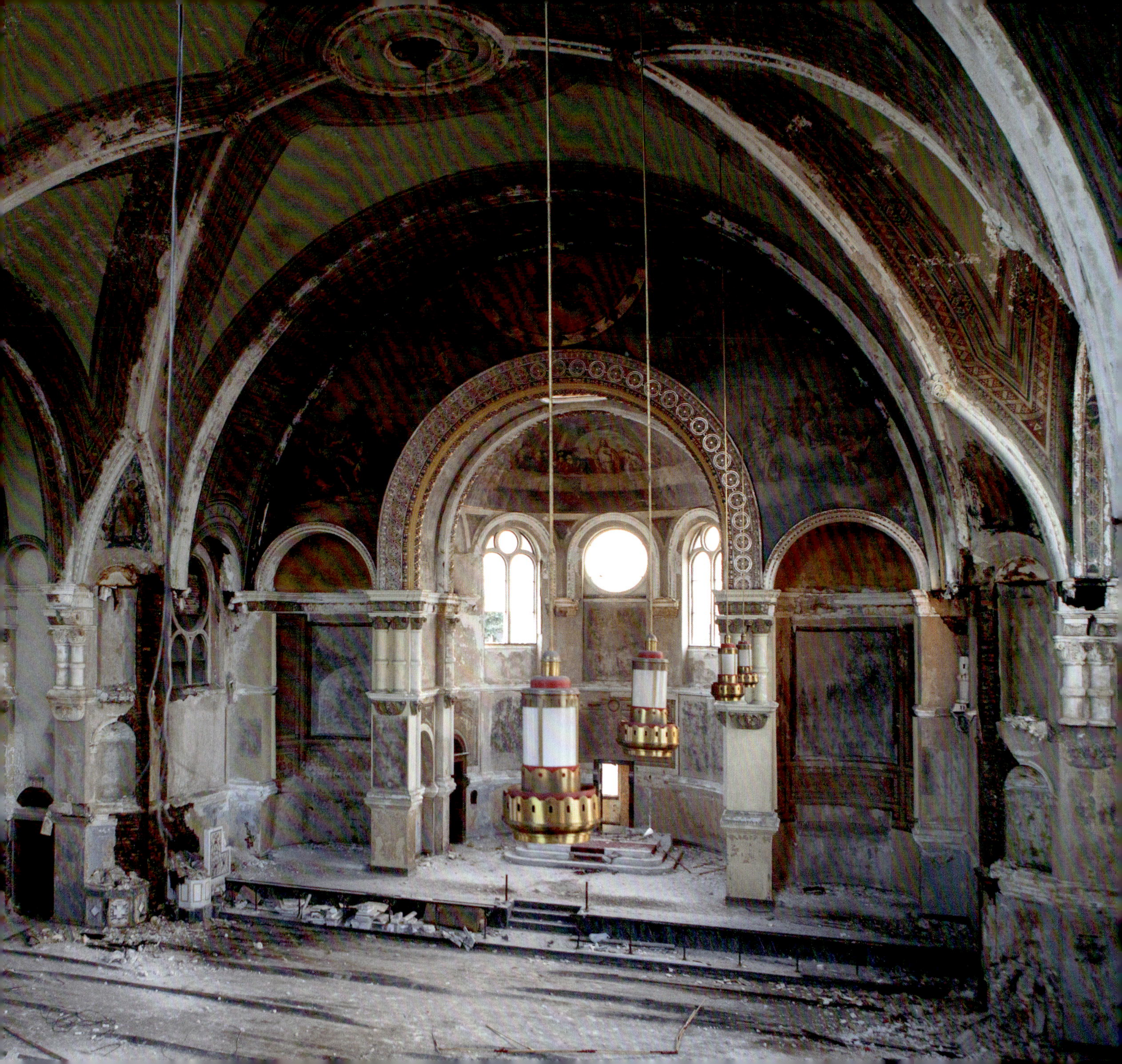

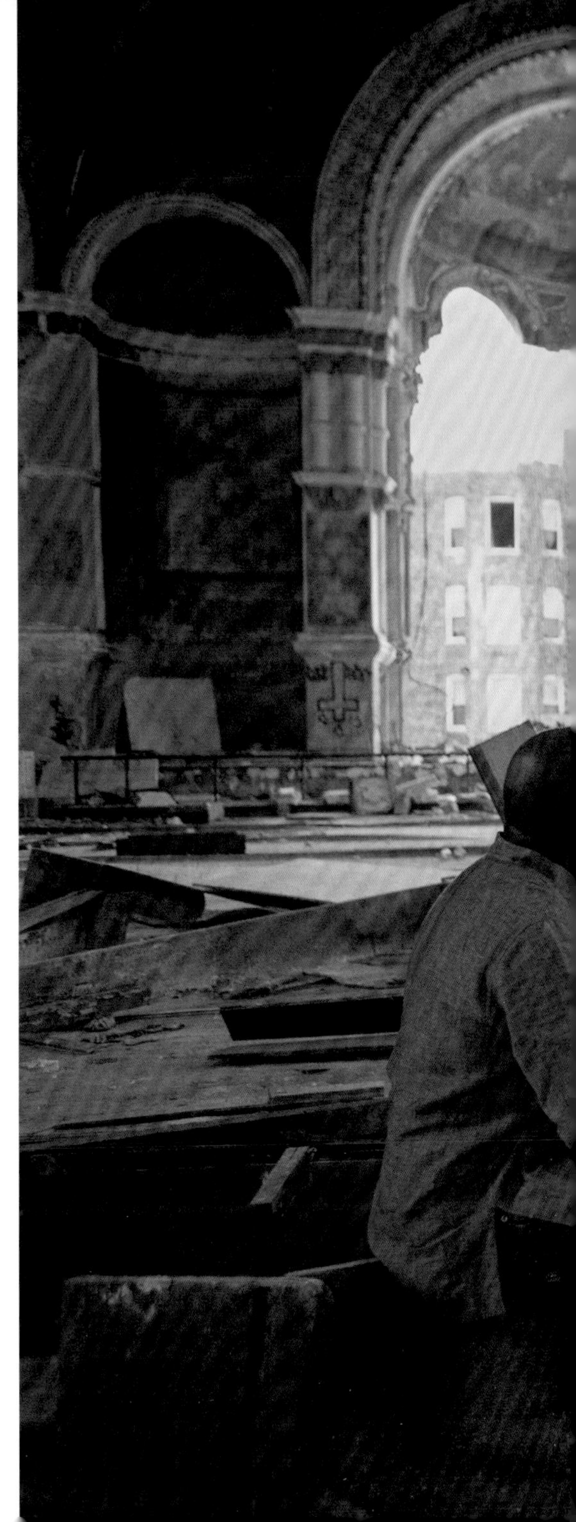

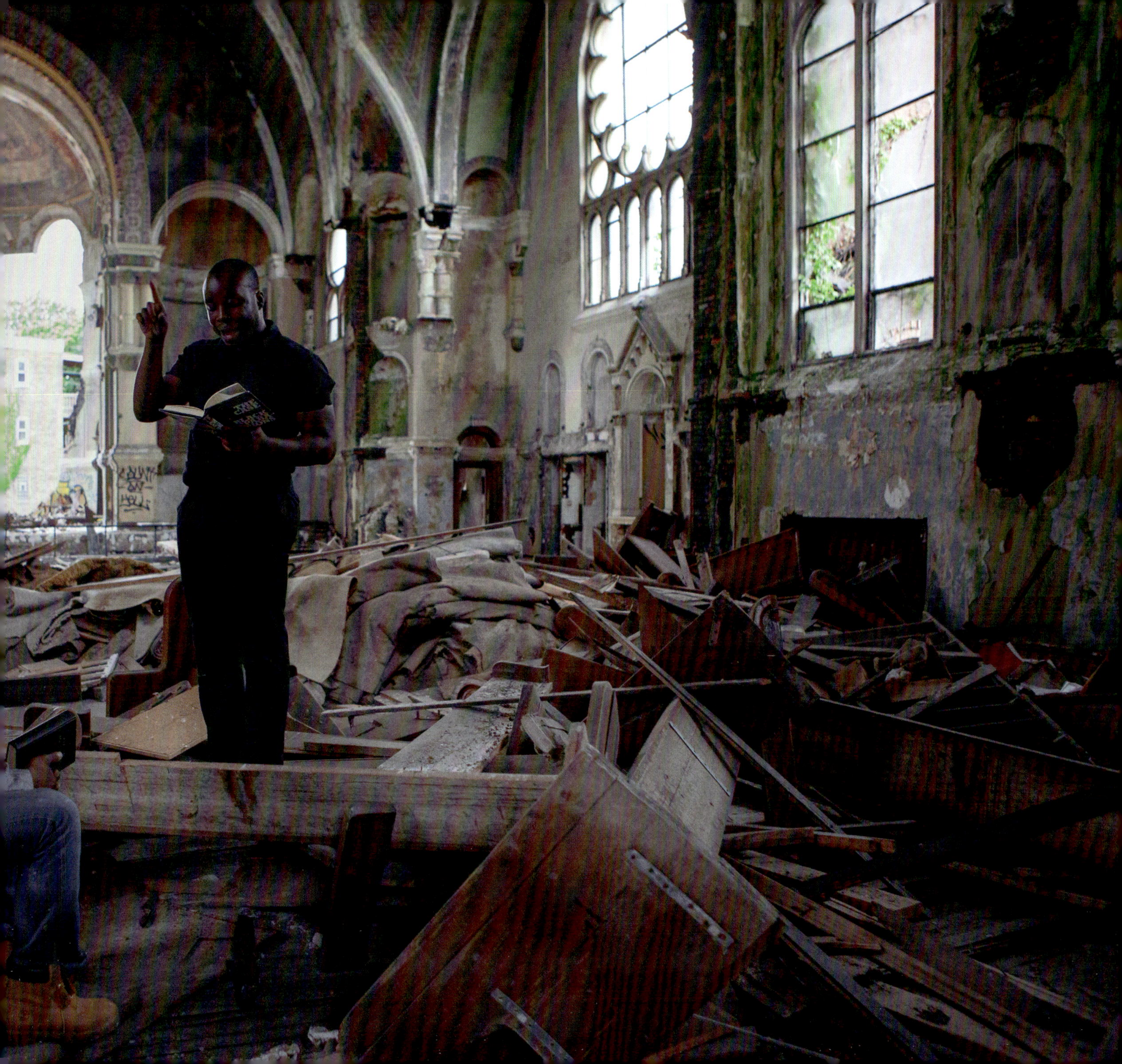

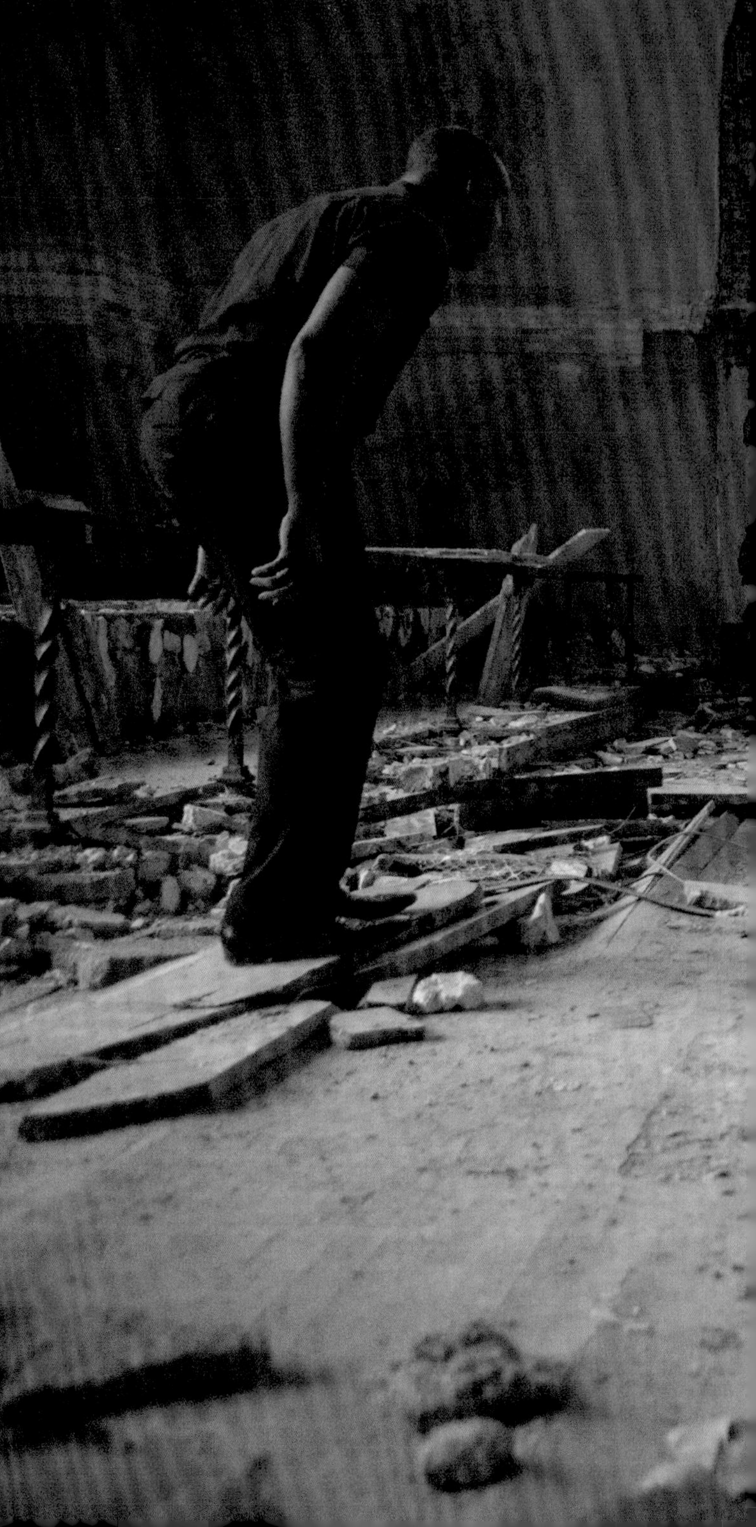

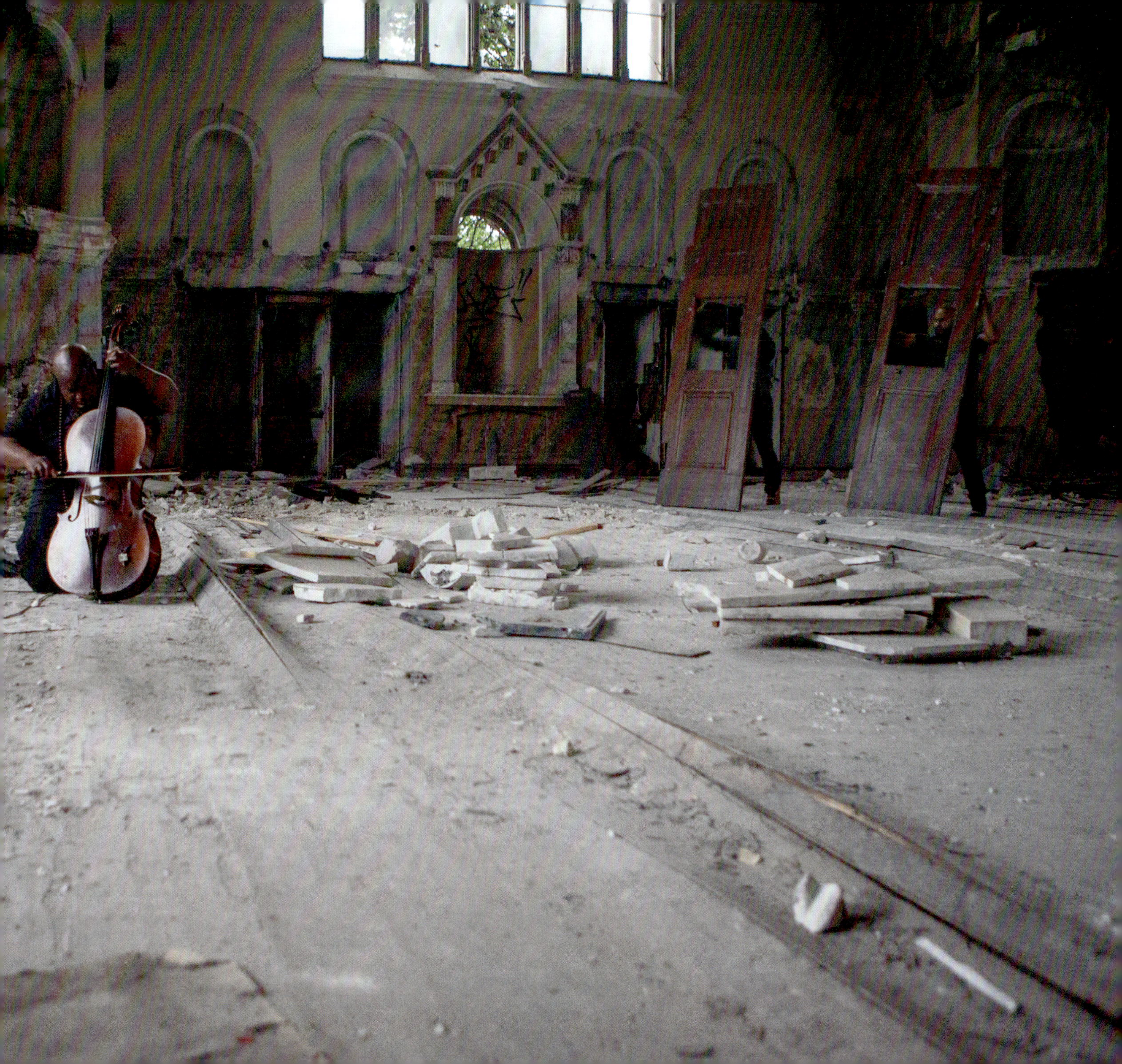

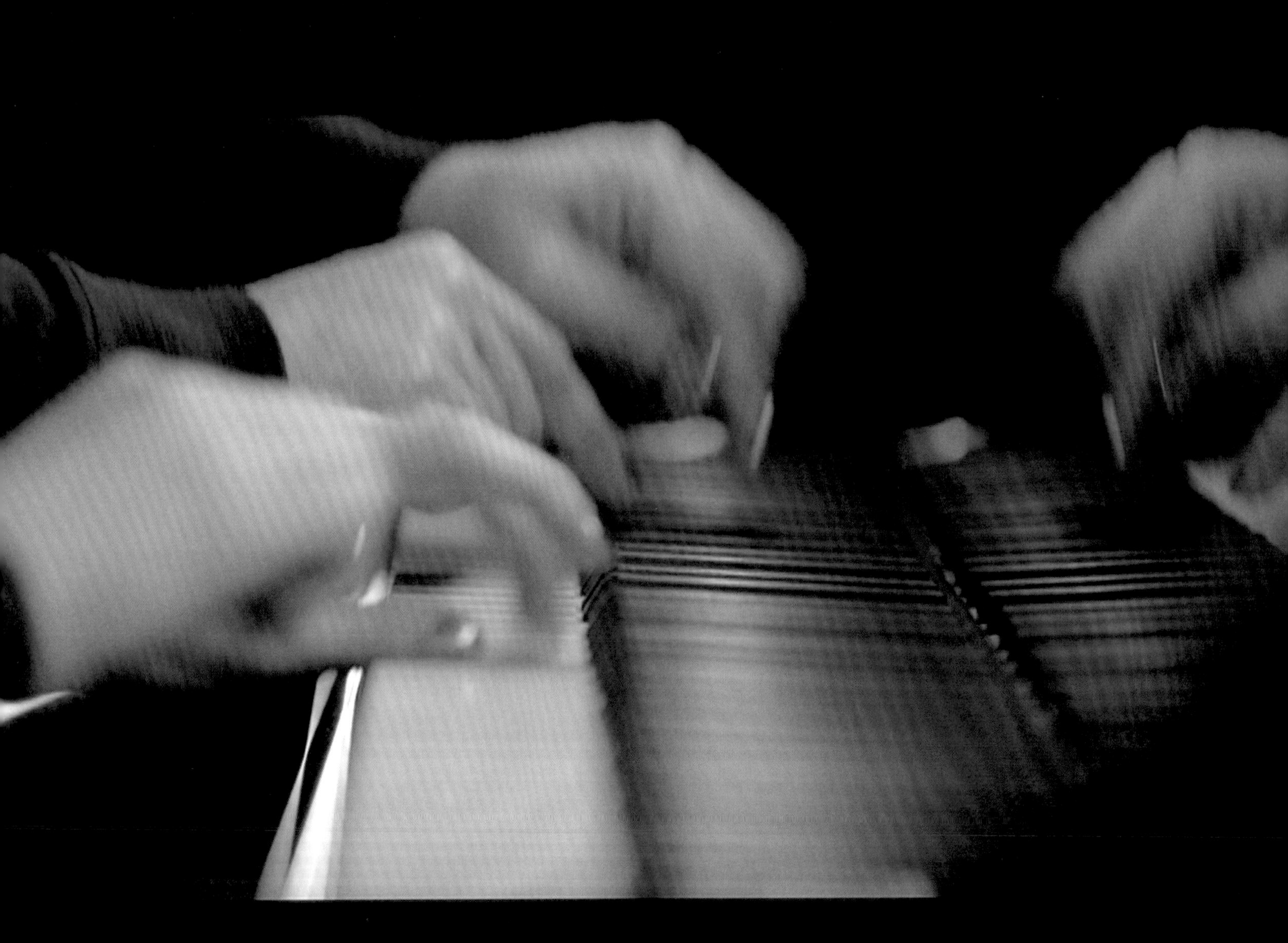

TEMPO

TEMPO

TEMPO

TEMPO

TEMPO

TEMPO

TEMPO

TEMPO

TEMPO

TEMPO

TEMPO

TEMPO

TEMPO

TEMPO

TEMPO

TEMPO

TEMPO

TEMPO

TEMPO

LÊ QUAN
NINH

LÊ QUAN
NINH

LÊ QUAN
NINH

LÊ QUAN
NINH

LÊ QUAN
NINH

LÊ QUAN

More than twenty years ago, I was setting up my instrumentarium on the first day of rehearsal for a new project when the drummer Jean-Pierre Arnoux (1946–2002) asked me: "Are you more *tempo* or more *ambiance*?" Not knowing how to answer, I just kept working until Arnoux, observing my equipment, declared: "Ambiance!" Today this anecdote lives on as a joke shared between me and the saxophonist Michel Doneda, another participant in the project. But despite its broadly generalizing binarism, the question had been introduced: *tempo* or *ambiance*? Did these two concepts have to be separated by an exclusionary *or*? Did they originate in two different chapters of a theory of music previously unknown to me? Back then I could not imagine giving two different names to terms that seemed to belong to a single gesture. Nor could I imagine that a strict distinction could be maintained between the brusque antonyms of *tempo* and *ambiance*, as though definitively naming two antagonistic visions of the function of the percussionist within a band without allowing for other alternatives.

But perhaps Arnoux's question articulated a concern I still have today, namely: to discover a musical practice that would relinquish both *tempo* and *ambiance*, as if to return to a personal origin where sonic activity is not yet lexically dispersed.

If *tempo* is synonymous with *beat*, then perhaps to relinquish *tempo* is to relinquish music itself, for the musical beat has primacy everywhere in the world. This smallest common denominator, exerting the least possible energy, attests to our need for order in the elastic sensation of time, permitting us to organize different speeds specific not only to daily tasks, but also to each individual's different characteristics. Music, according to this shared metric, would allow for the construction of a world that is at last regulated, where what happens happens *in time* and not in unpredictable ways.

Walking has a steady pace, which is necessary for economically covering long distances. If the *tempo* of walking was instead incessantly changeable, we'd expend energy that would lead to great physical fatigue: change is energy, as the physical sciences teach us. Thus *tempo* as regular beat provides a stable foundation that permits all kinds of events to occur, from the simplest to the most complex. *Tempo* reassures us of time's flow and direction, creating a kind of common ground underneath the innumerable rhythms and diverse velocities of daily life. Add frequency to the equation, and we find ourselves completely satisfied in our need to measure and circumscribe the flux of circumstances that follow so many vanishing points and incomprehensible paths.

Yet we could dedicate ourselves to a musical practice that would forget this common ground, forgo the shared beat on which sound material is established, in order to devote ourselves to the material of sound itself. Once freed from the duty of meter and of maintaining the instruments' consistent action, I realize the degree to which that action is voluntary and external to their resonance, imposing—through intervals of time—an order that doesn't inherently belong to instruments or to their breathing. What happens if I refuse the authority of this imposition? To make space instead for careful listening to the vibrations that are present? What I discover then are fluctuations that may be untimely and chaotic but nevertheless reveal much about the nature of sound. Where sound material indicates its own velocities, I find no measure. What is alive in sound manifests constantly, as unstable as a profound and unexpected trembling. From there, I easily slide toward relinquishing all measure, accepting chaos as it is, whereupon I must situate myself on the crest between the desire for music and abandonment to the sonic. *Tempo* is no longer a need or even a necessity: before *tempo*, there is so much to hear.

But this contemplation is indissociable from action. I must also render the action as inoffensive as possible, deploy it without exaggerating its deployment, and accompany its movement without guiding it. The engagement is not so much in the action but rather in what I perceive in the traversing of the moment—a moment that is no longer regulated by a fixed temporal frame but a return to the very origin of the sonic, before the beating of the first heart.

In this oscillation between action and contemplation, I can consider *tempo* not as the inevitable foundation of music in its ensemble, but as an object, a correlated part that can reappear as fragments, like so many neutral objects issuing from an ephemeral music theory whose necessity is annulled as soon as it is applied. *Tempo* appears as an element taking place in a space through the intervention of a non-dominating form of will among all other forms of will and abandonment, allowing for both sudden relief and the possibility of assuming different positions in the sonic landscape. The fragment is recognized as such: not as an obligation but as information, offered up with eyes wide open.

In the end, what occurs is only a change in regime: from immobility to a frantic race, many possible instantaneities of contingent and simultaneous velocities. If its reality will survive, *tempo* must see itself as an alternation between observation and non-observation, attention and inattention, but also between the capacity to follow the movements of sonorous material and what that material produces in a space and the desire to follow an idea.

There are so many possible *tempi* that
there is no longer any *tempo*: proximity
with sonorous material paradoxically
creates a distance from which it is no
longer possible to clearly distinguish all
the velocities you confront.

What are the consequences of an attitude that refuses the offer of stability?
Does the renunciation of what seems to
belong to the human condition and to
human culture make another aesthetic
spontaneously appear? How to envision
the unpredictable at the very heart of the
unpredictability of sonorous material
when it is no longer subjected to time's
simplified measure? And further, how
to make each sonorous object legible in
its particular chaos? Such are the ques-
tions that call for discipline—and play.

As for *ambiance*, that's another subject
entirely …

*Lê Quan Ninh is a classically trained
percussionist based in Paris who has
been active since the early 1980s in
the field of contemporary music interpretation and free improvisation.*

Translated by Youna Kwak.

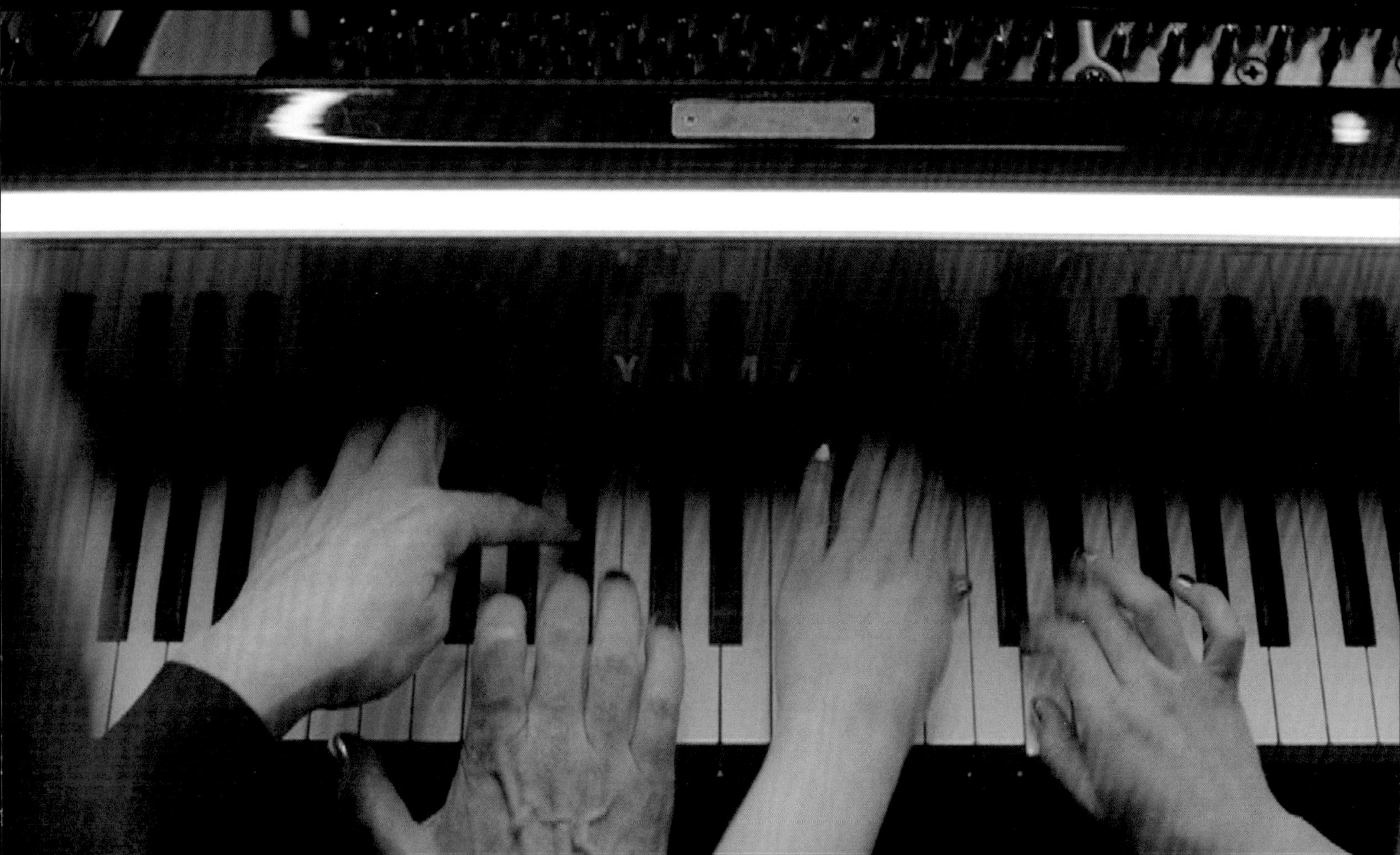

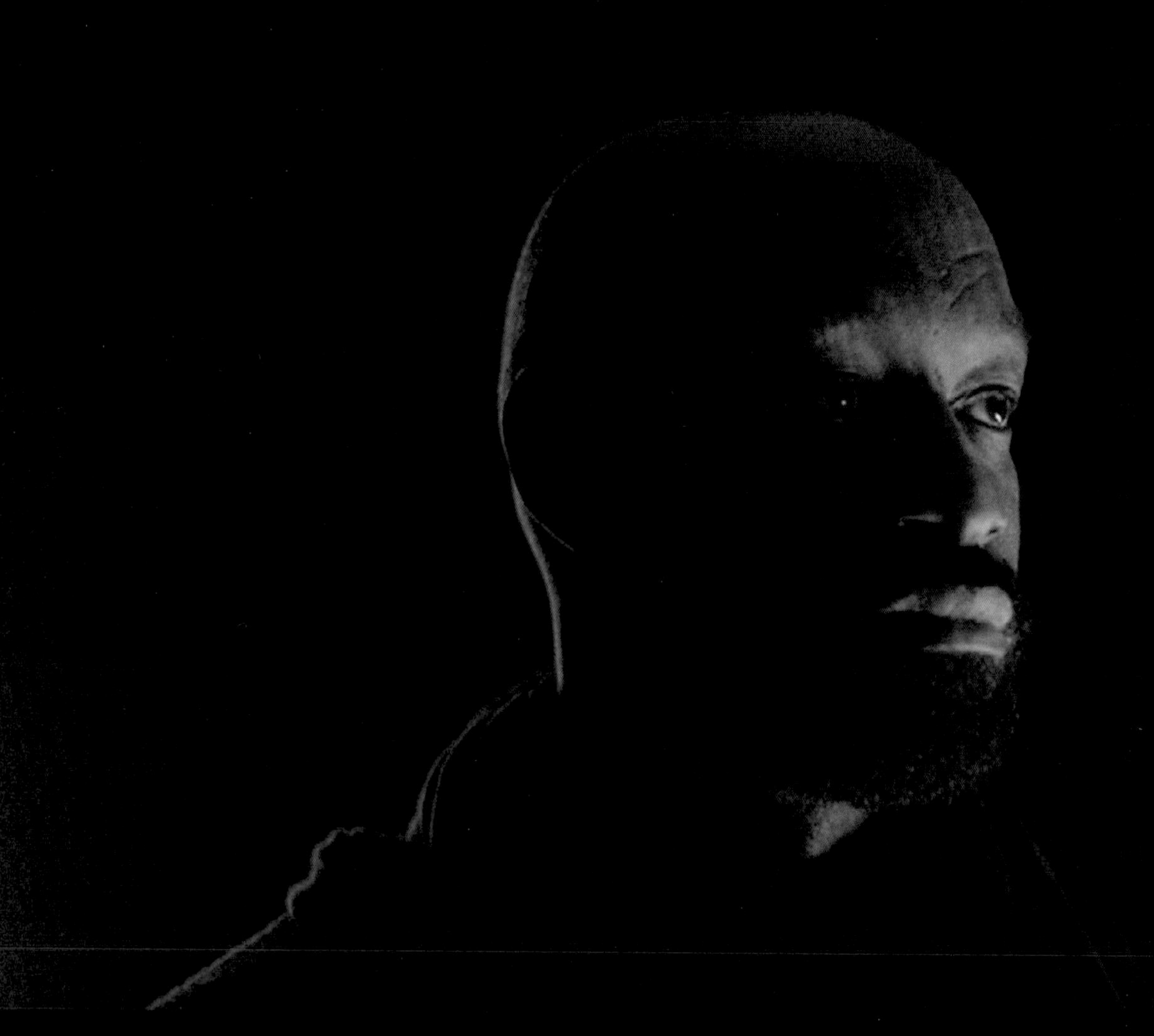

or in The Otolith Group's filmed staging of Julius Eastman's militant minimalism, via a piano's "88 drums."

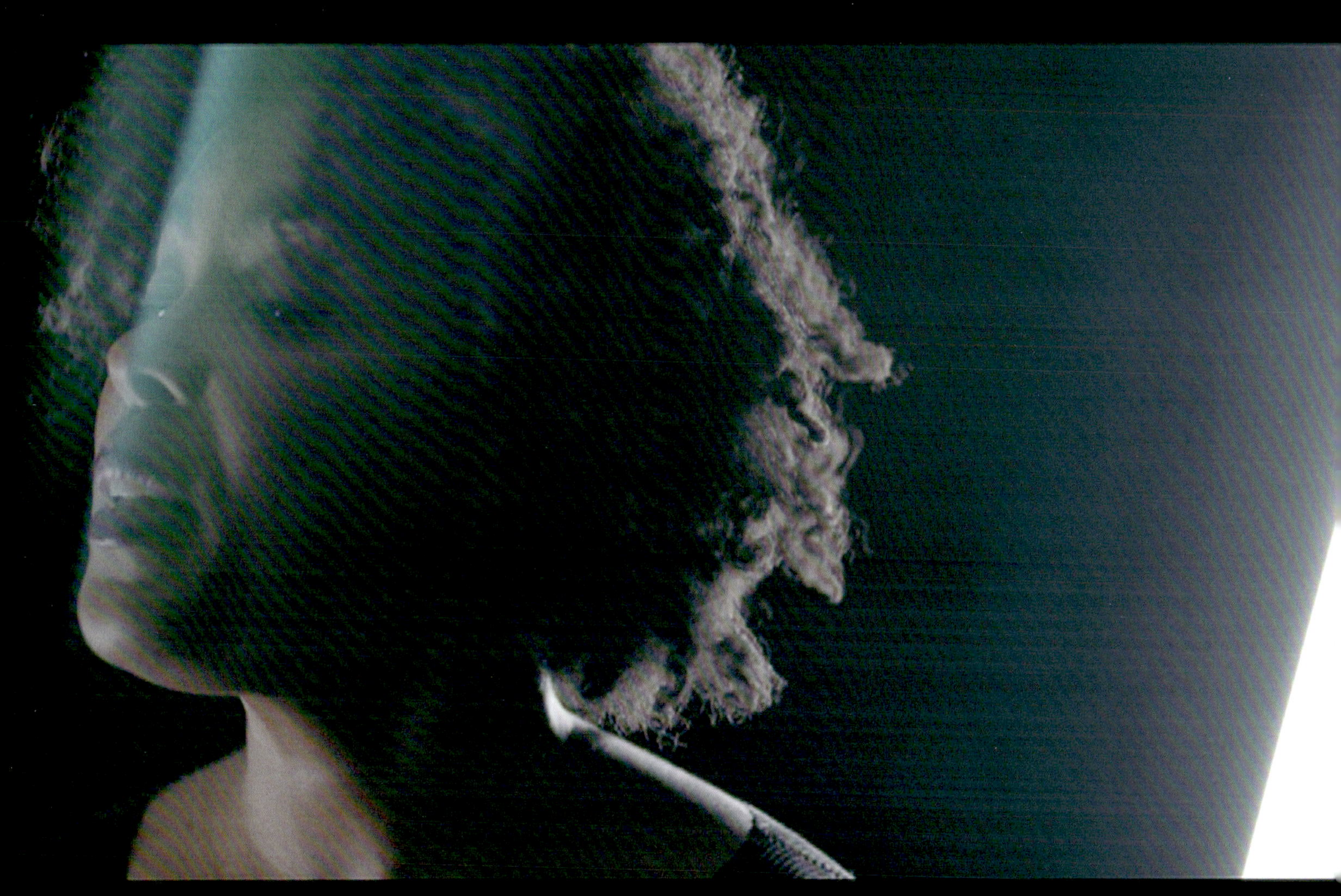

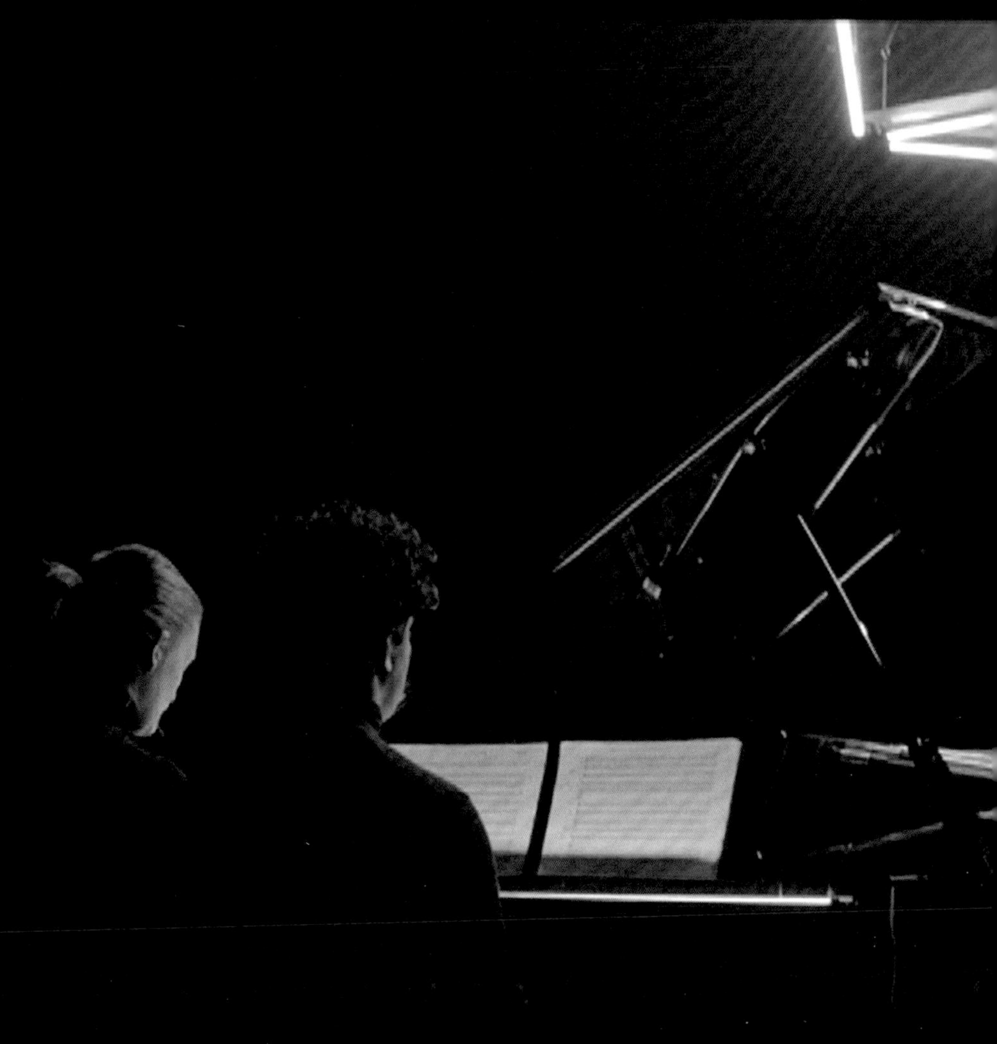

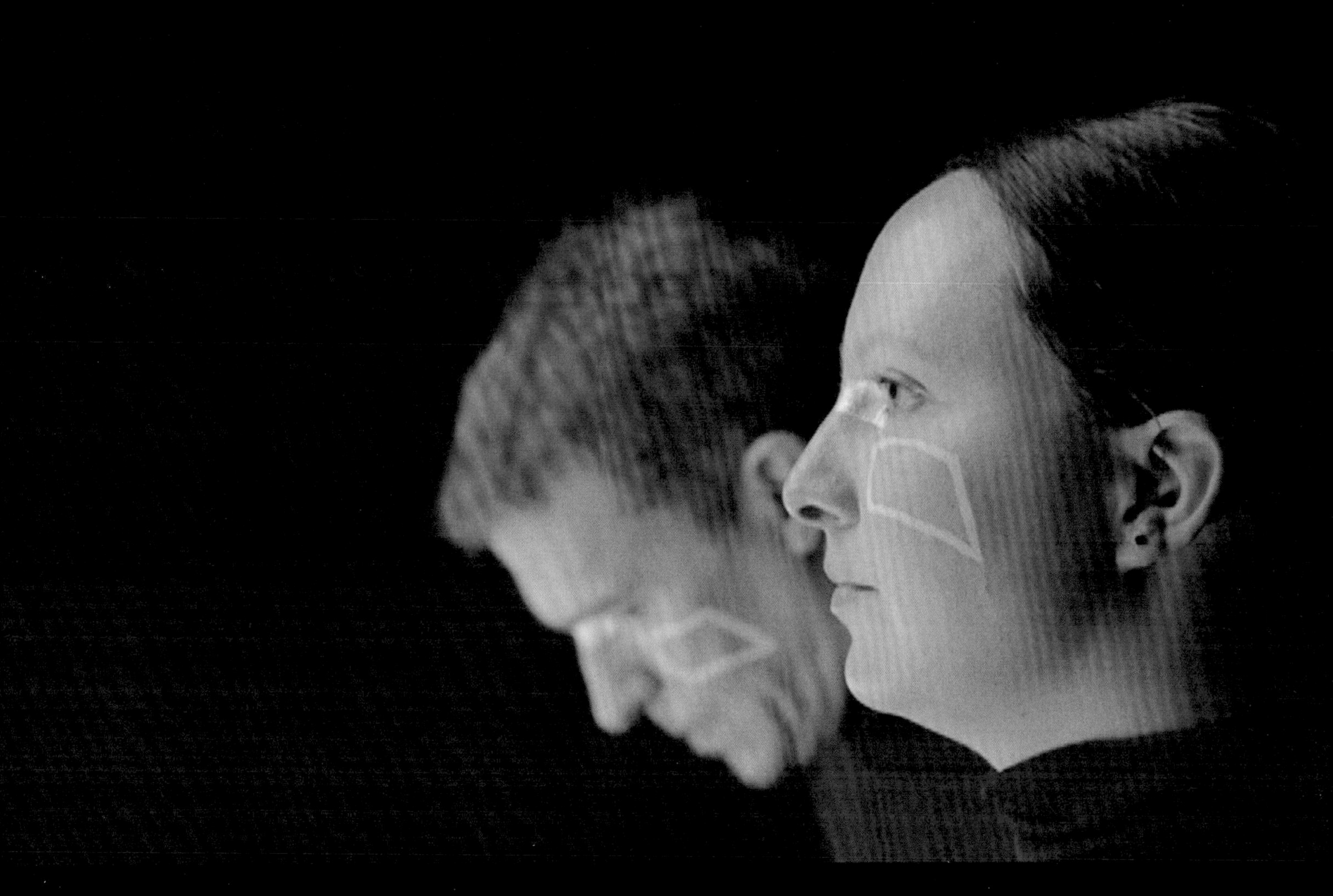

Printed on an army blanket, Raven Chacon's graphic score tells the creation story of the founding of the United States of America, one filled with violence and erasure, and is meant to be performed using coins, axe and wood, a police whistle, and a match.

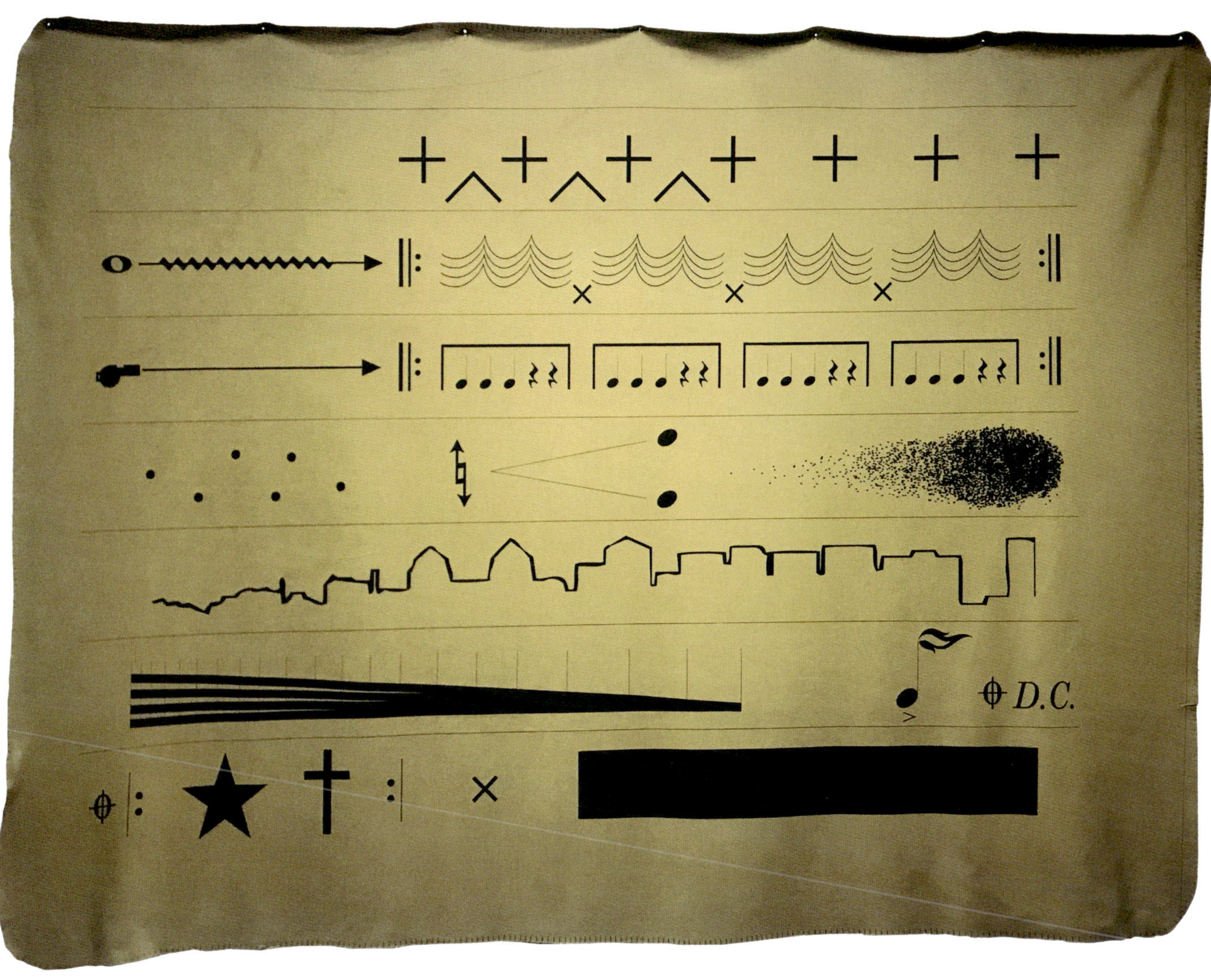

Aren't these prints remarkable? Inuit (Utkuhikhalingmiut) artist Luke Anguhadluq shares the ceremony of drum dancing, where a shaman would put an entire community in a trance by drawing a series of circles—the circle of the drum, the circle of the community that gathers around the drum, and the circles of the eyes under trance;

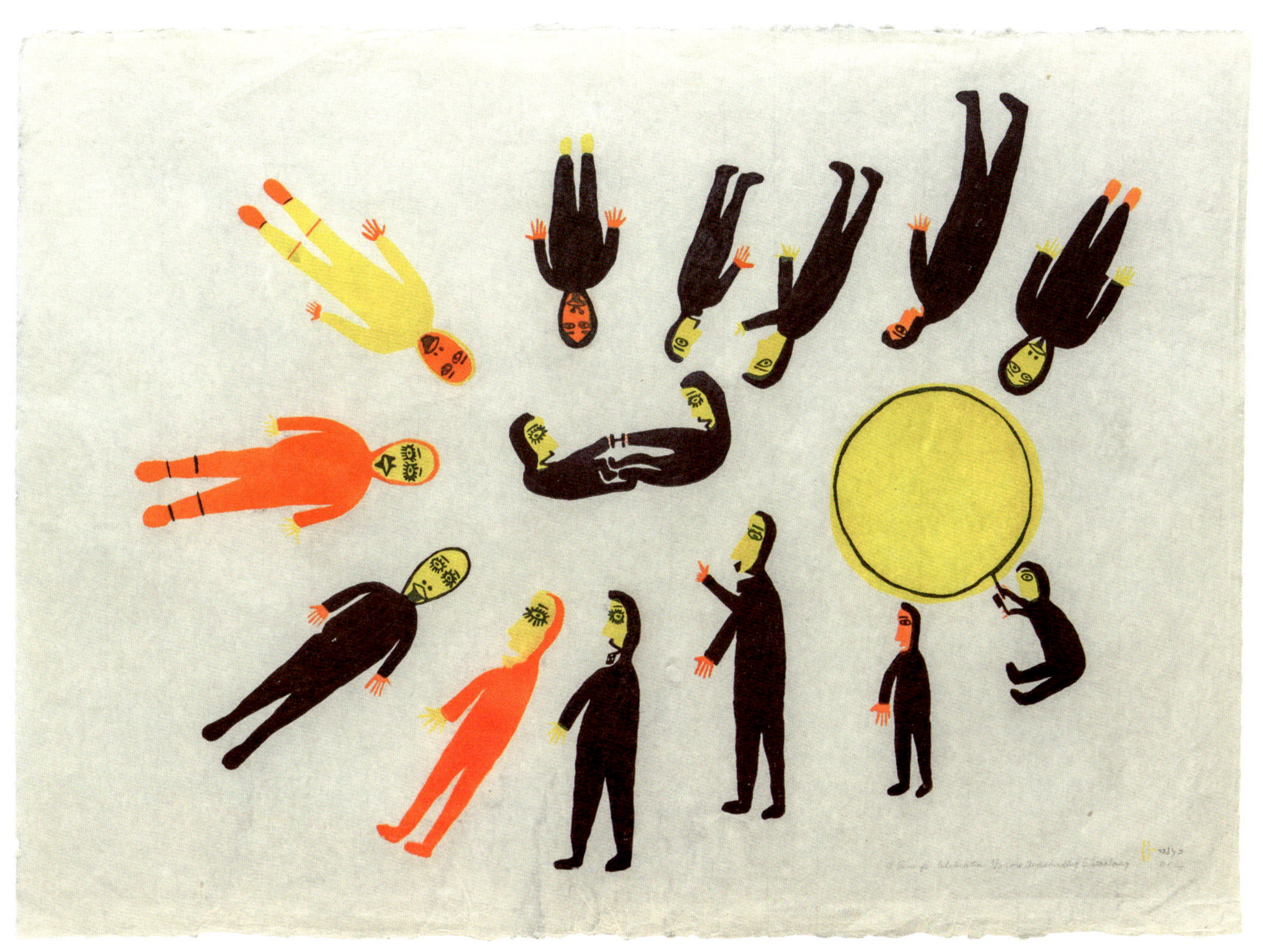

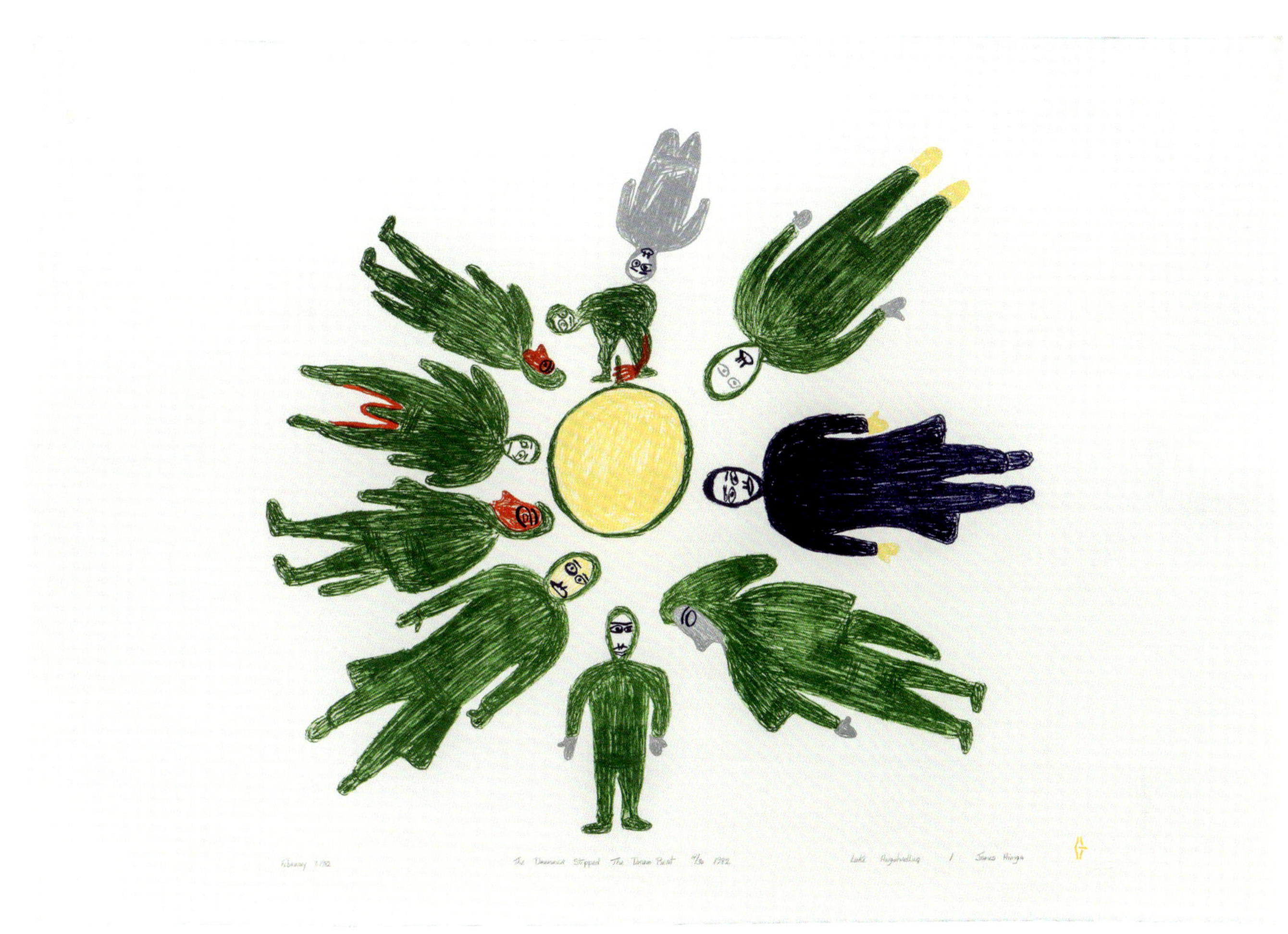

February 1982
The Dancers Stopped The Drum Beat   12/50 1982
Luke Anguhadluq   /   James Hinga

and Marcos Ávila
Forero, working with anthropologists and ethnomusicologists, reintroduces
a community of Afro-Colombians along the Atrato river to their own ancestral
practice of water-drumming, long lost and forgotten.

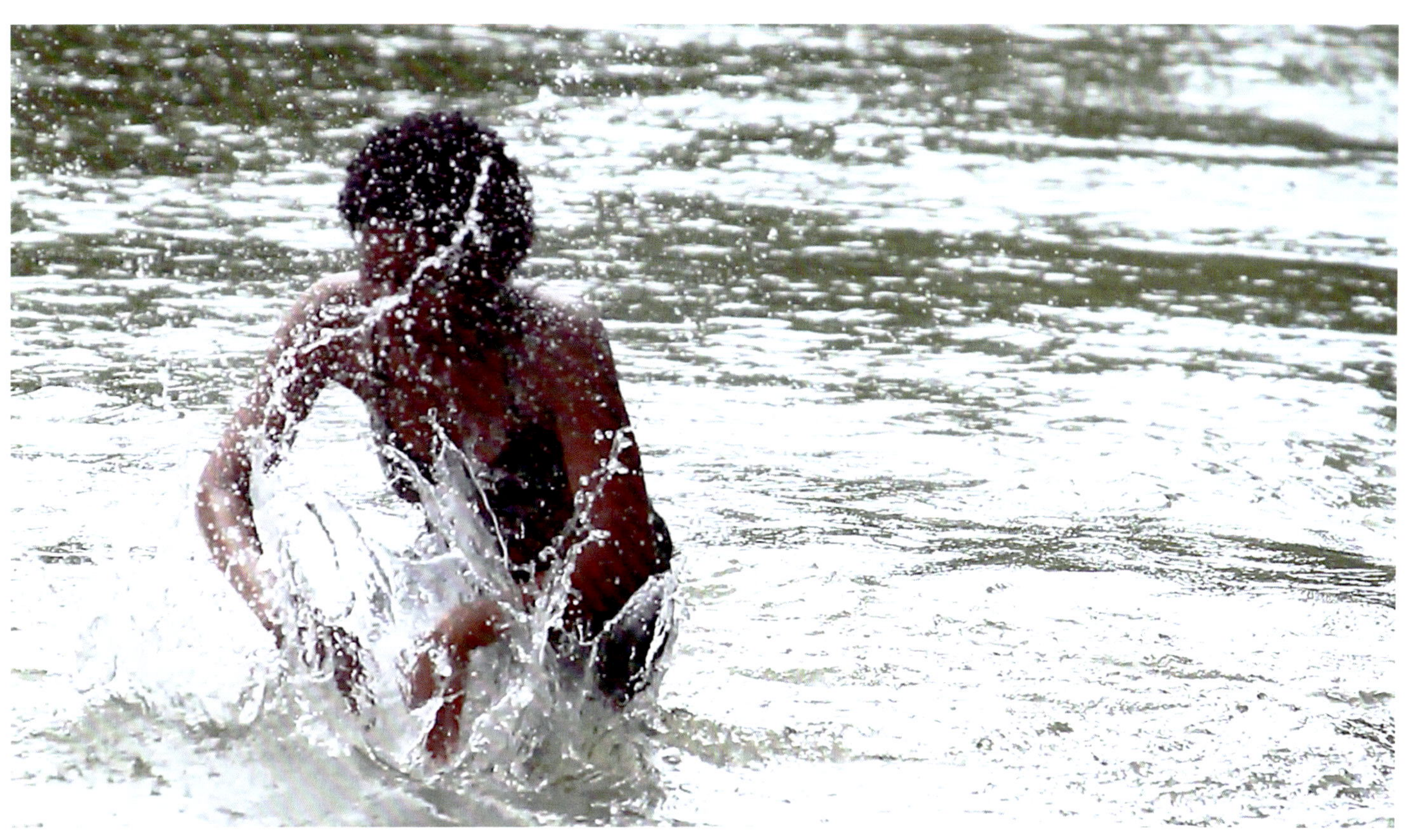

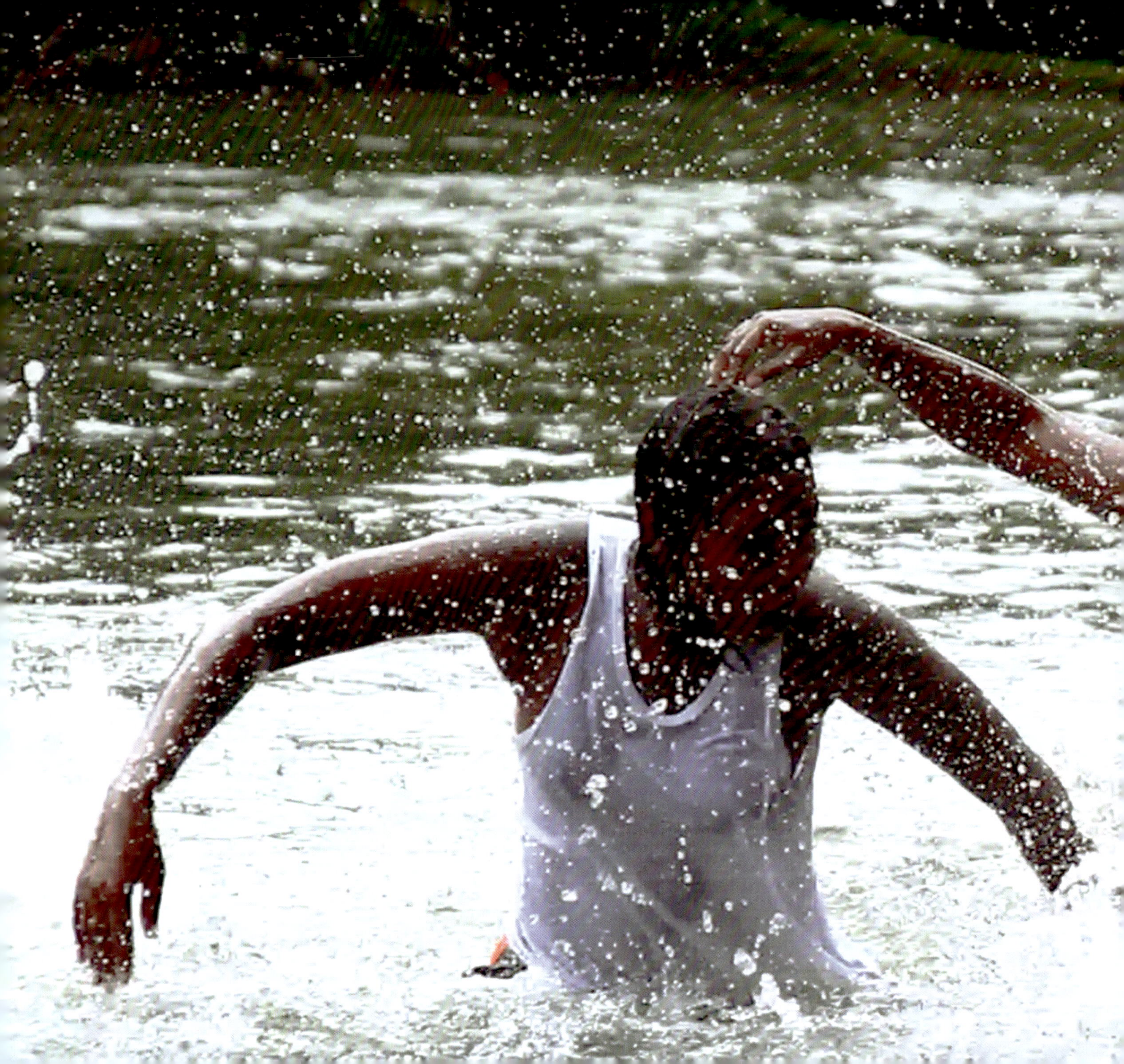

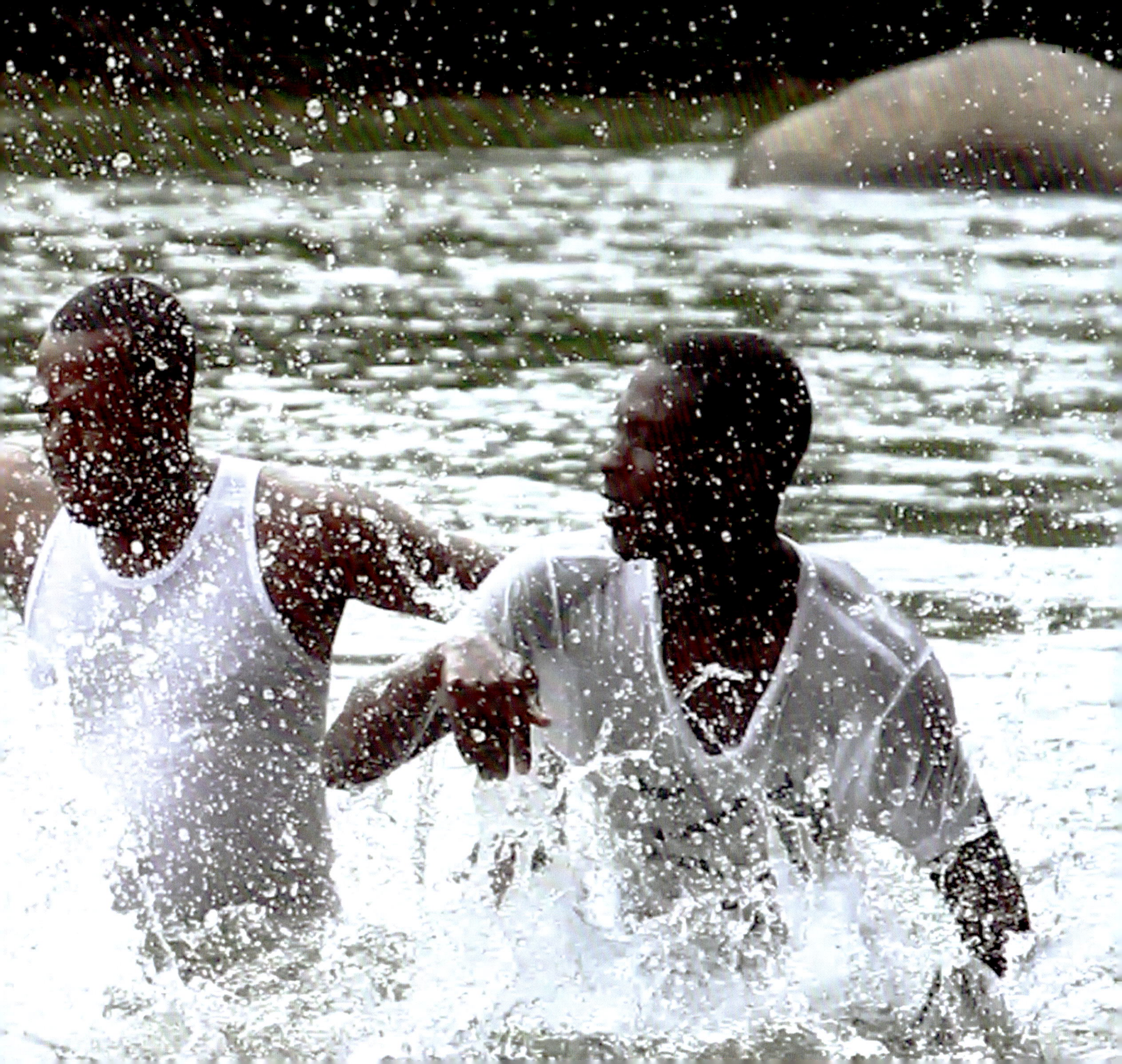

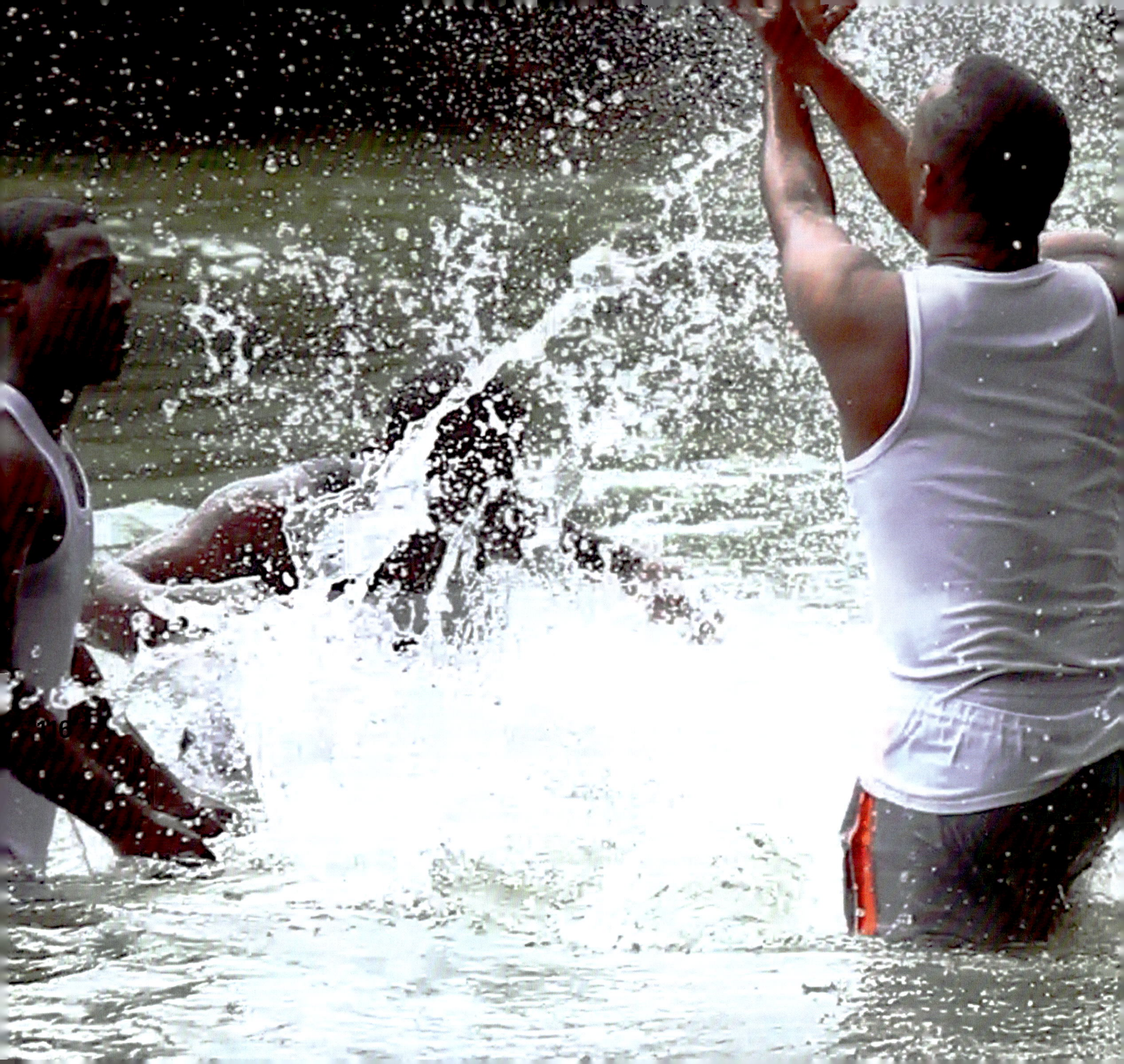

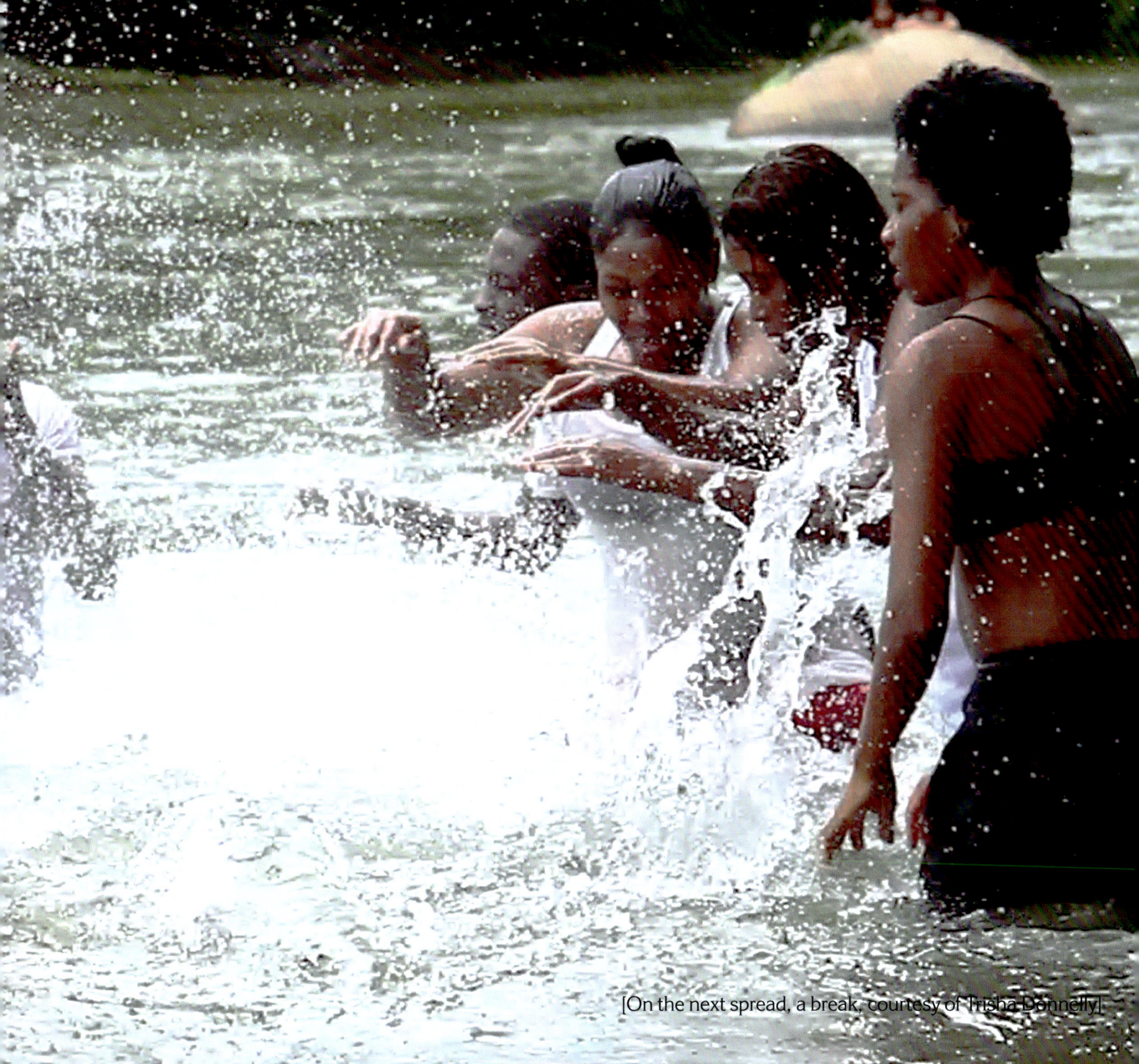

[On the next spread, a break, courtesy of Trisha Donnelly]

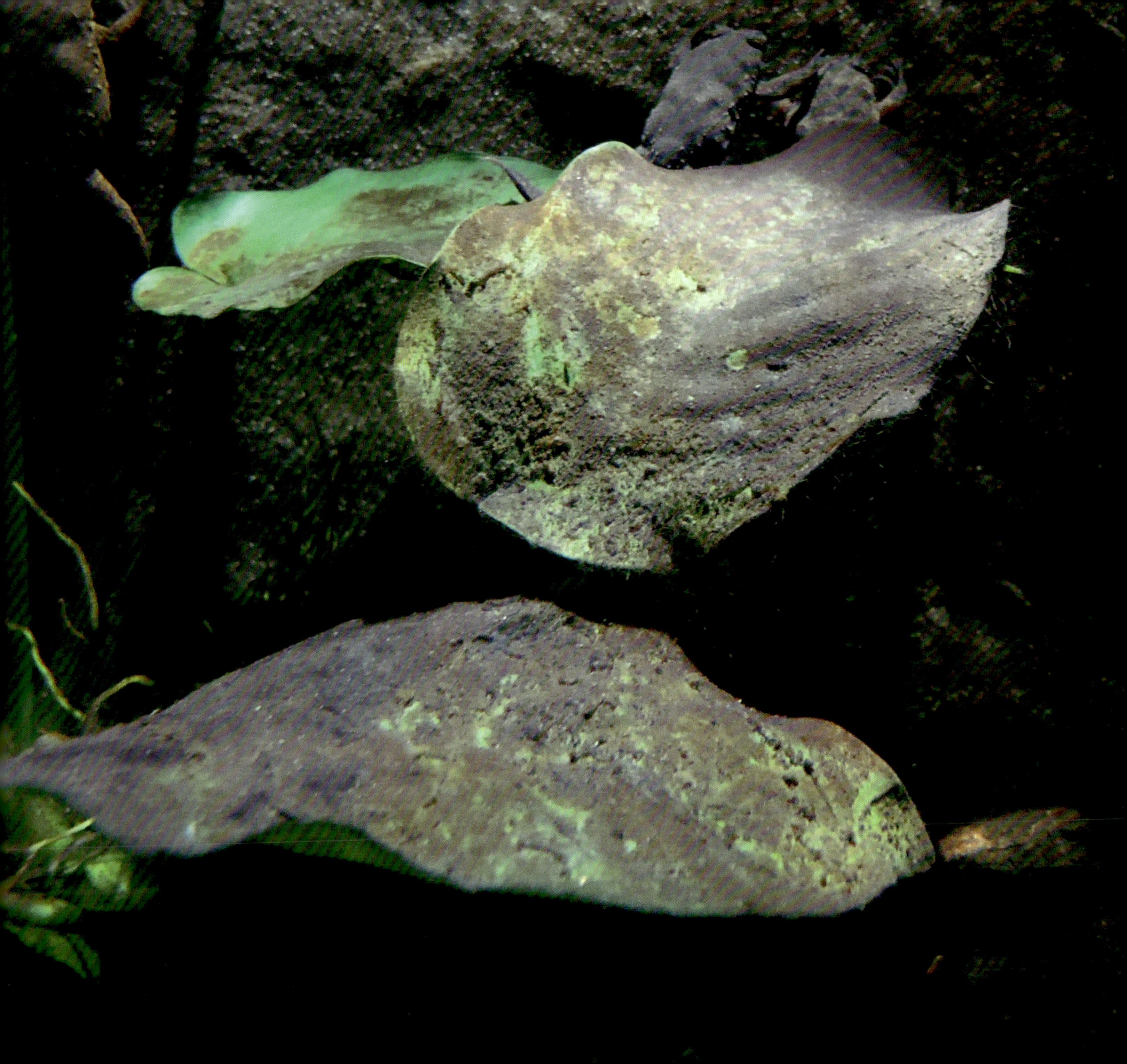

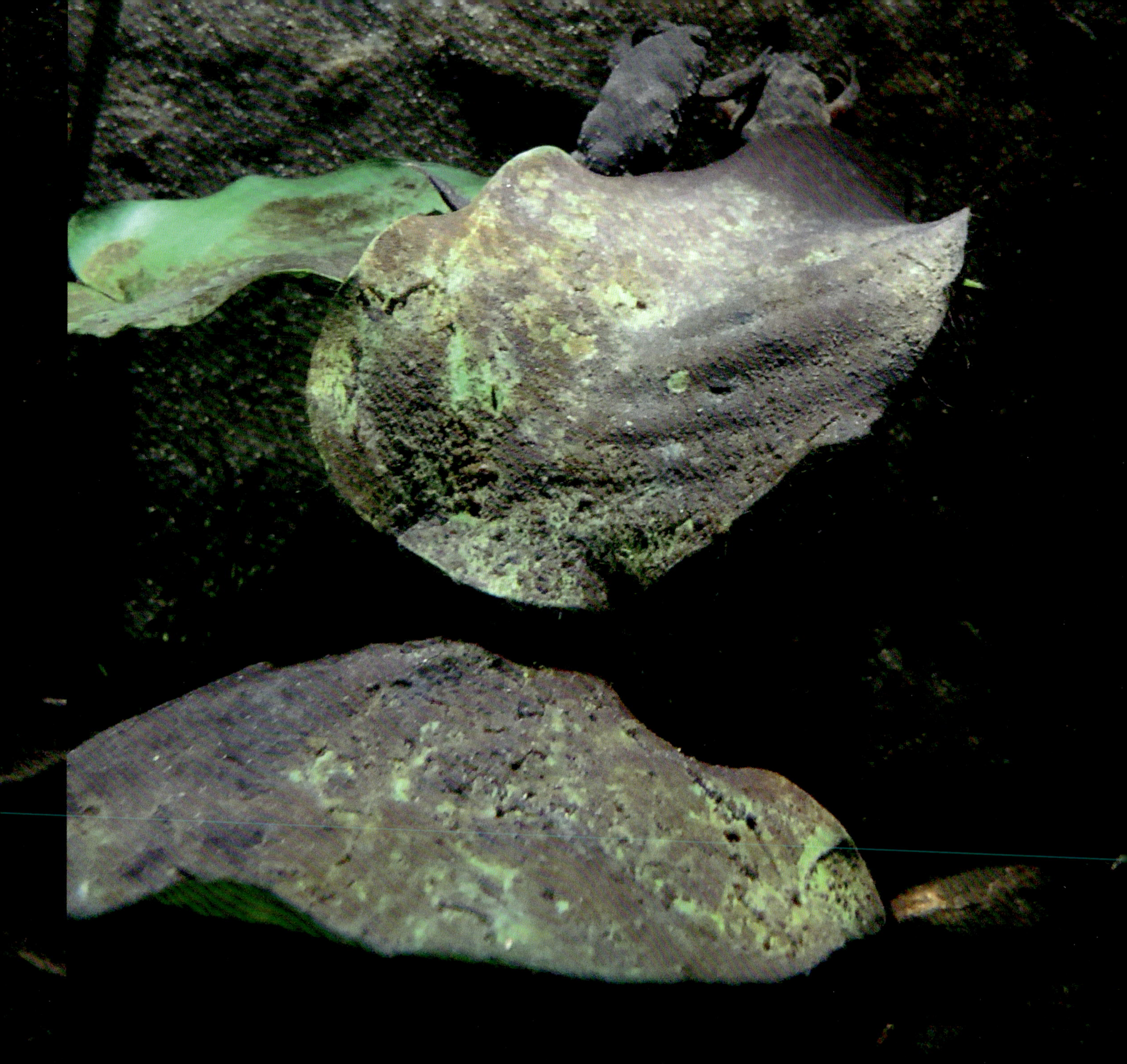

The ritual and the
healing properties of vibration inspired both Guadalupe Maravilla's sculptures,
which he calls "disease throwers,"

124

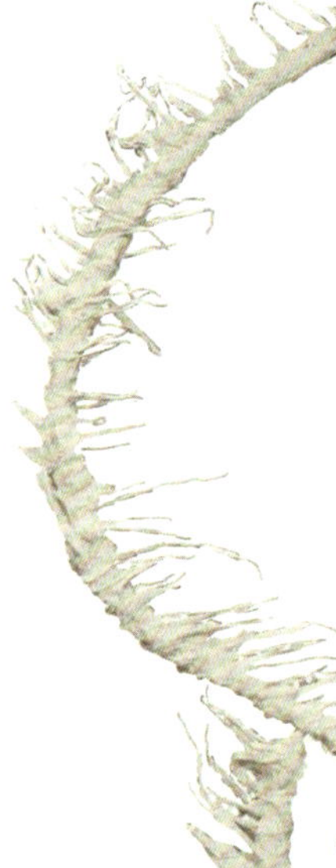

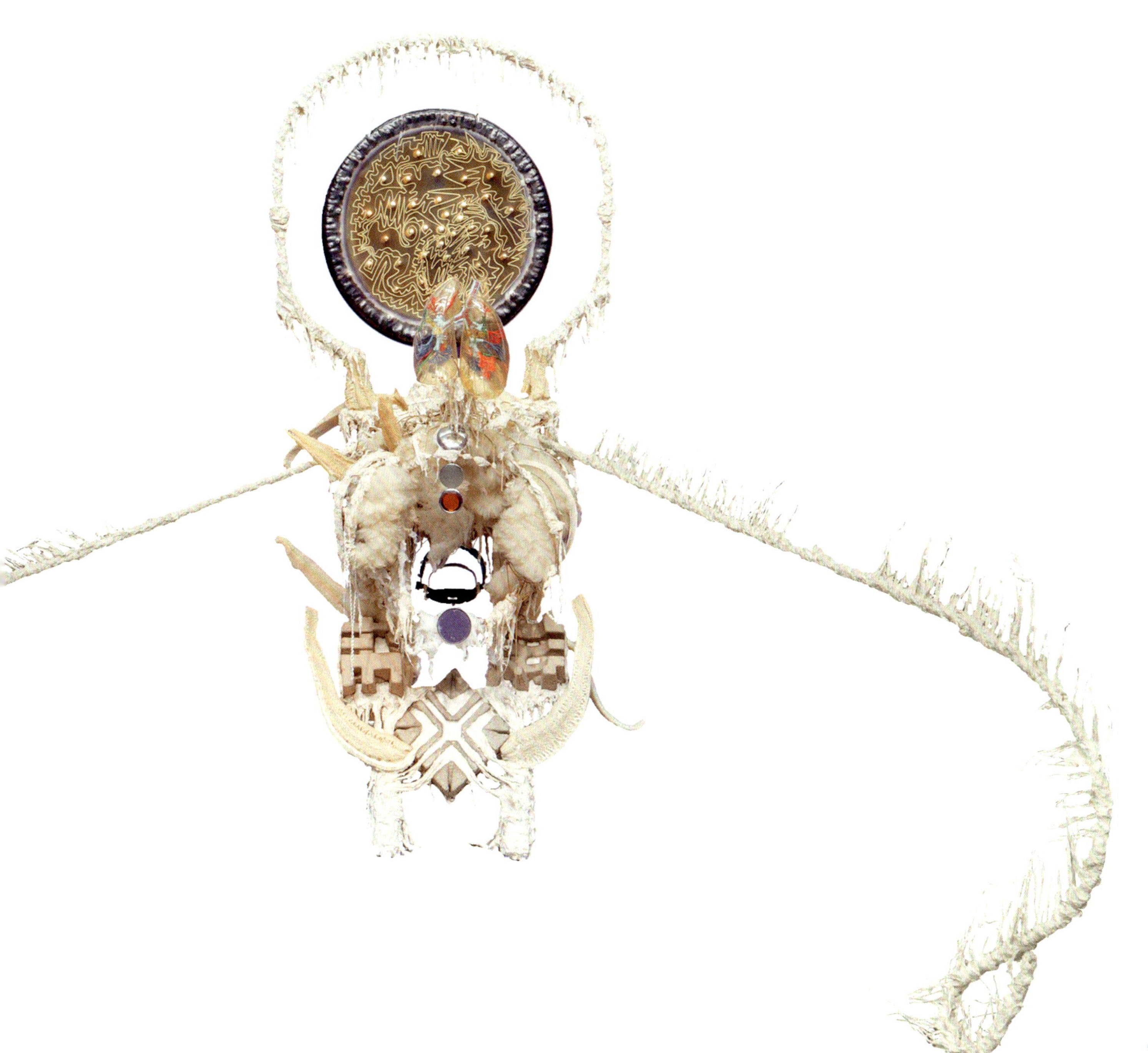

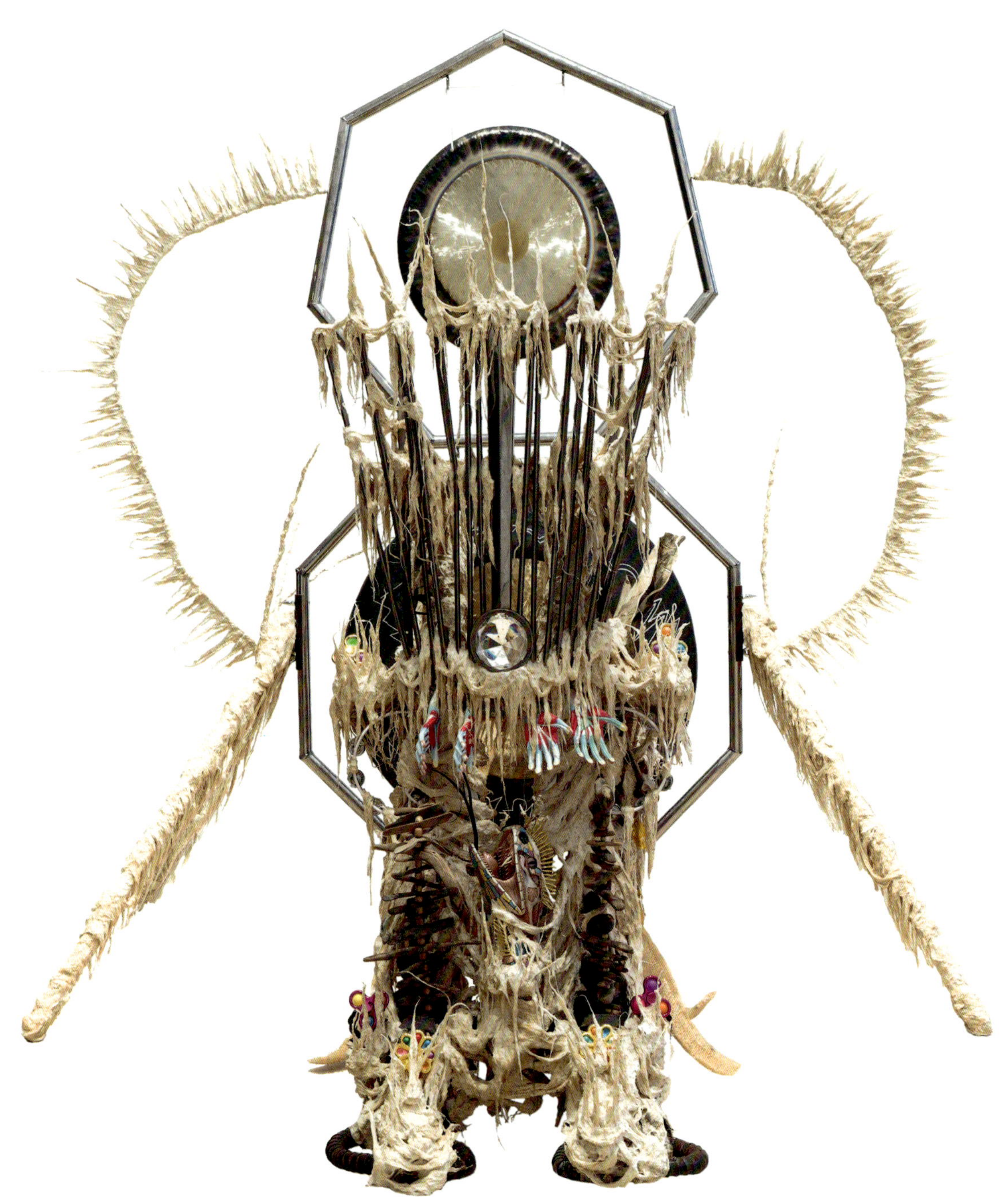

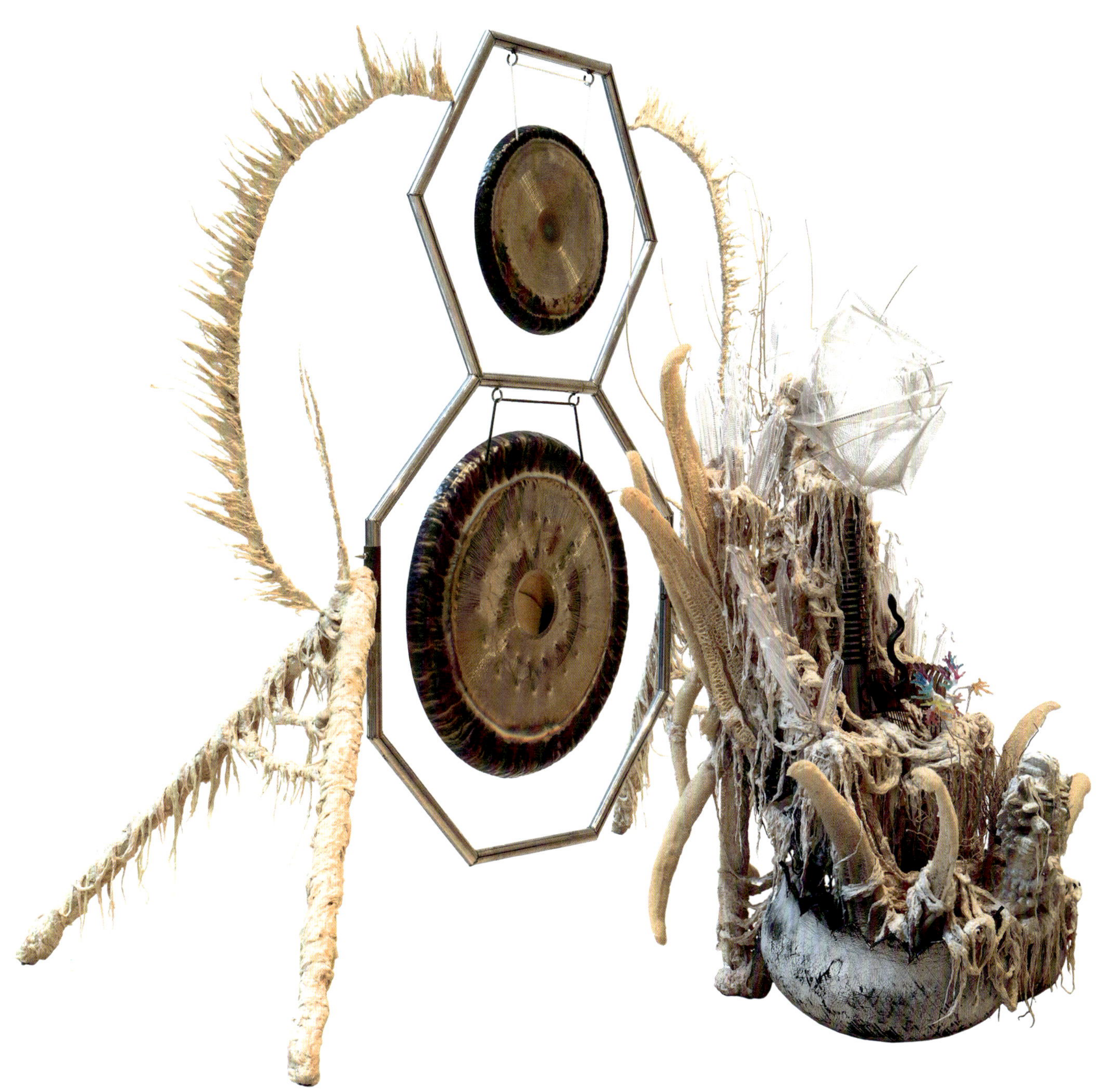

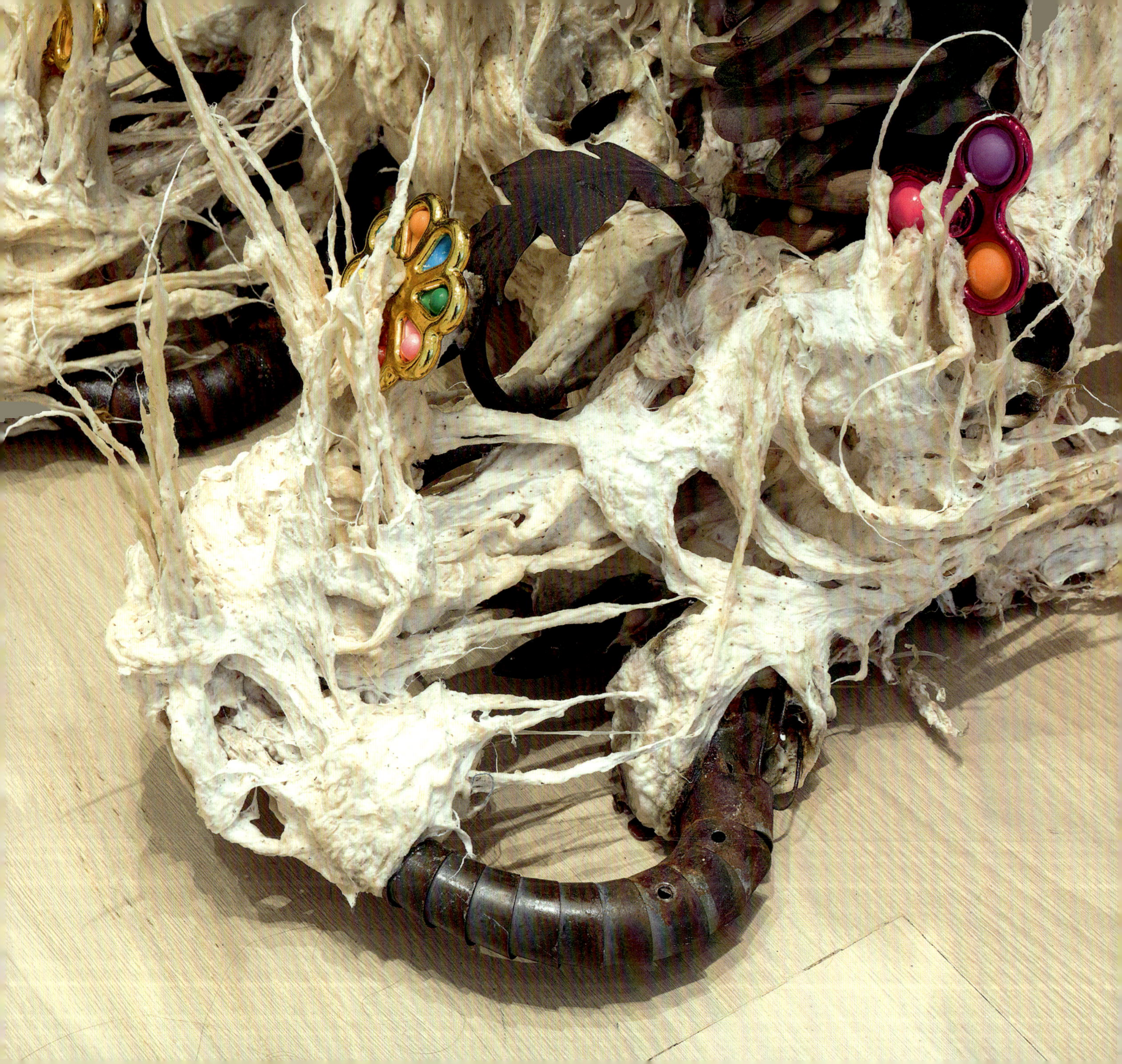

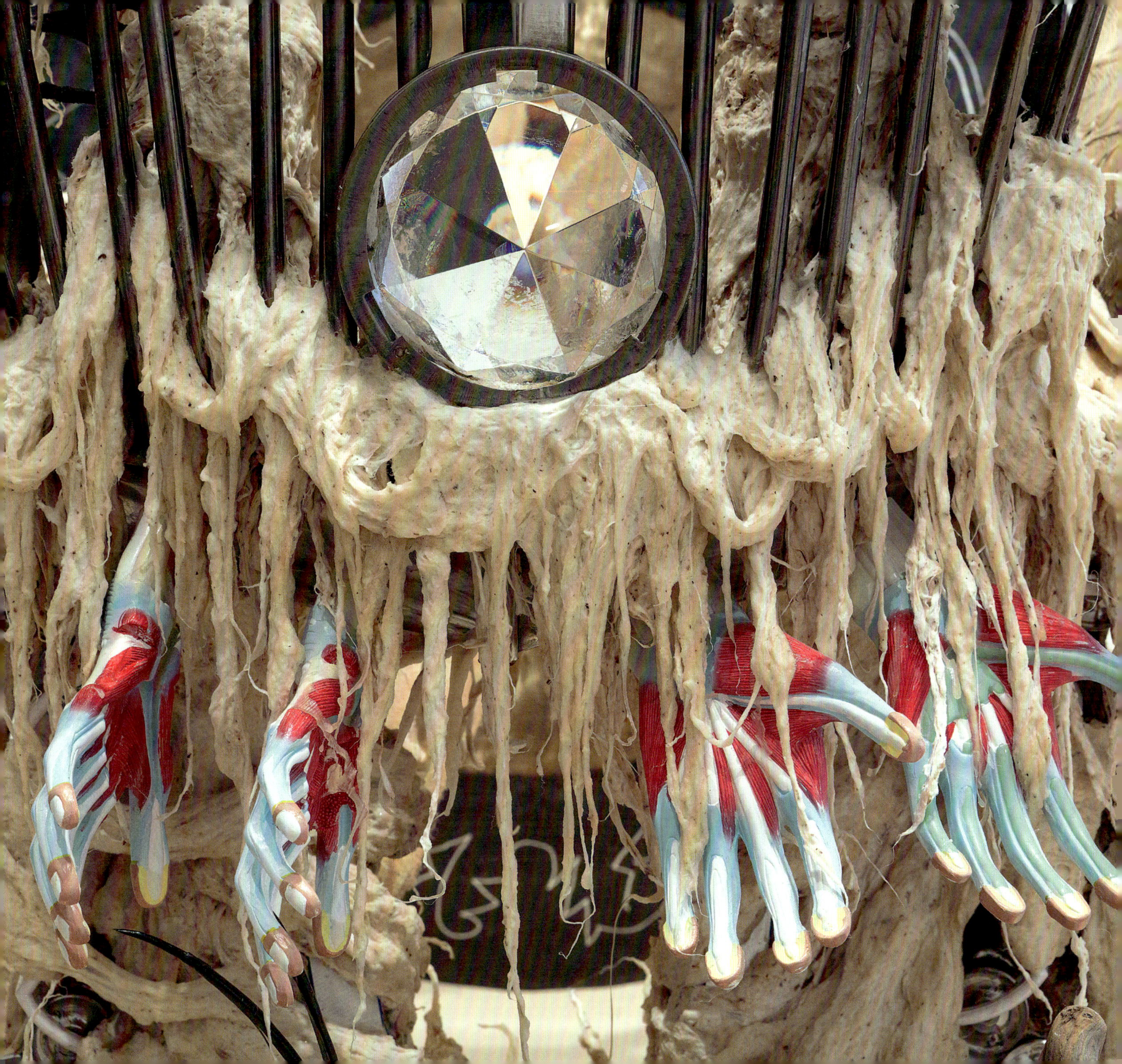

as well as Em'kal Eyongakpa's cave-like installation of water drips, resonant surfaces, and beat generators.

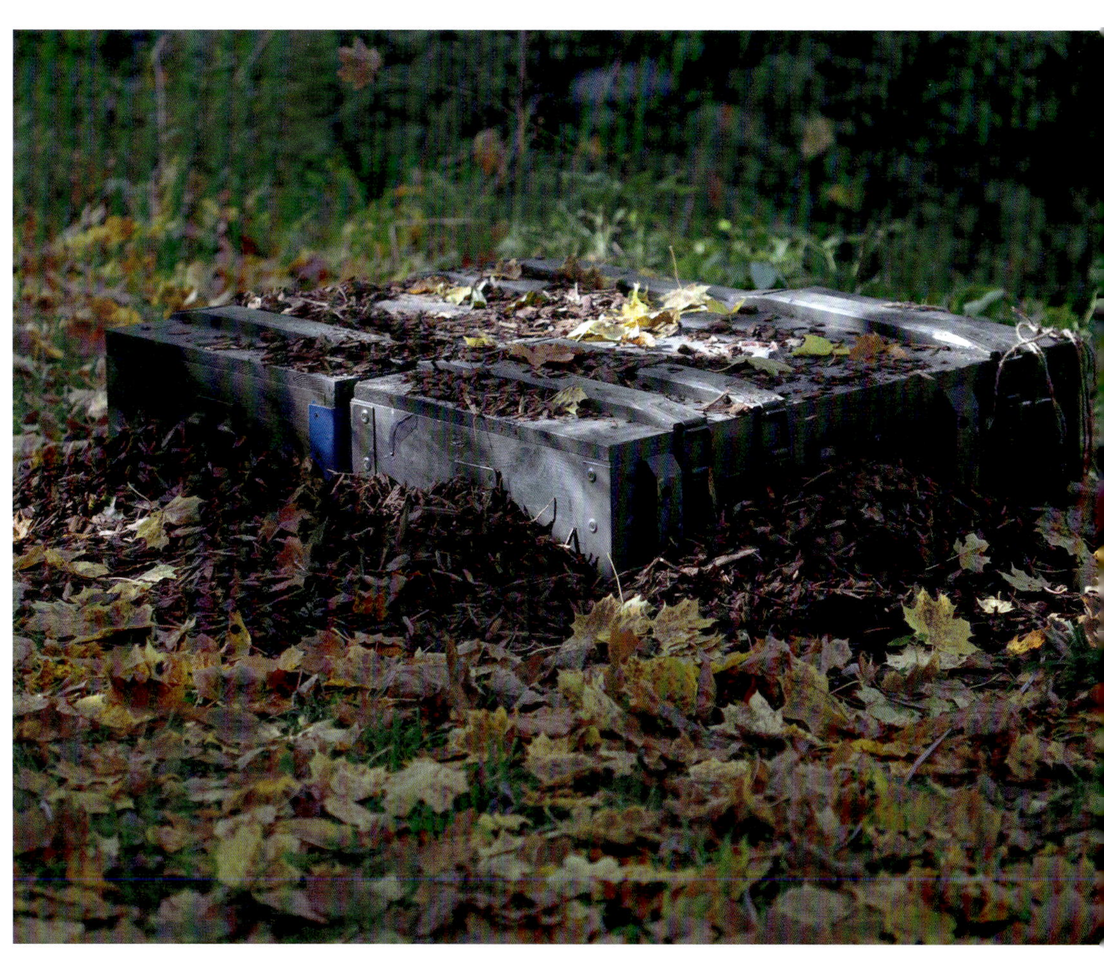

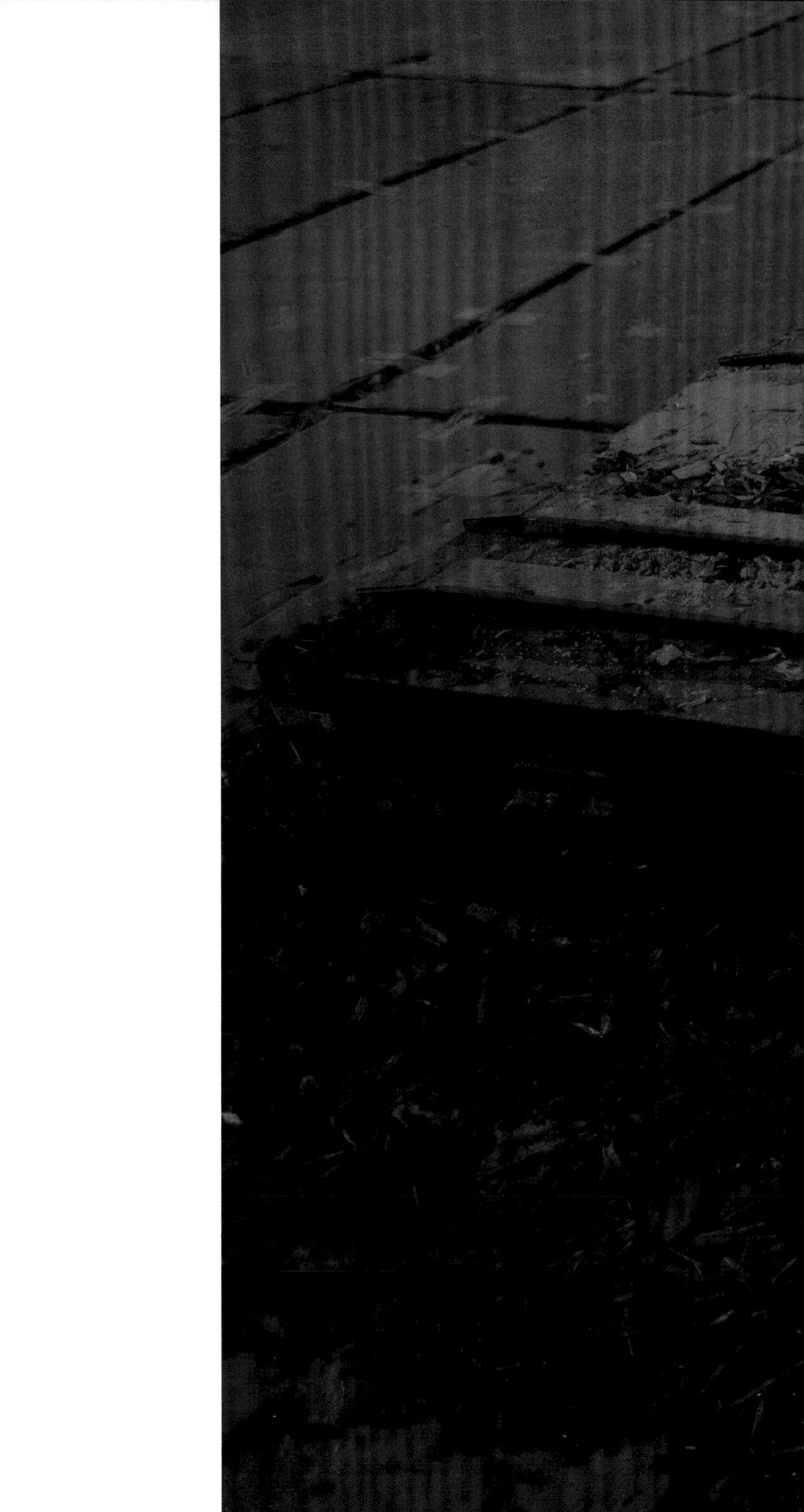

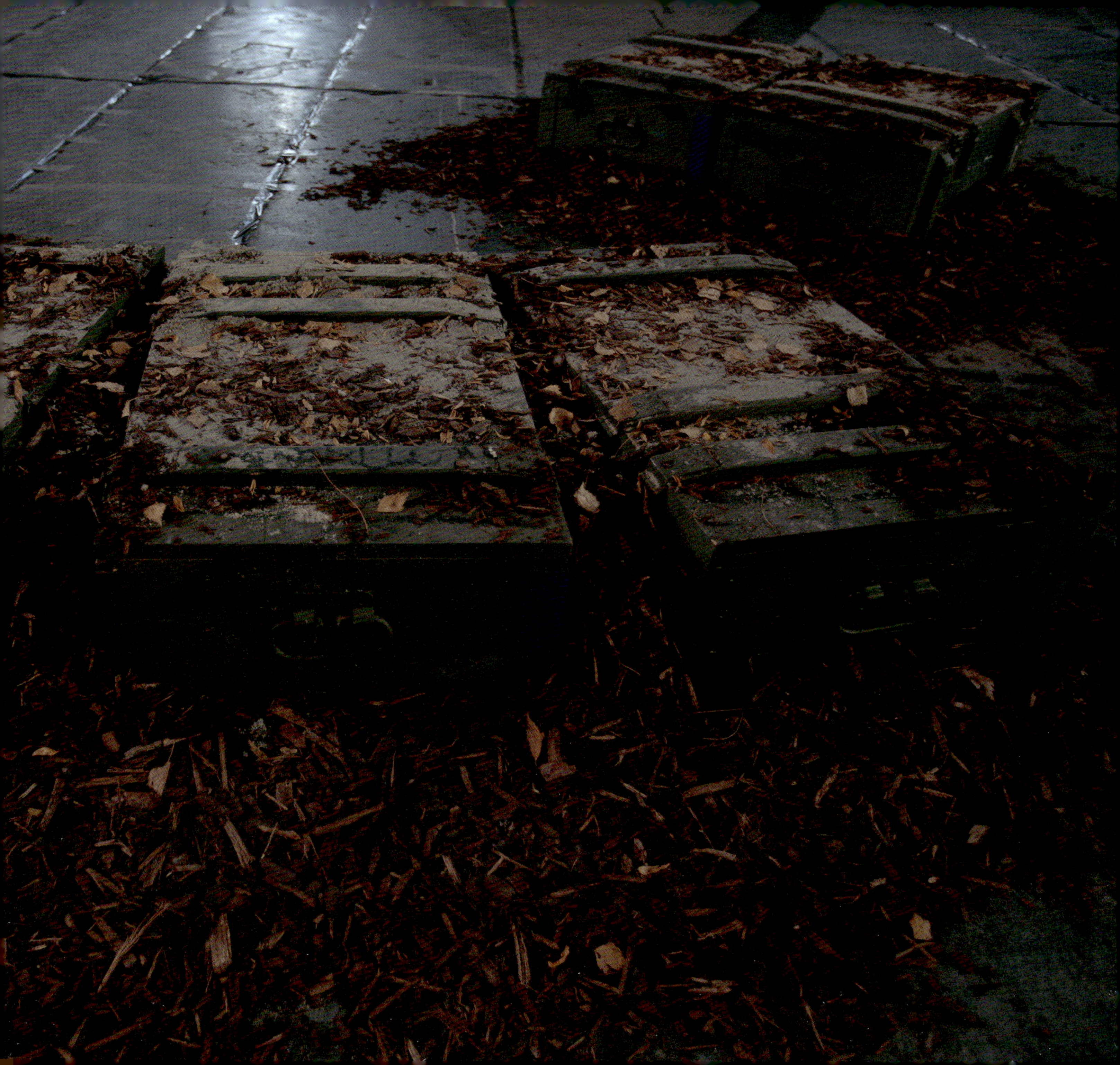

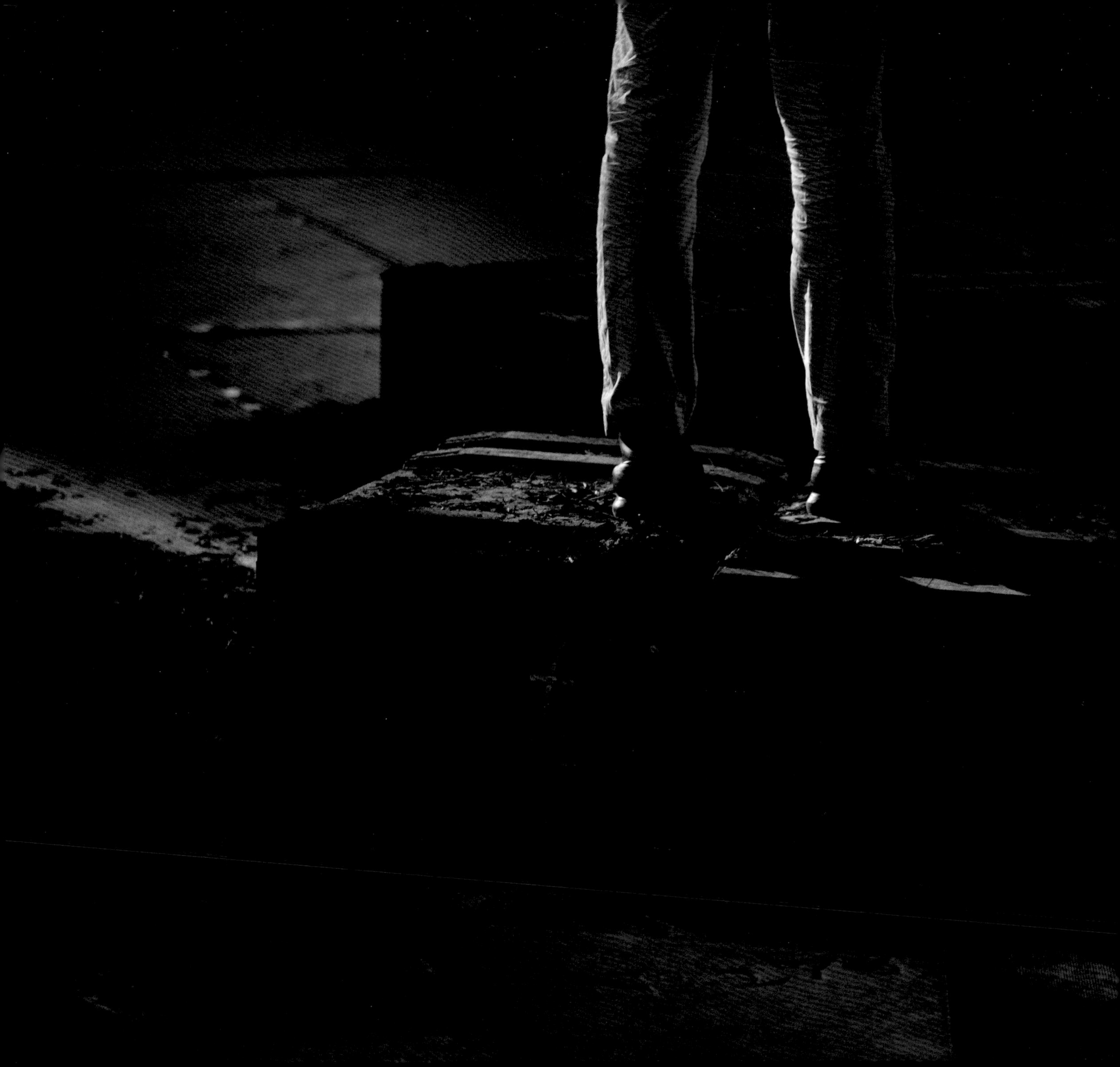

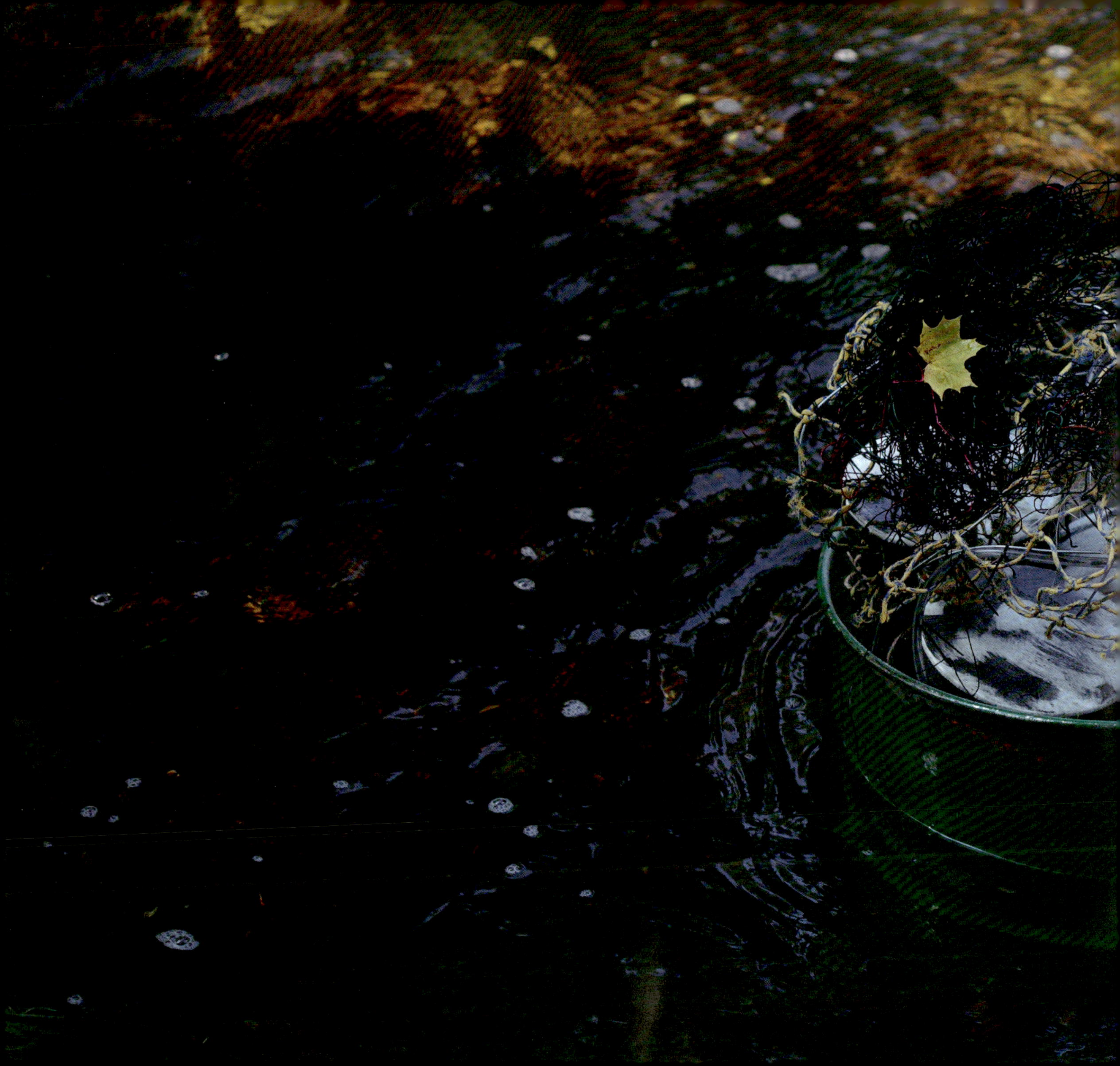

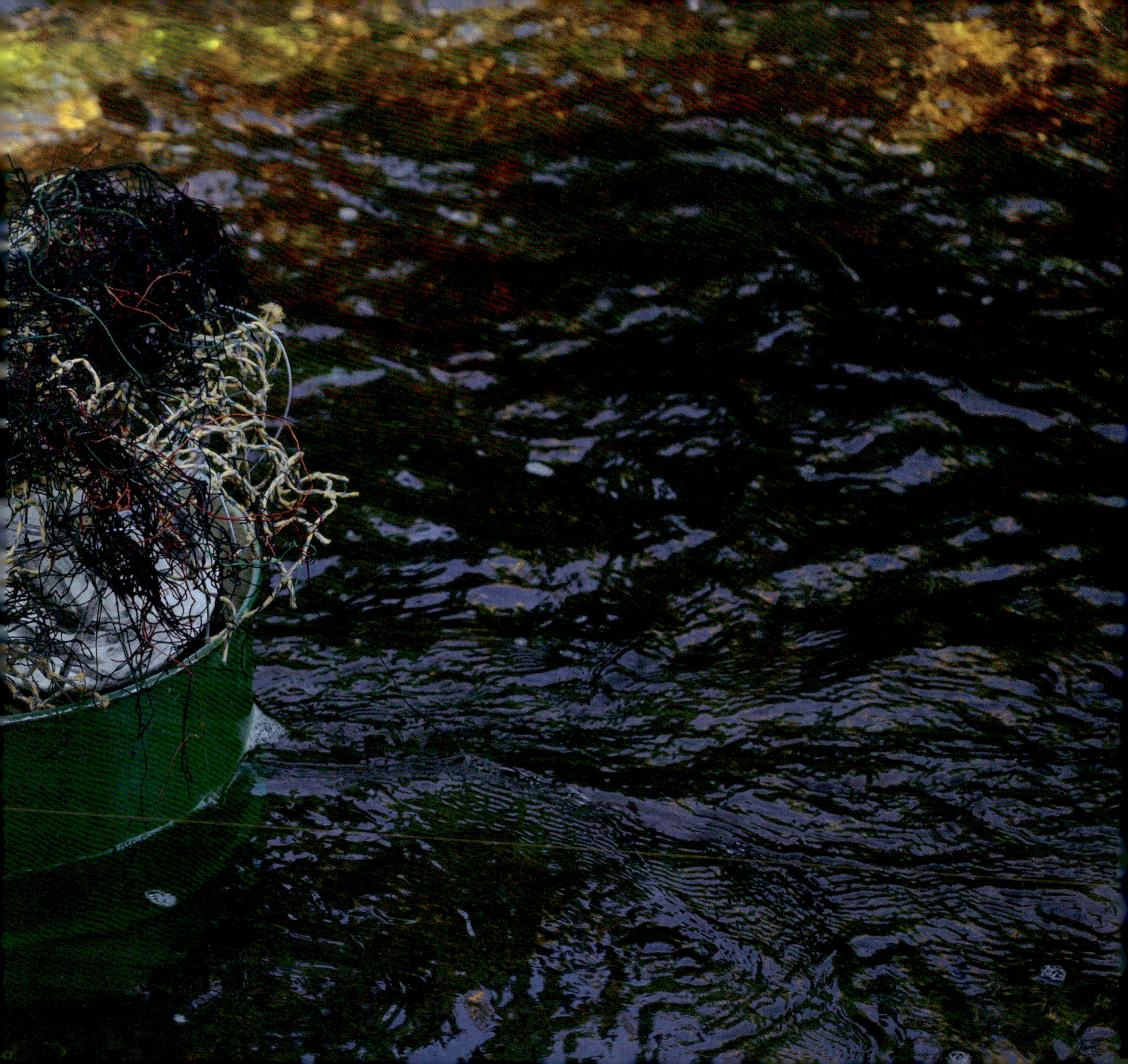

Or, witnessing
a scene many of us see everyday, David Hammons joins a construction crew
on a city street, adding his own instrument to the mix and transforming the site
into an improvised orchestra. While funny and playful, it has bite: it's not about
shaping noise into music, but about contesting the world that calls it noise.[2]

2 Jack Halberstam, "The Wild Beyond: With and for the Undercommons," in Stefano Harney and Fred Moten, The Undercommons: *Fugitive Planning & Black Study* (New York: Minor Compositions, 2013), 8.

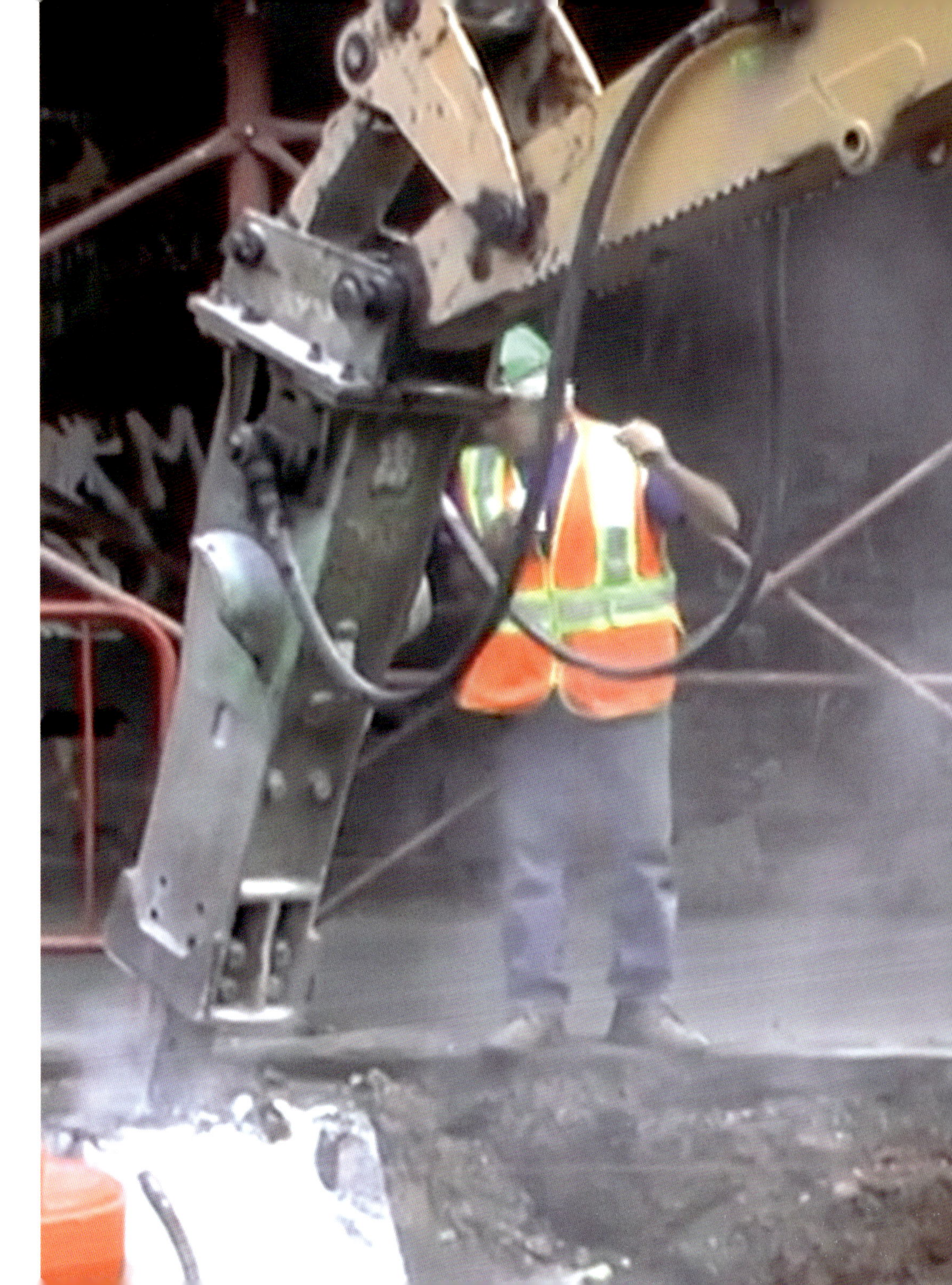

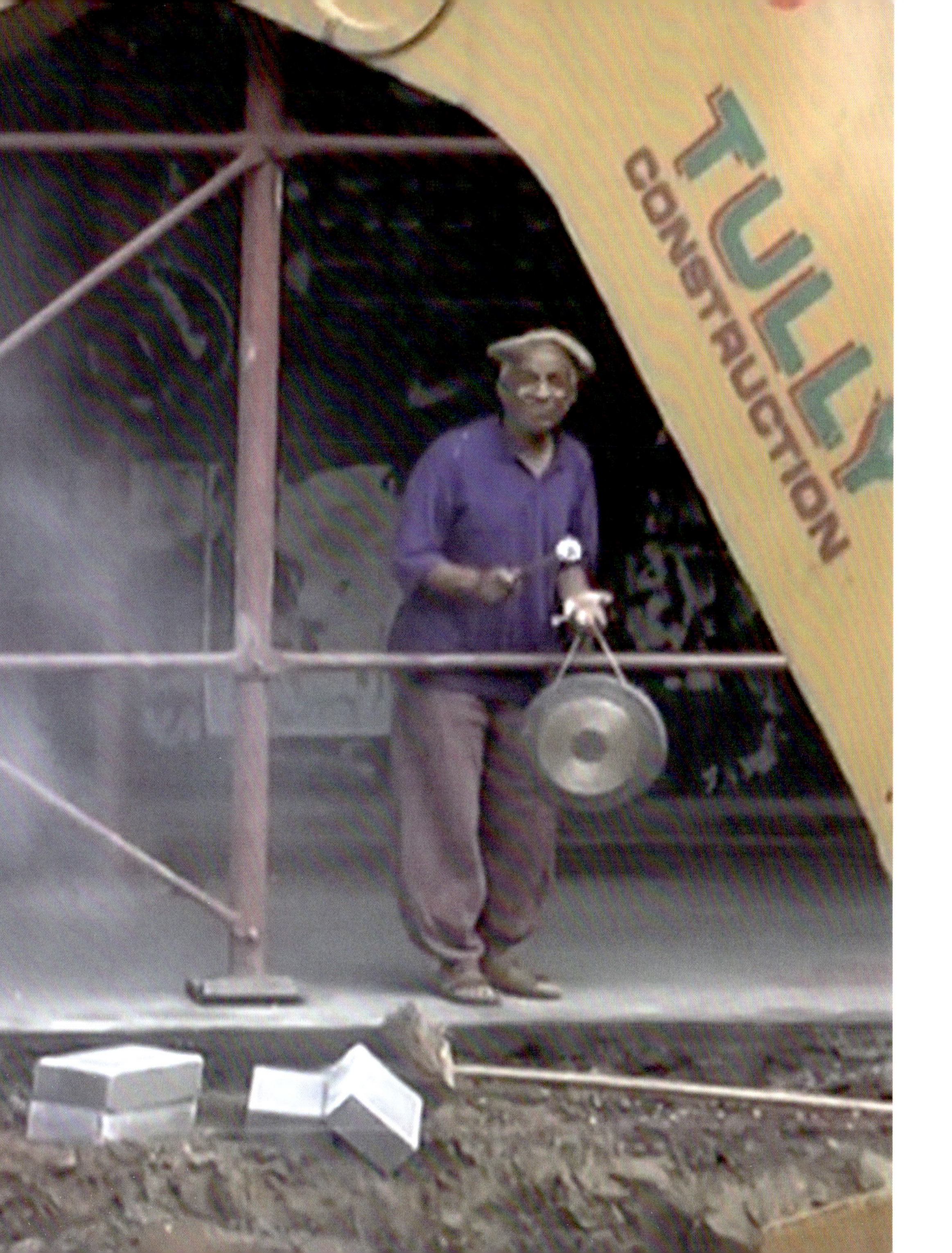

TULLY
CONSTRUCTION

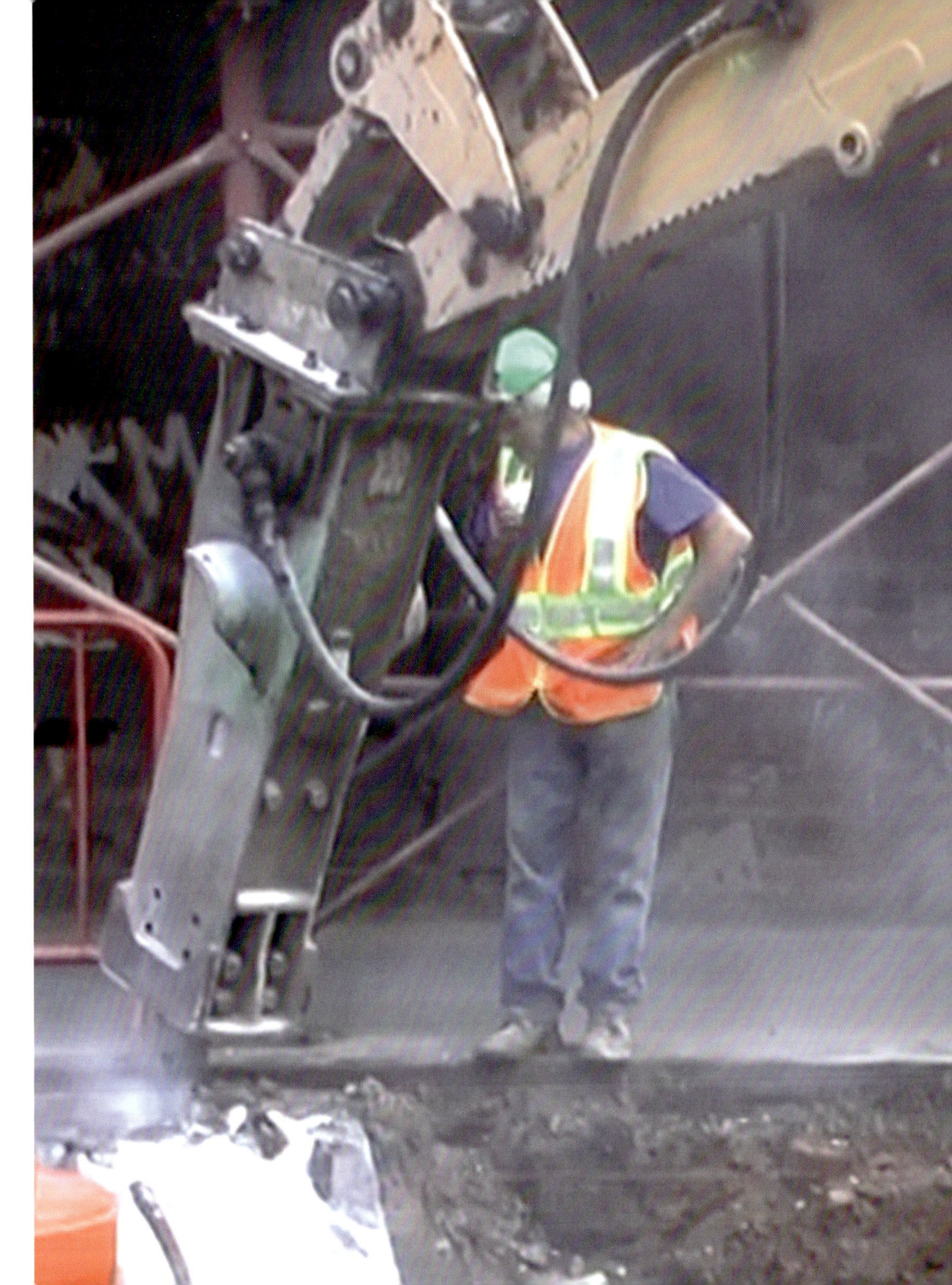

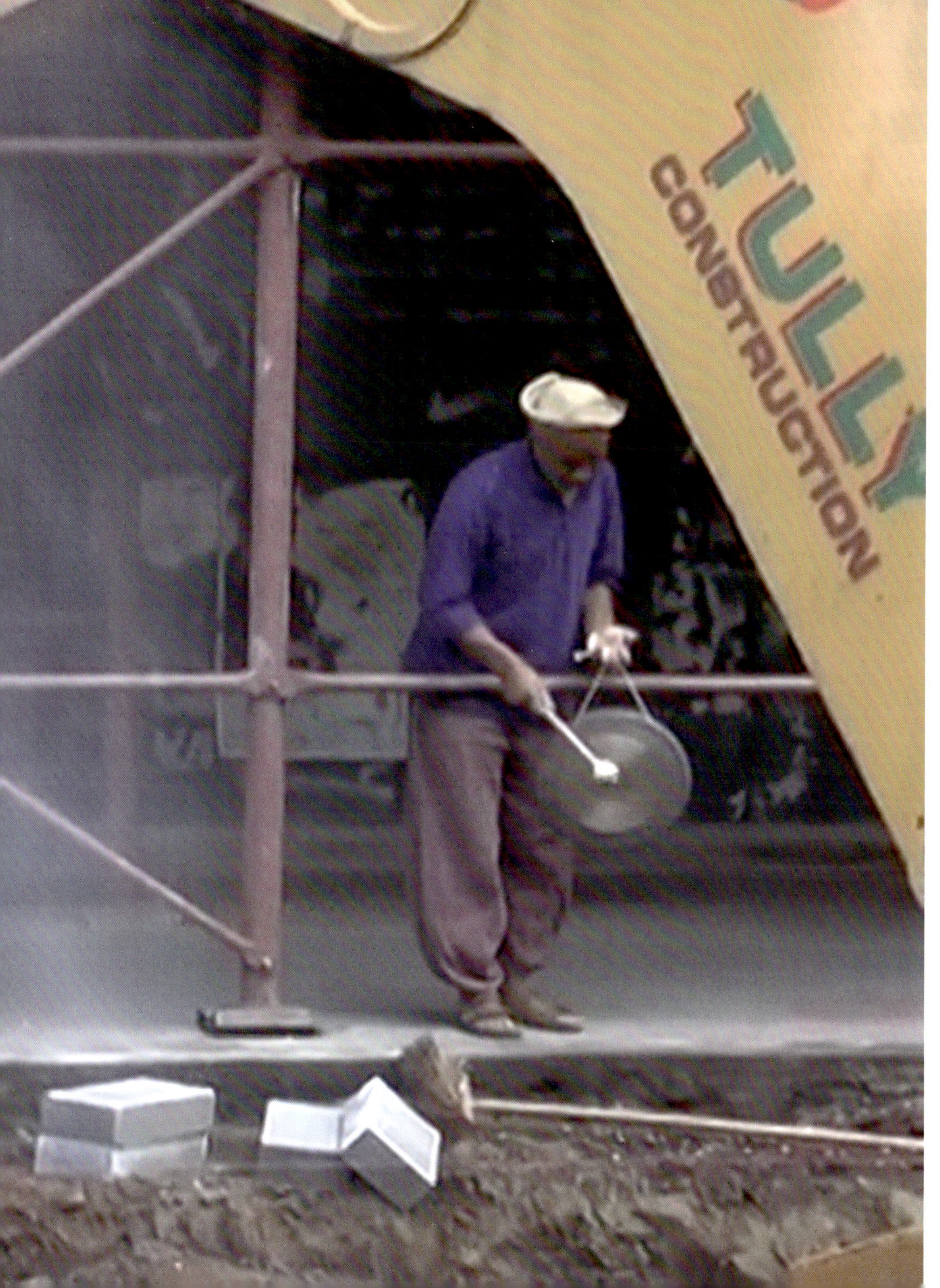
TULLY
CONSTRUCTION

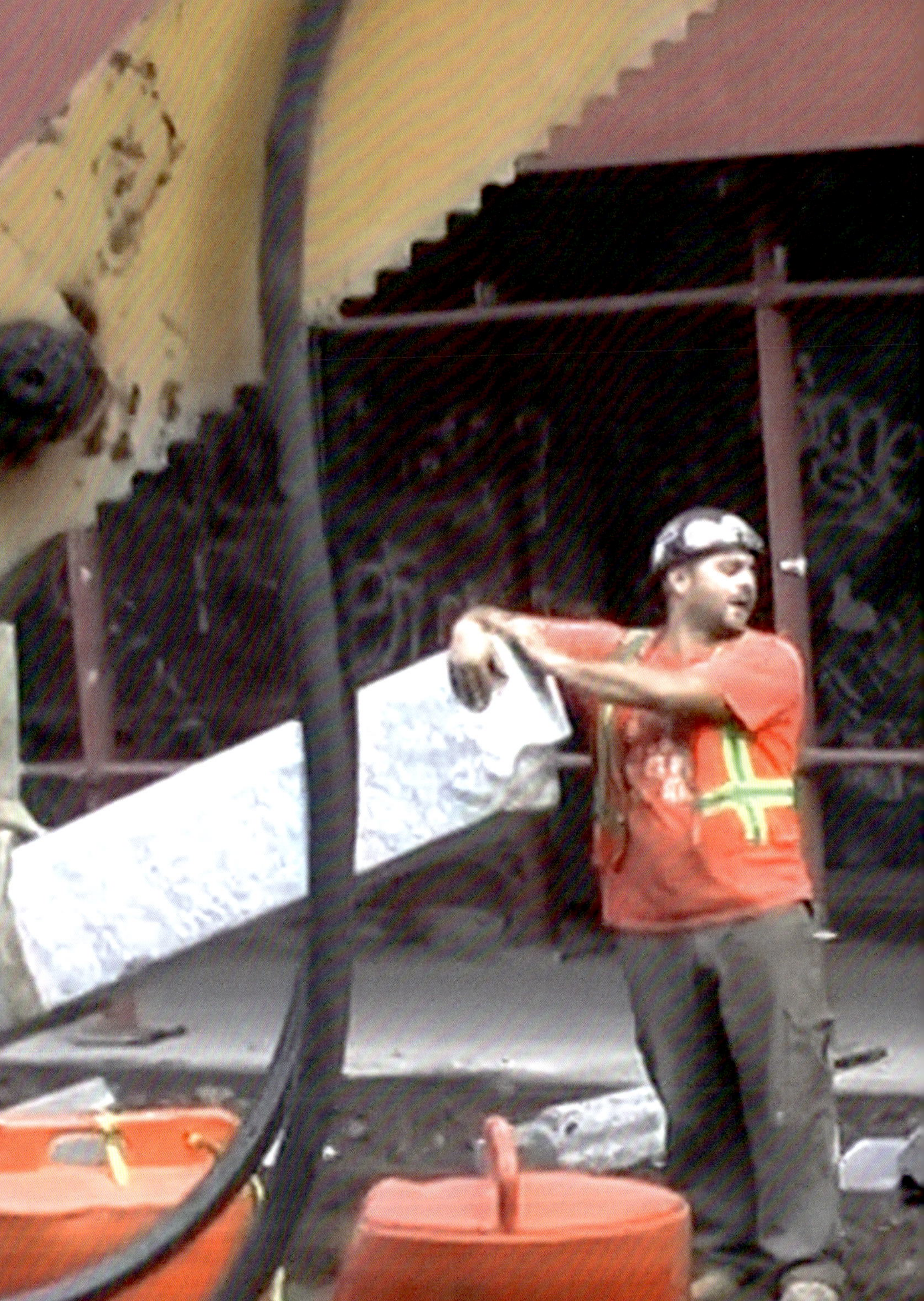

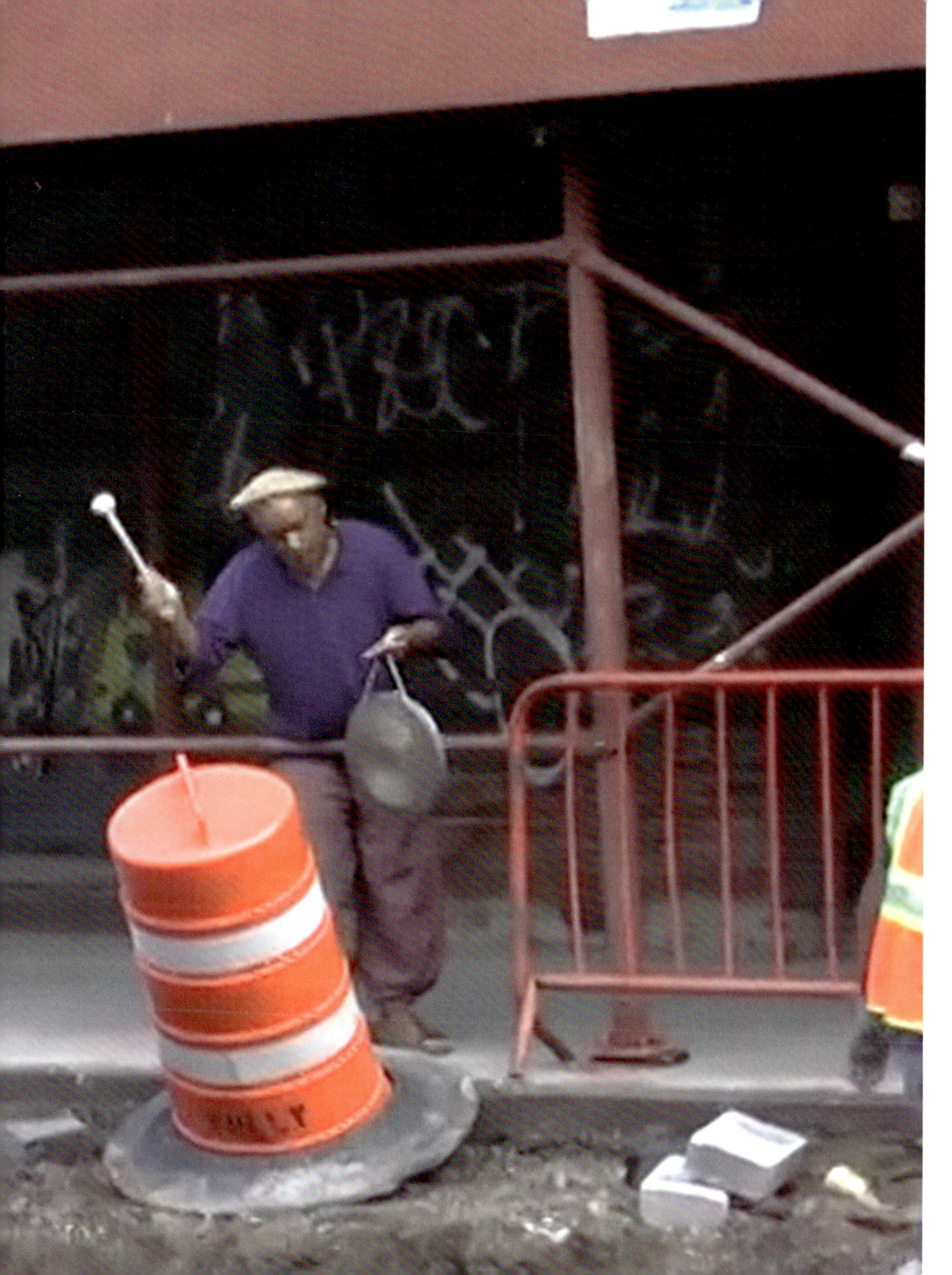

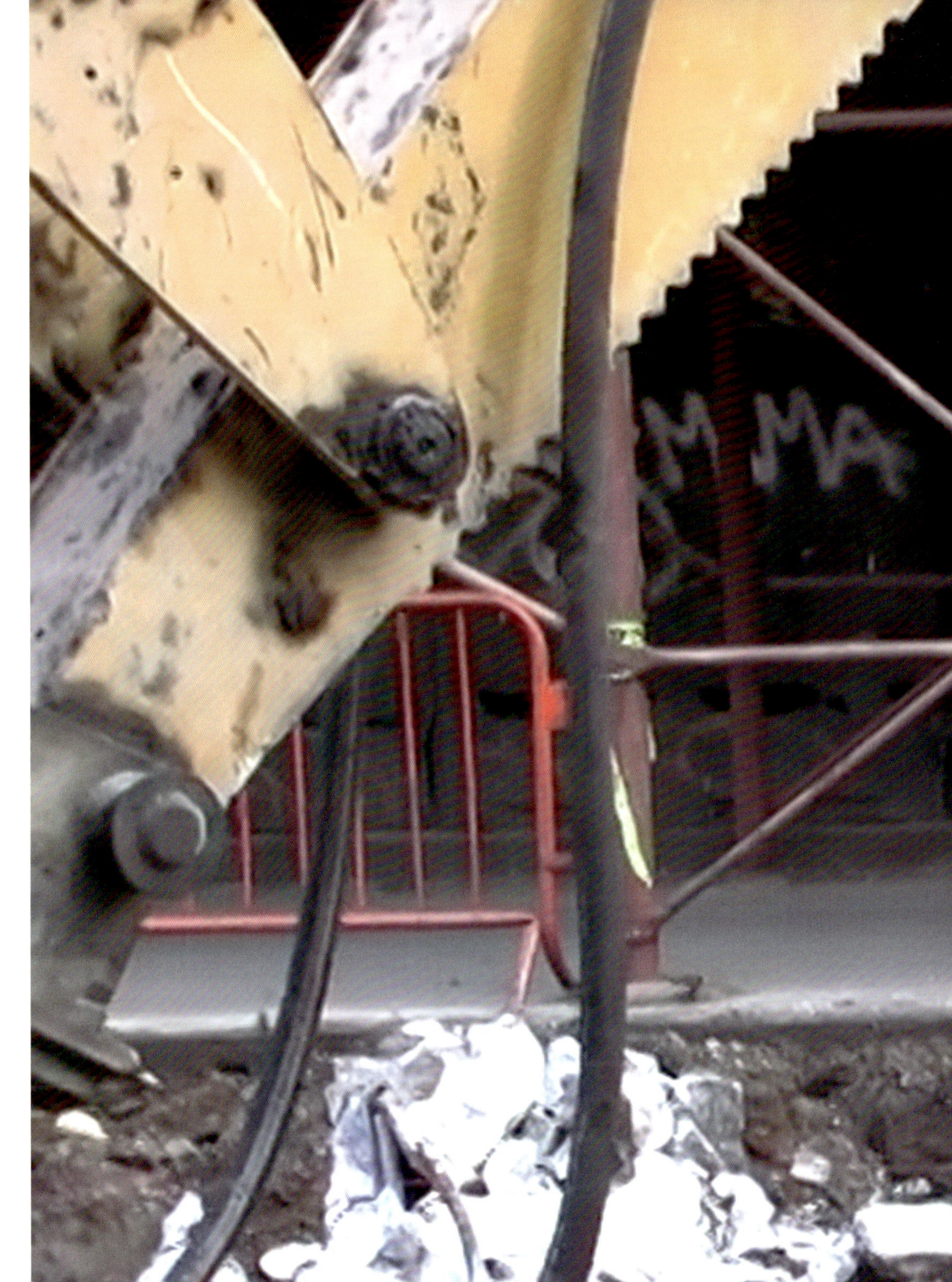

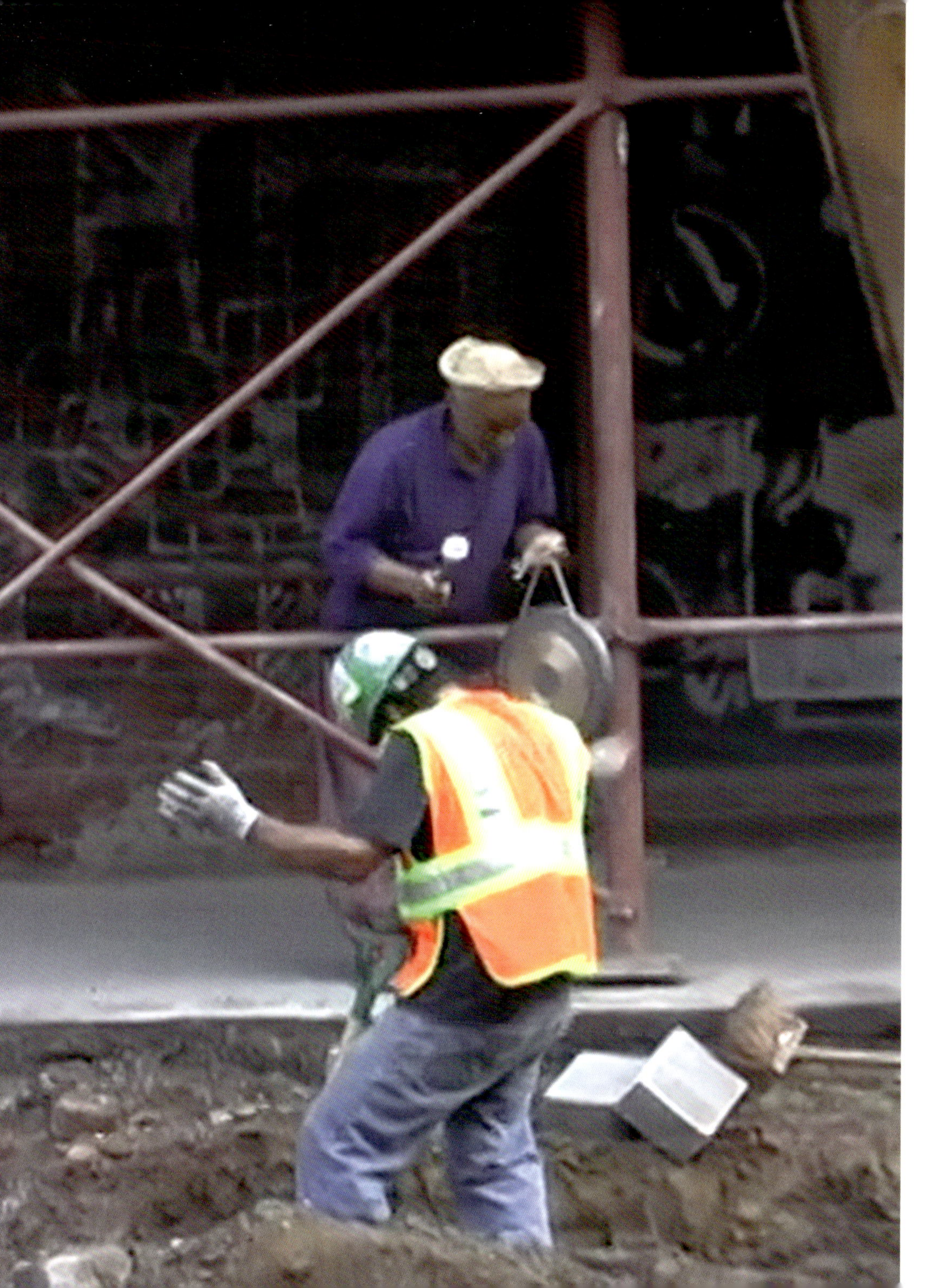

In a more subtle form of impact, Rie Nakajima connects everyday objects to simple mechanical triggers—a small motorized device makes a tin can hit a wall over and over; another rotates a cardboard box so that a tiny ball inside rolls around in a series of small thuds—to create a meditative ecosystem of material, machine, and cricket-like tapping.

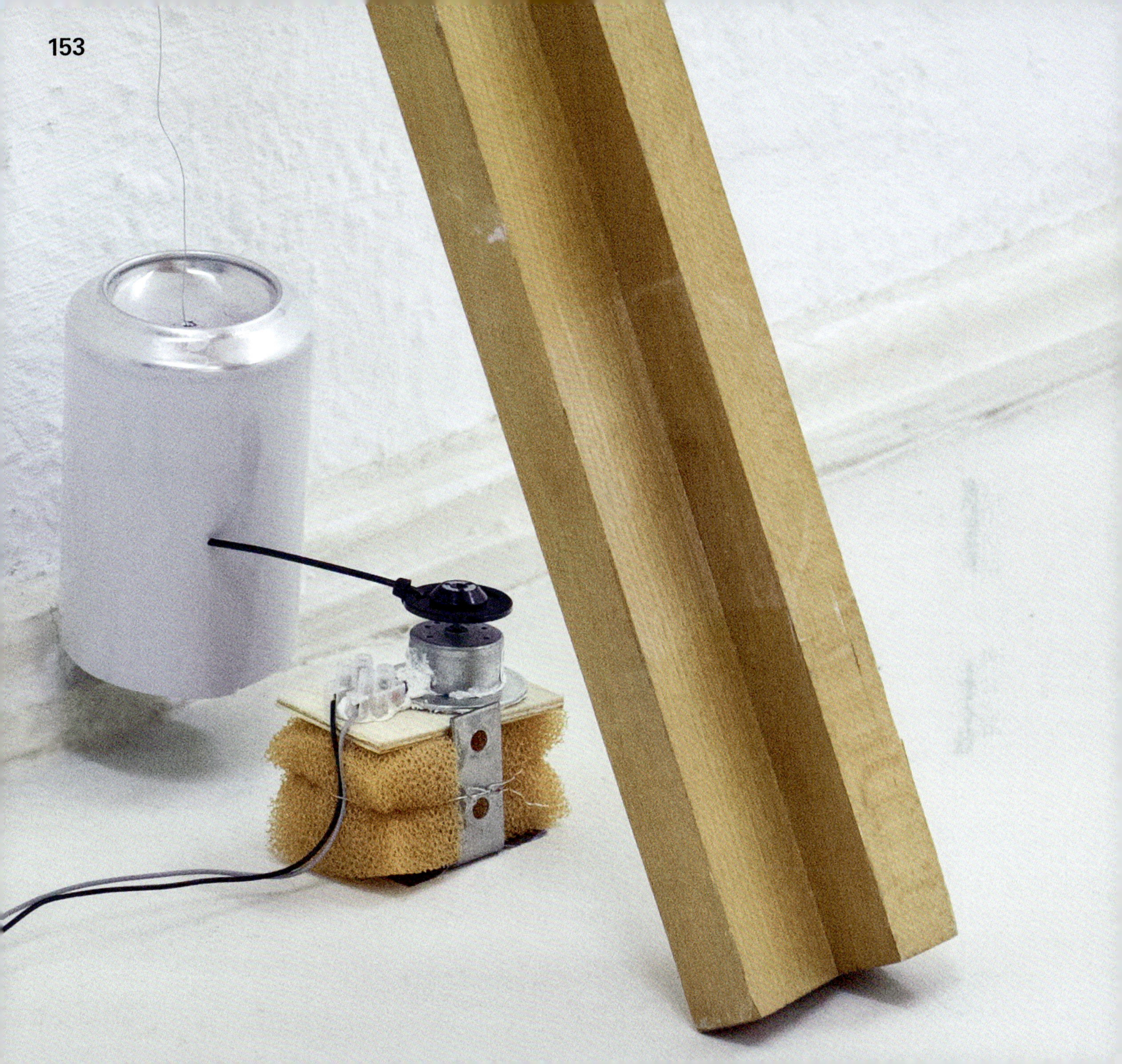

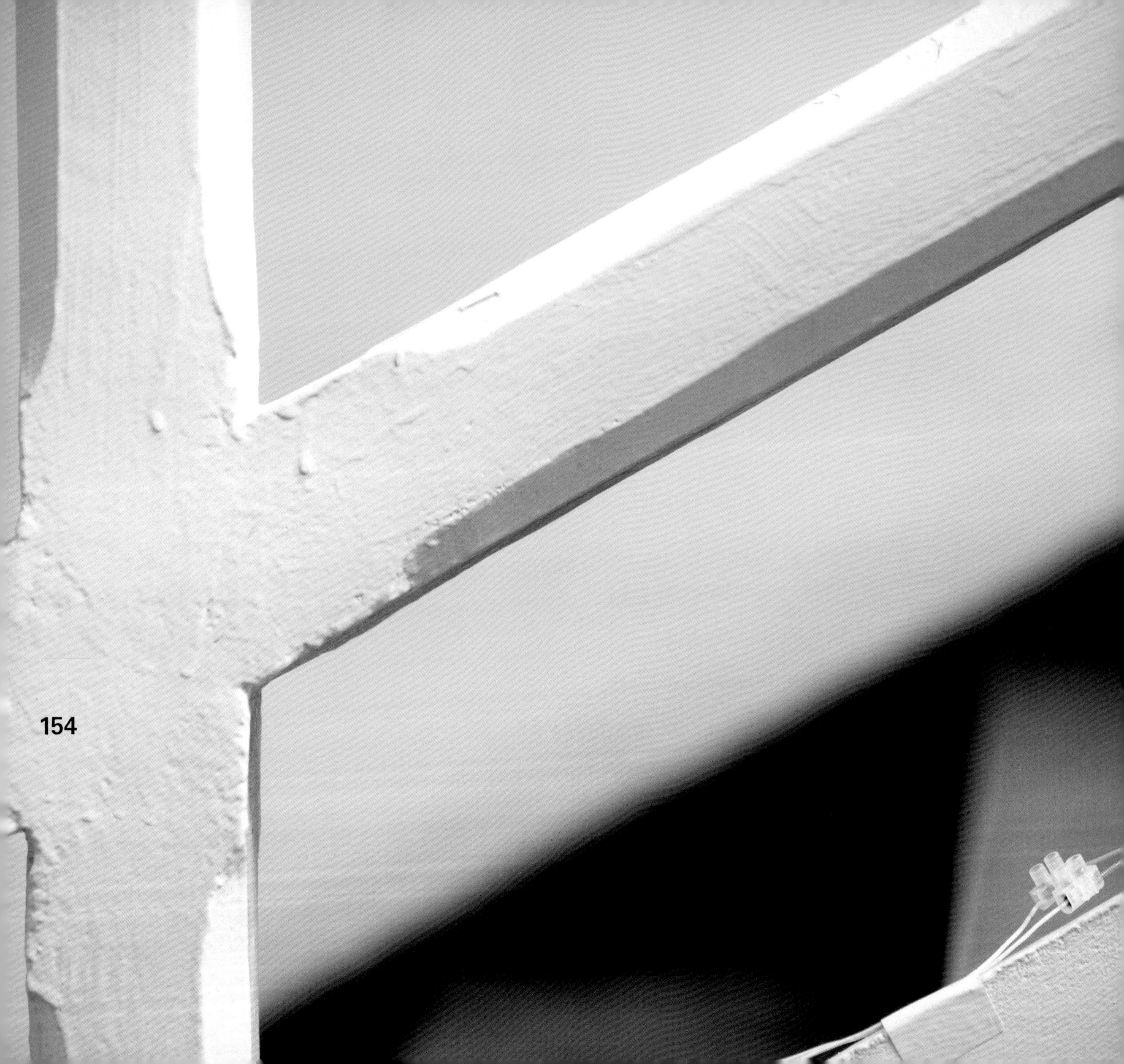

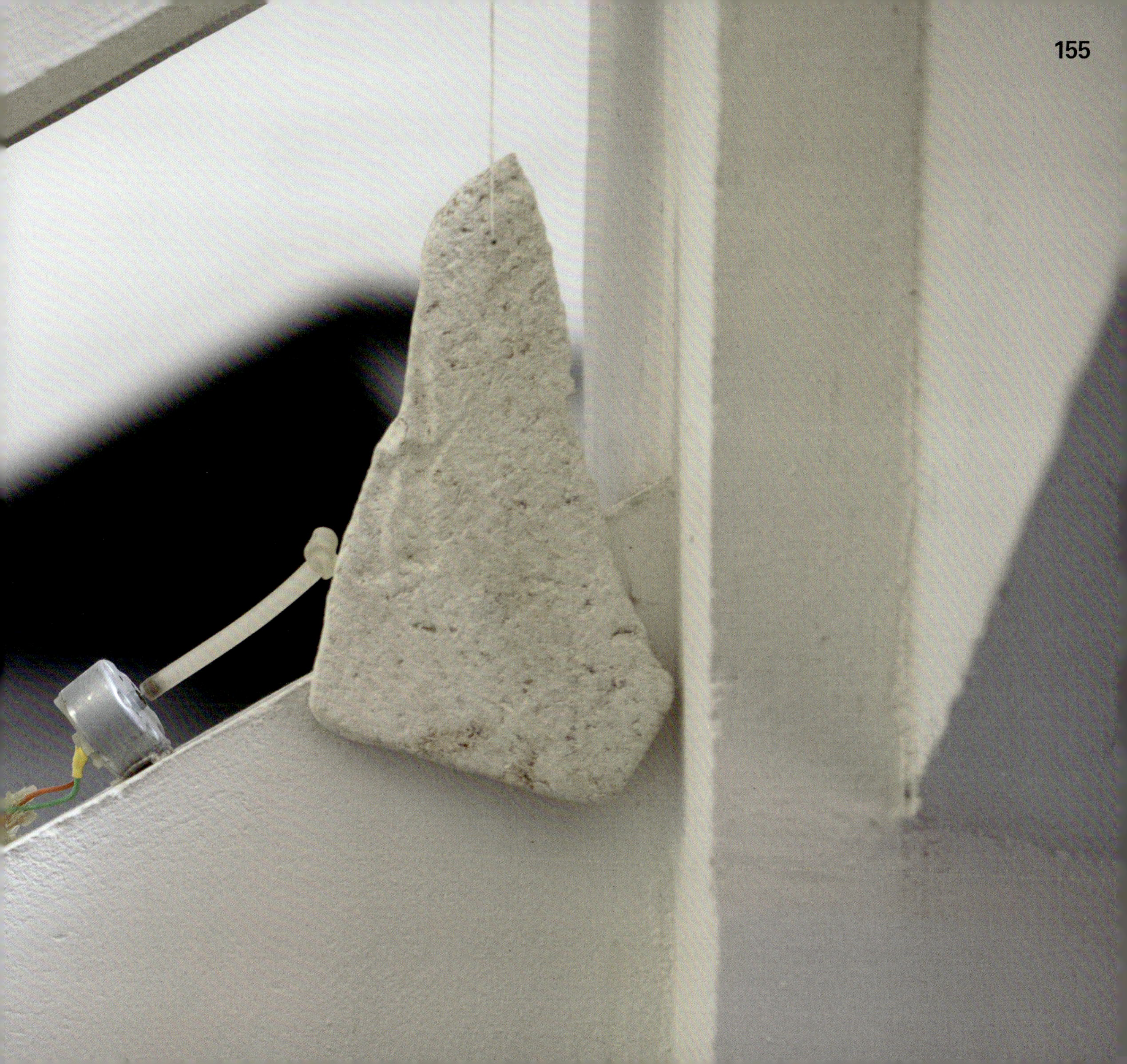

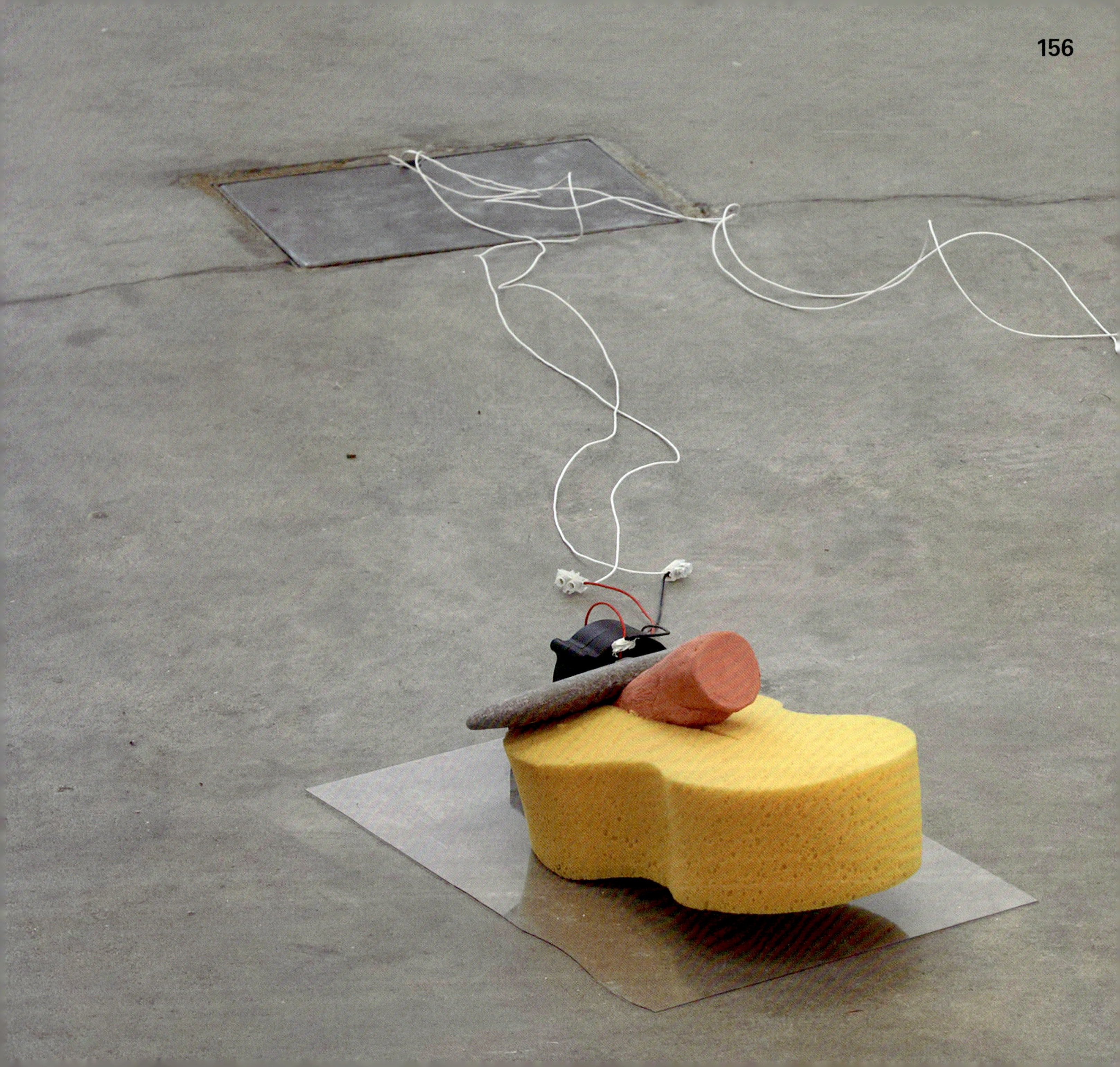

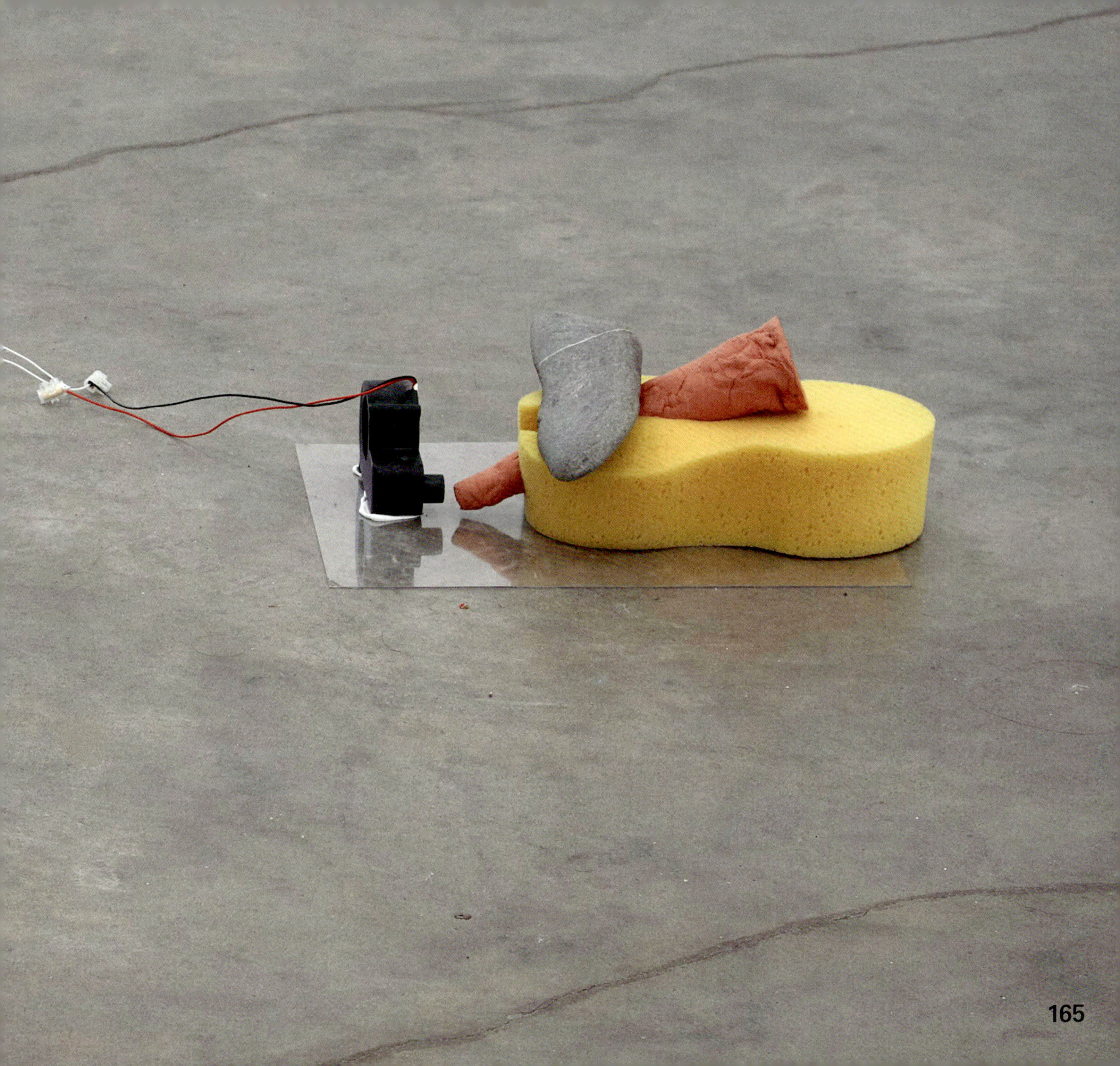

NIC Kay channels their childhood
memories of table drumming on school desks to give shape to a choreographic
composition—because where the drum is, dance is never far behind.

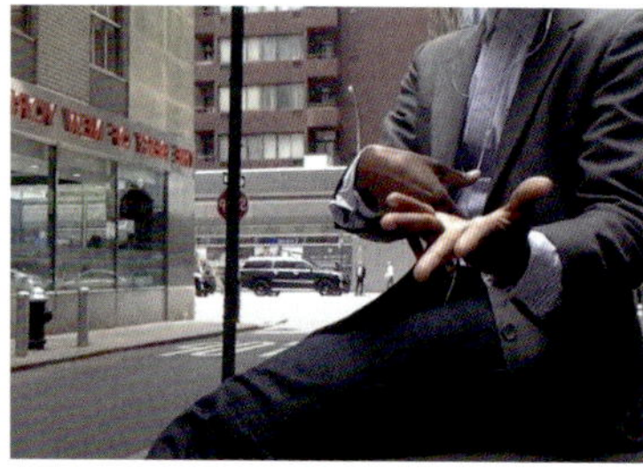

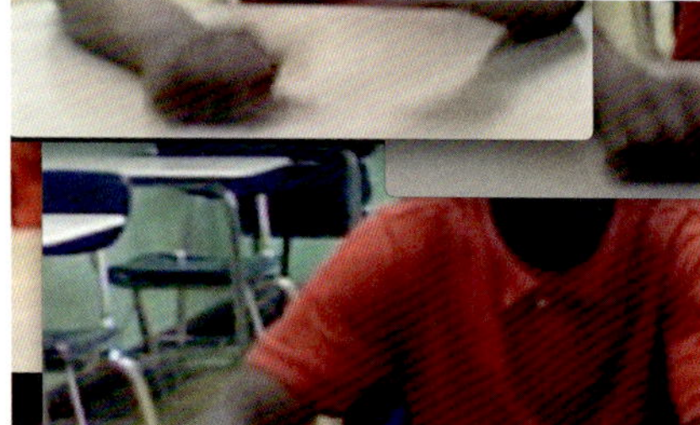

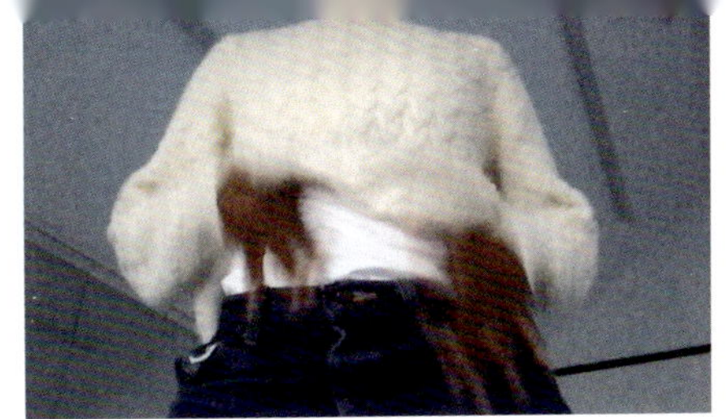

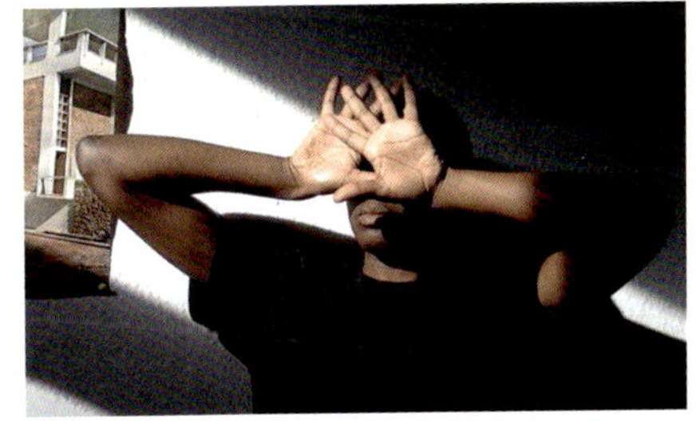

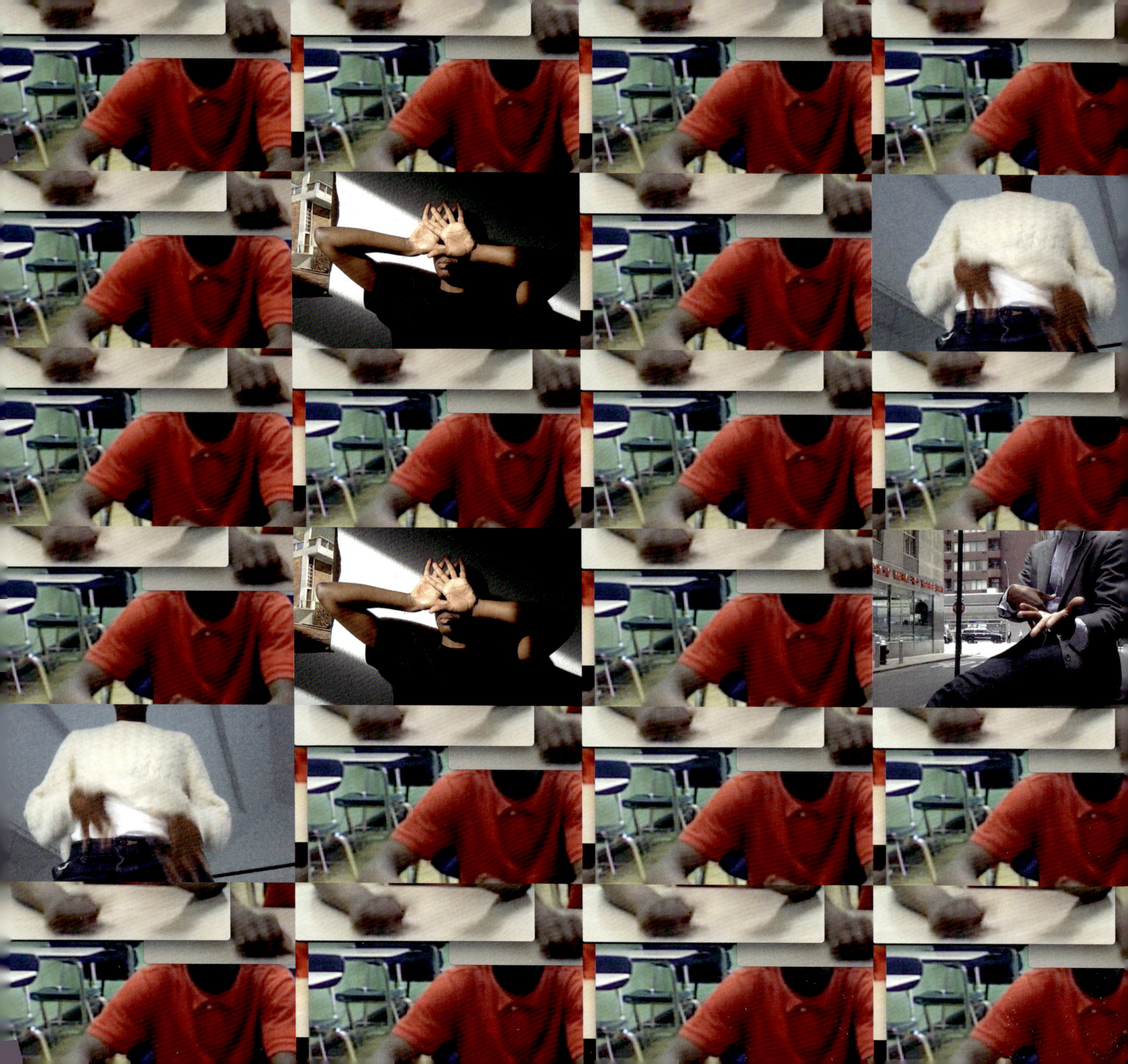

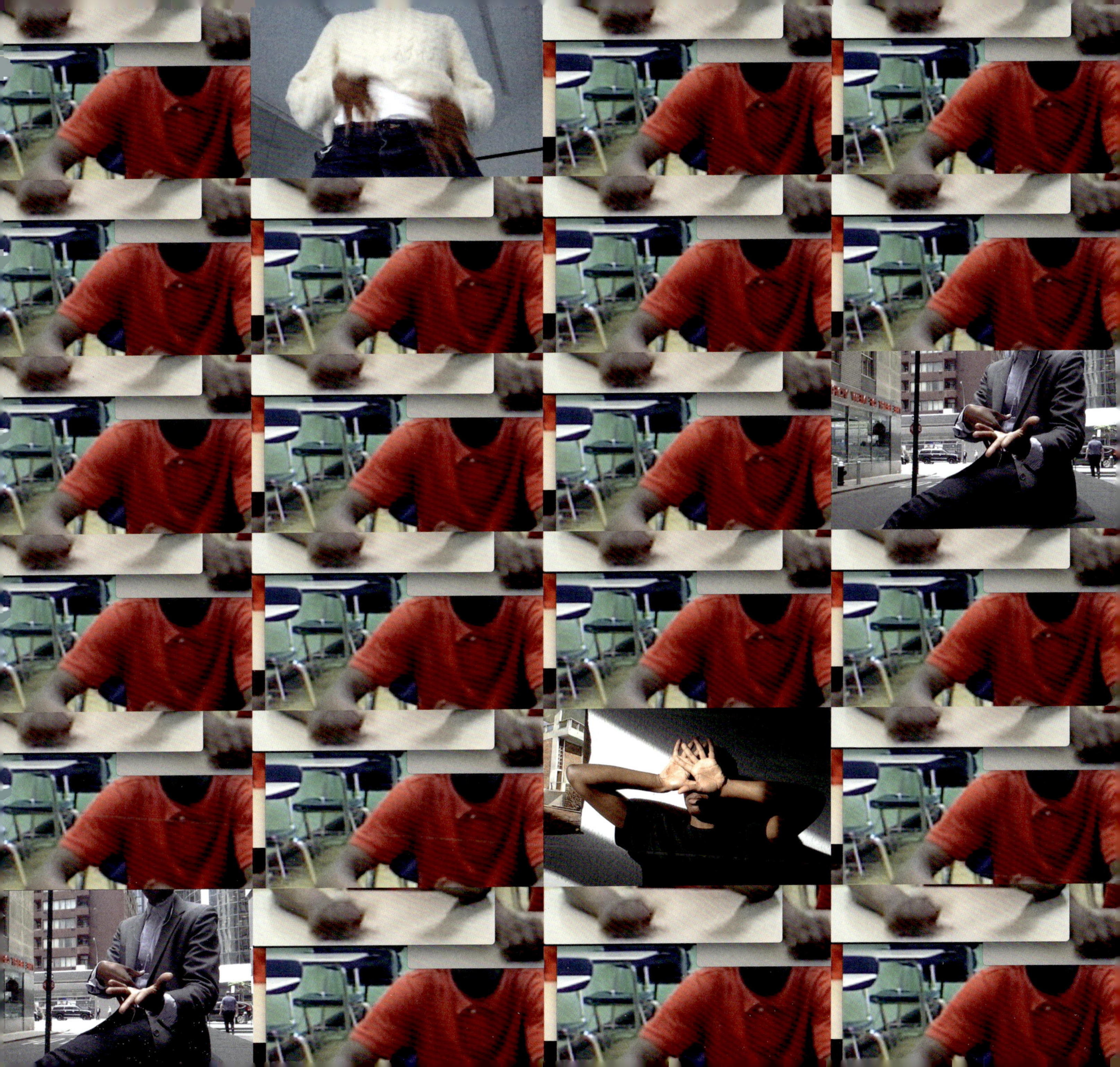

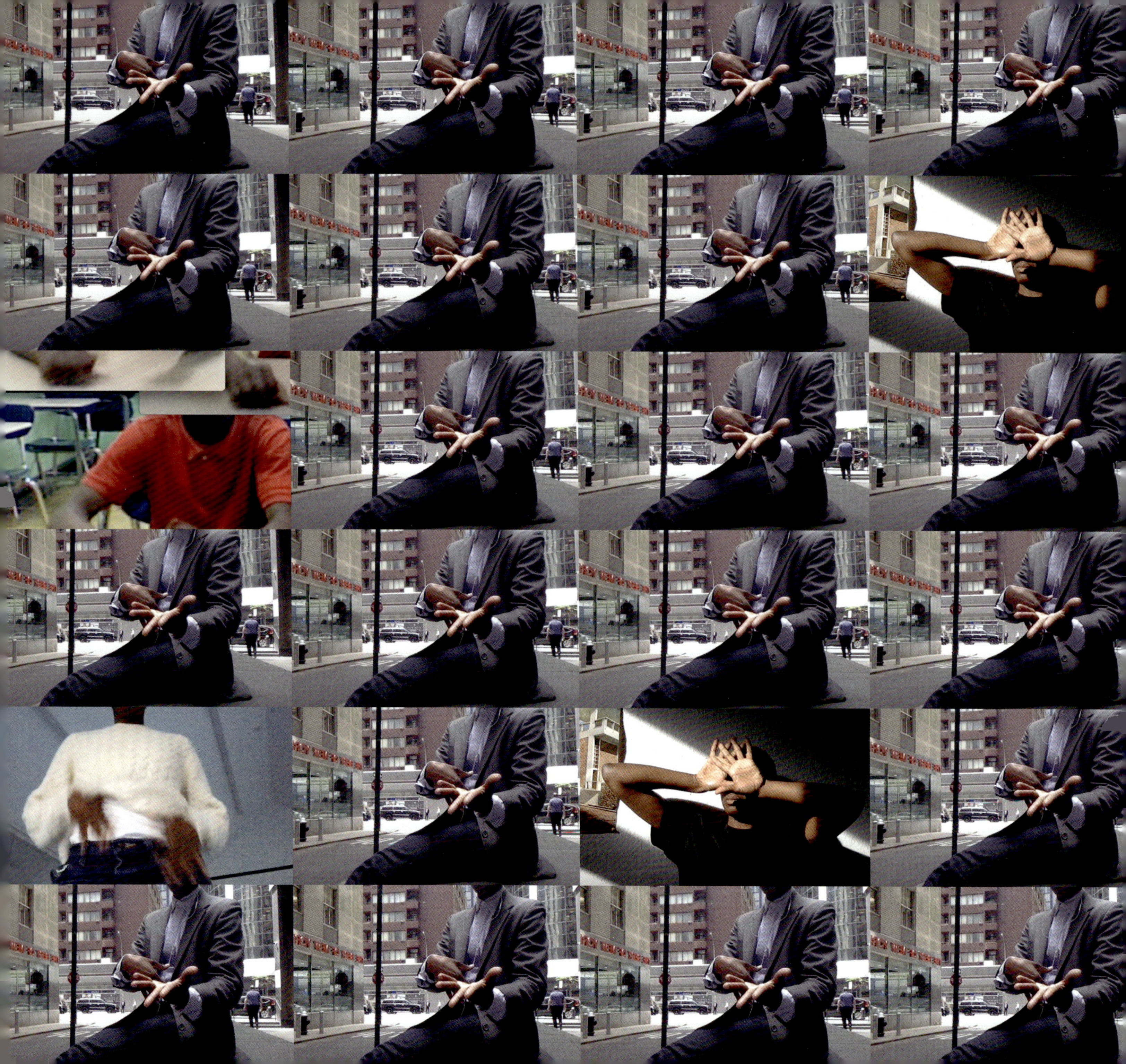

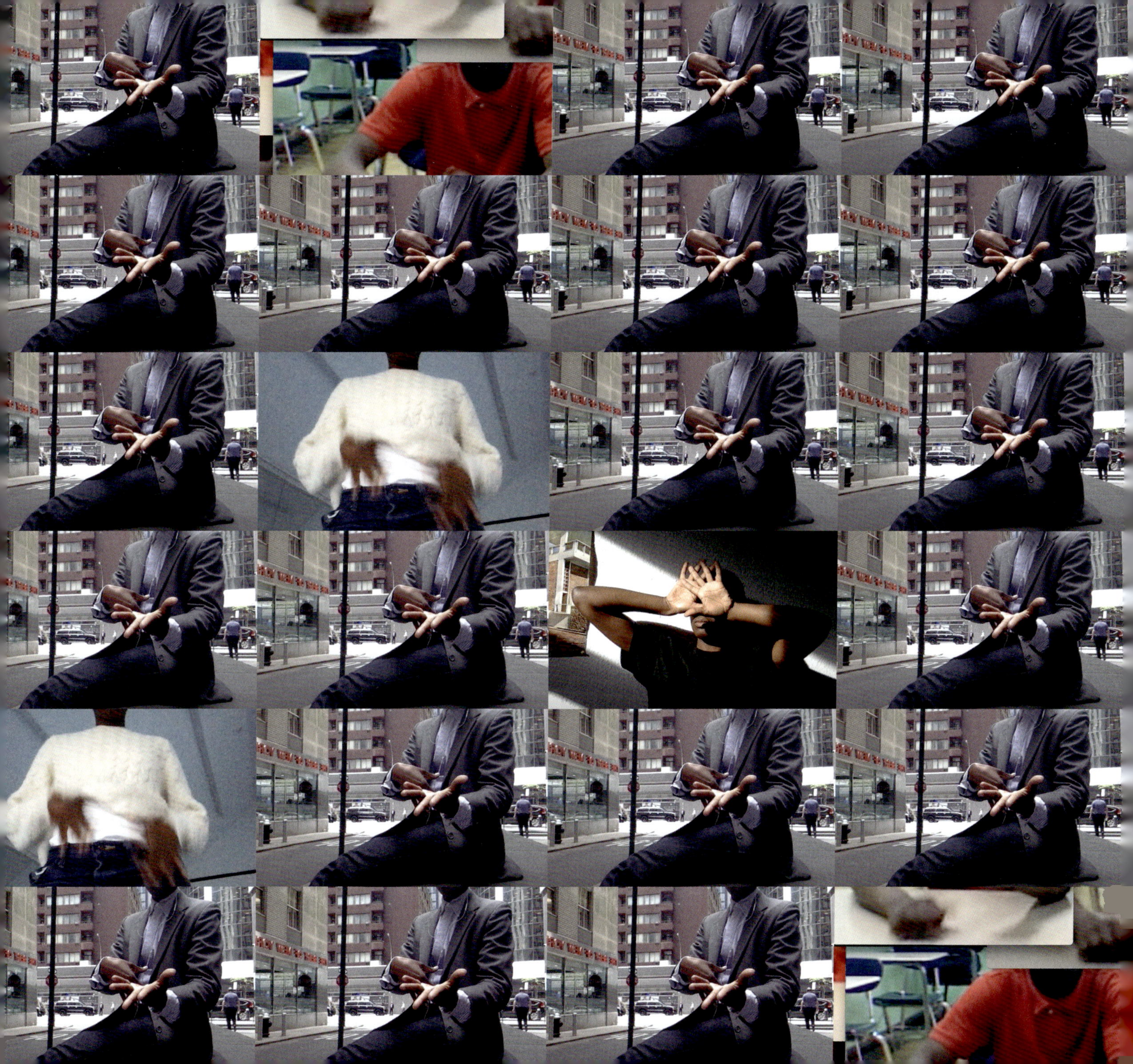

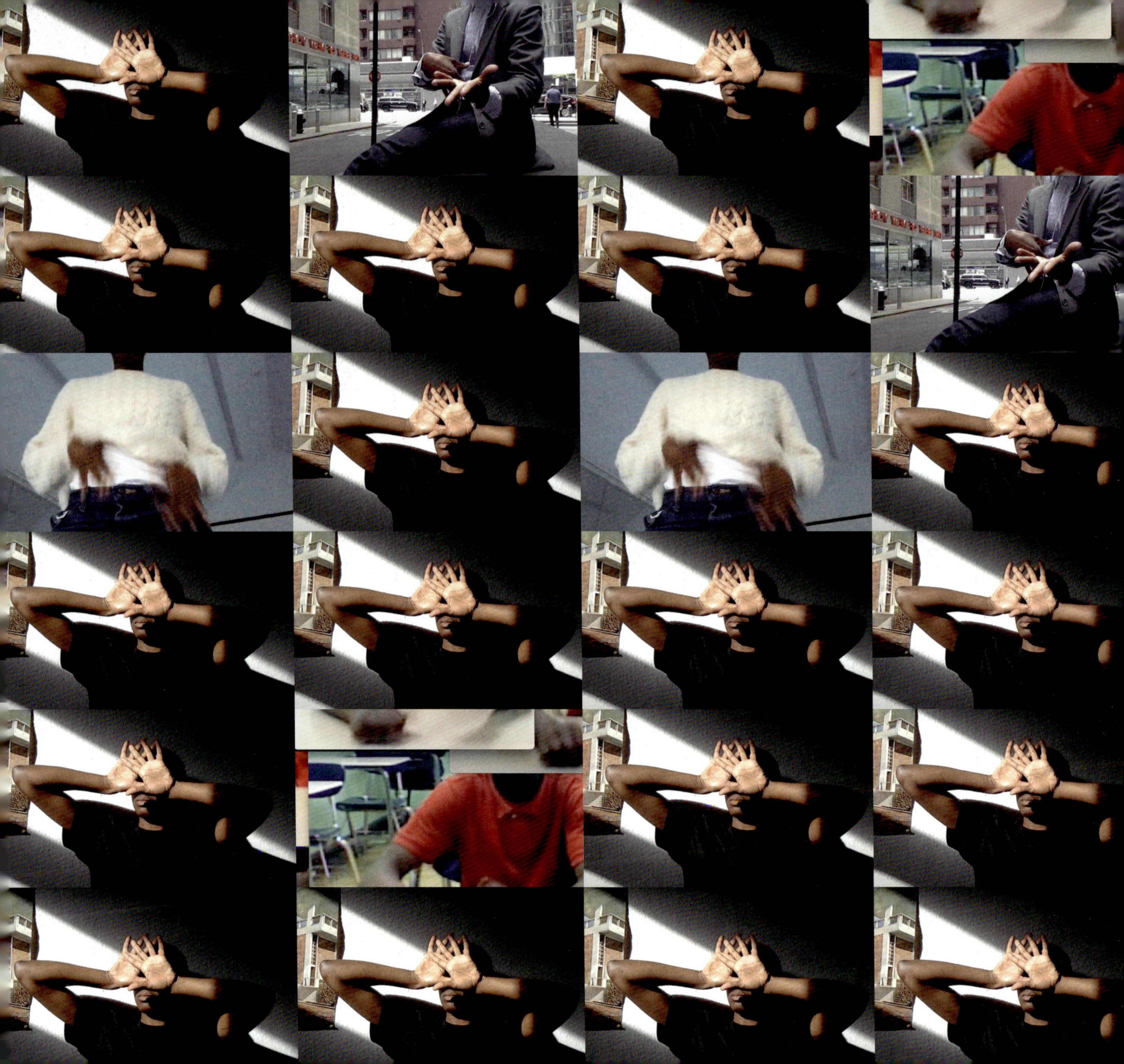

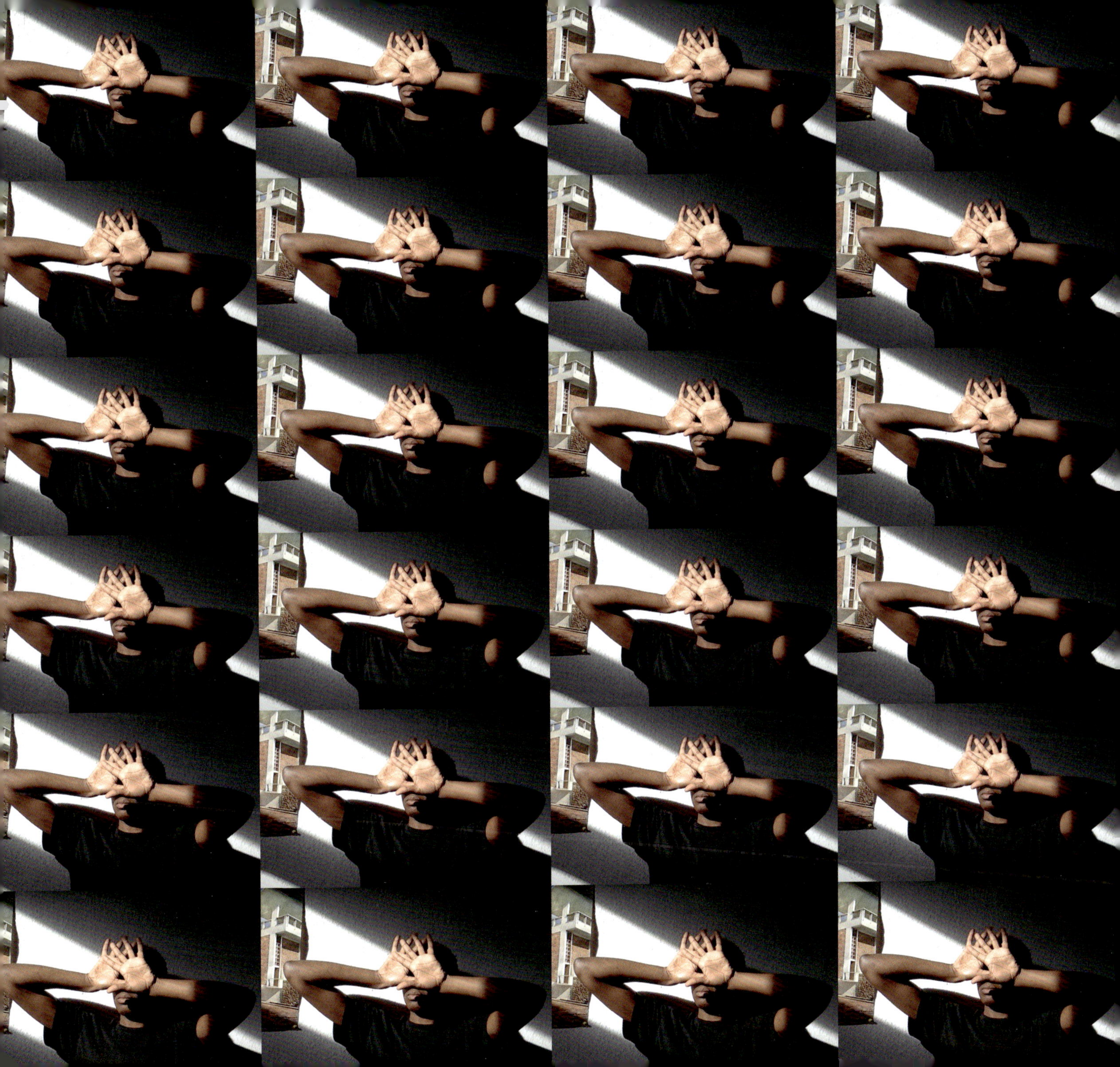

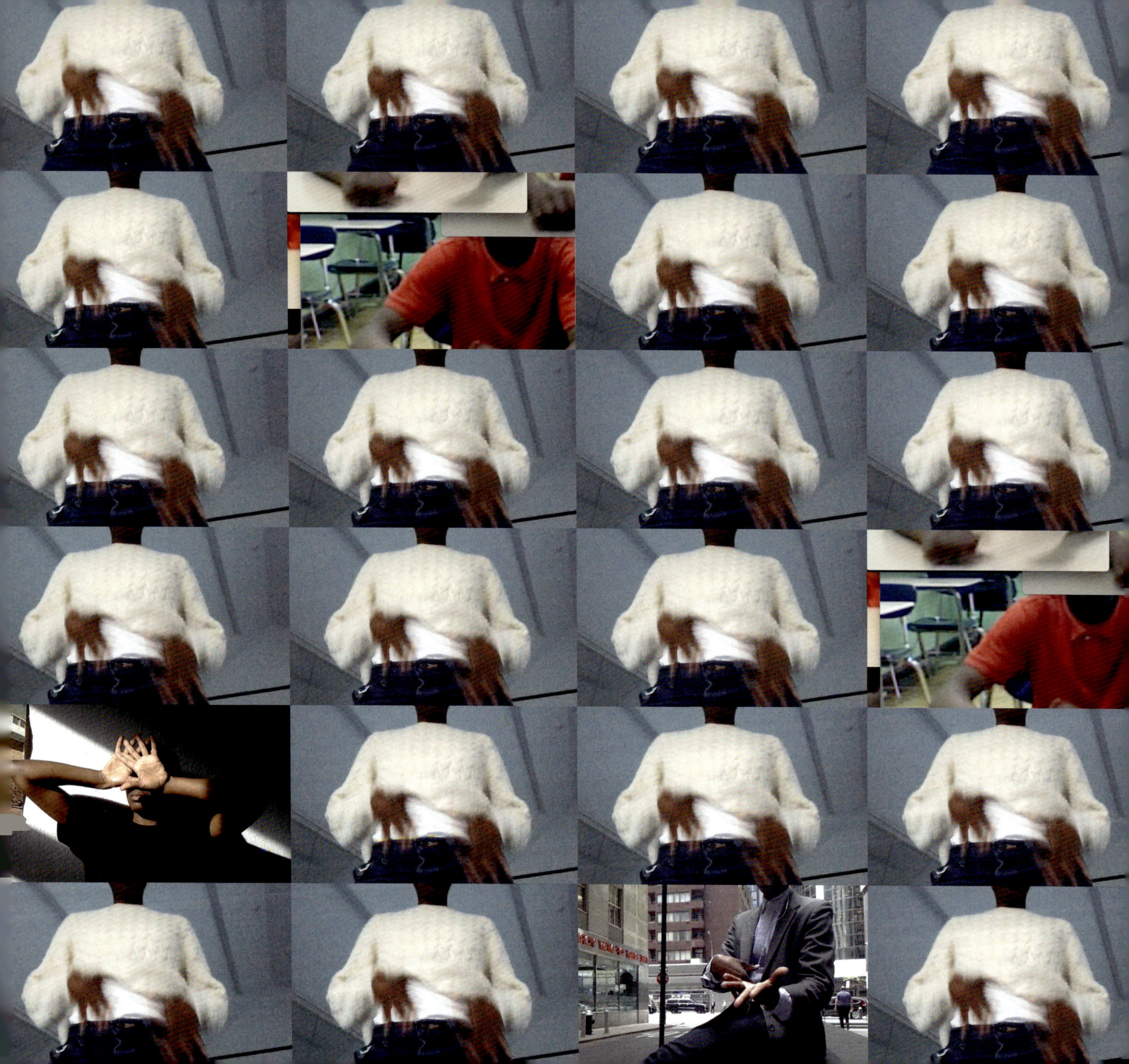

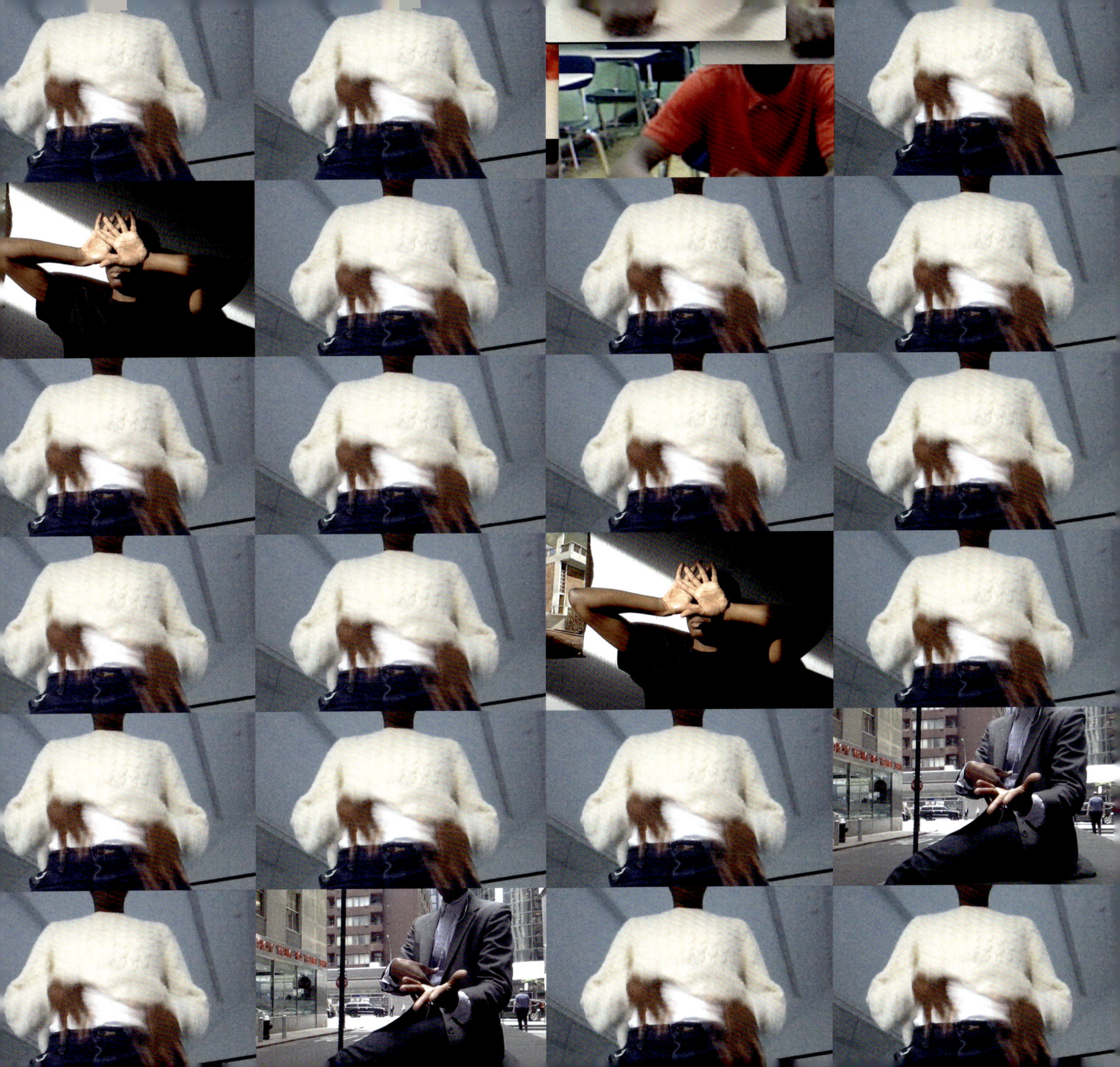

                                                        Francis Alÿs
instructs individual British guards, in uniform, to wander the streets and link up with
other guards whenever they happen to cross paths. What begins as a chaotic but
emancipated polyrhythm gradually becomes a single disciplined beat.

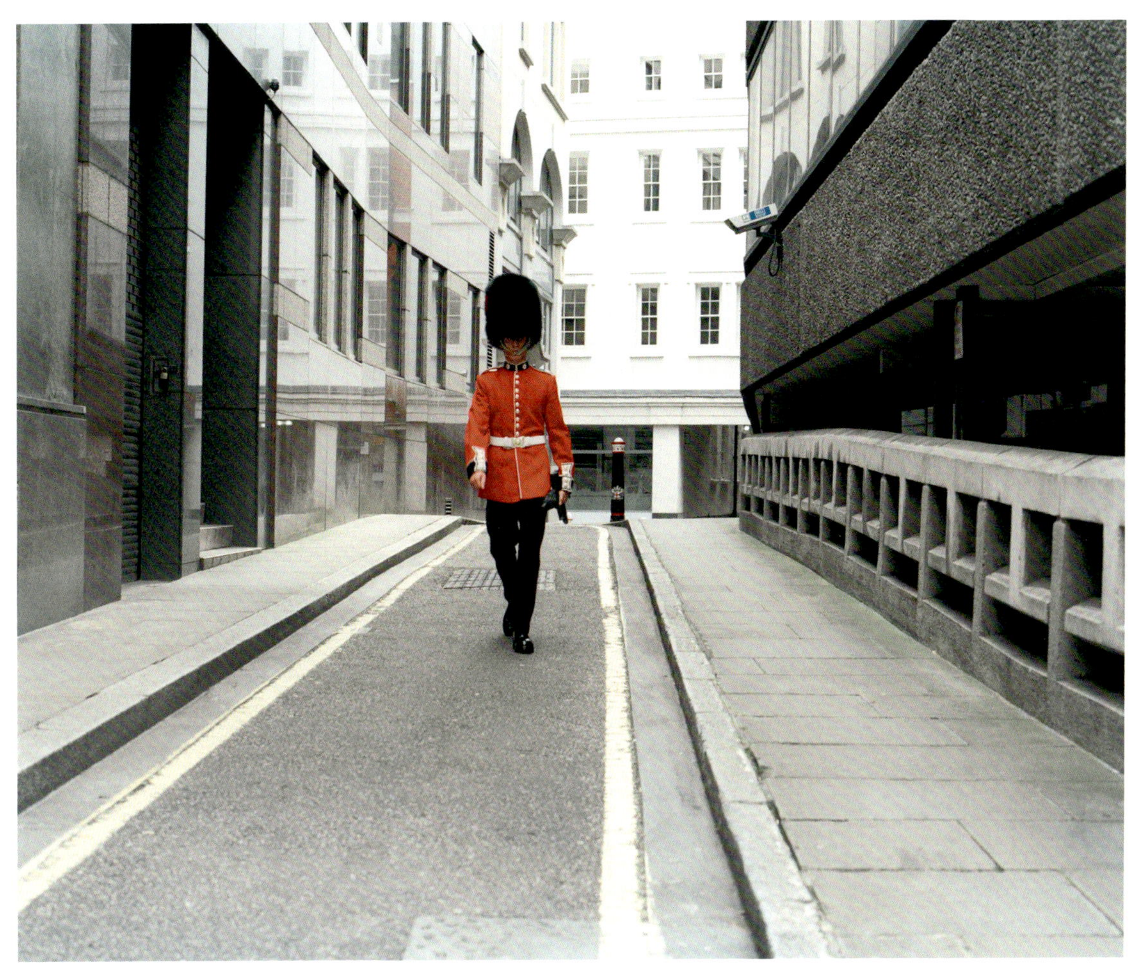

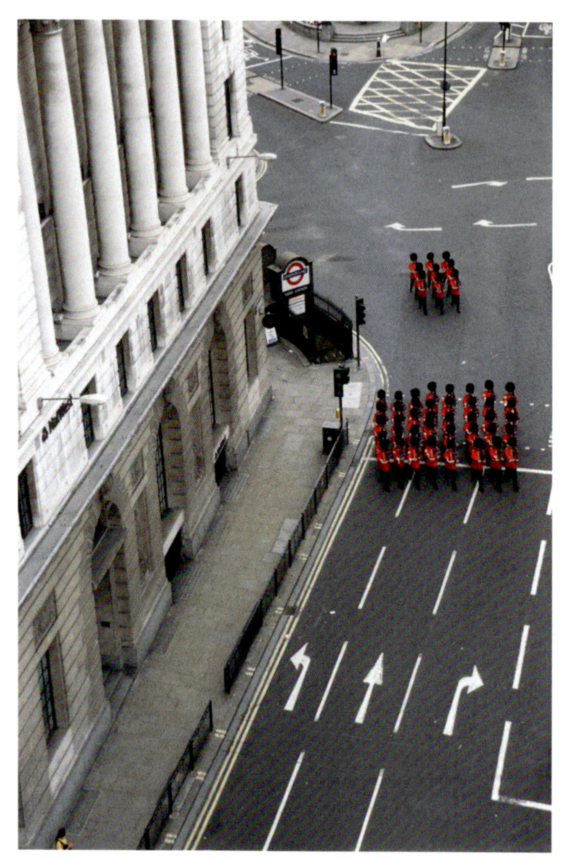

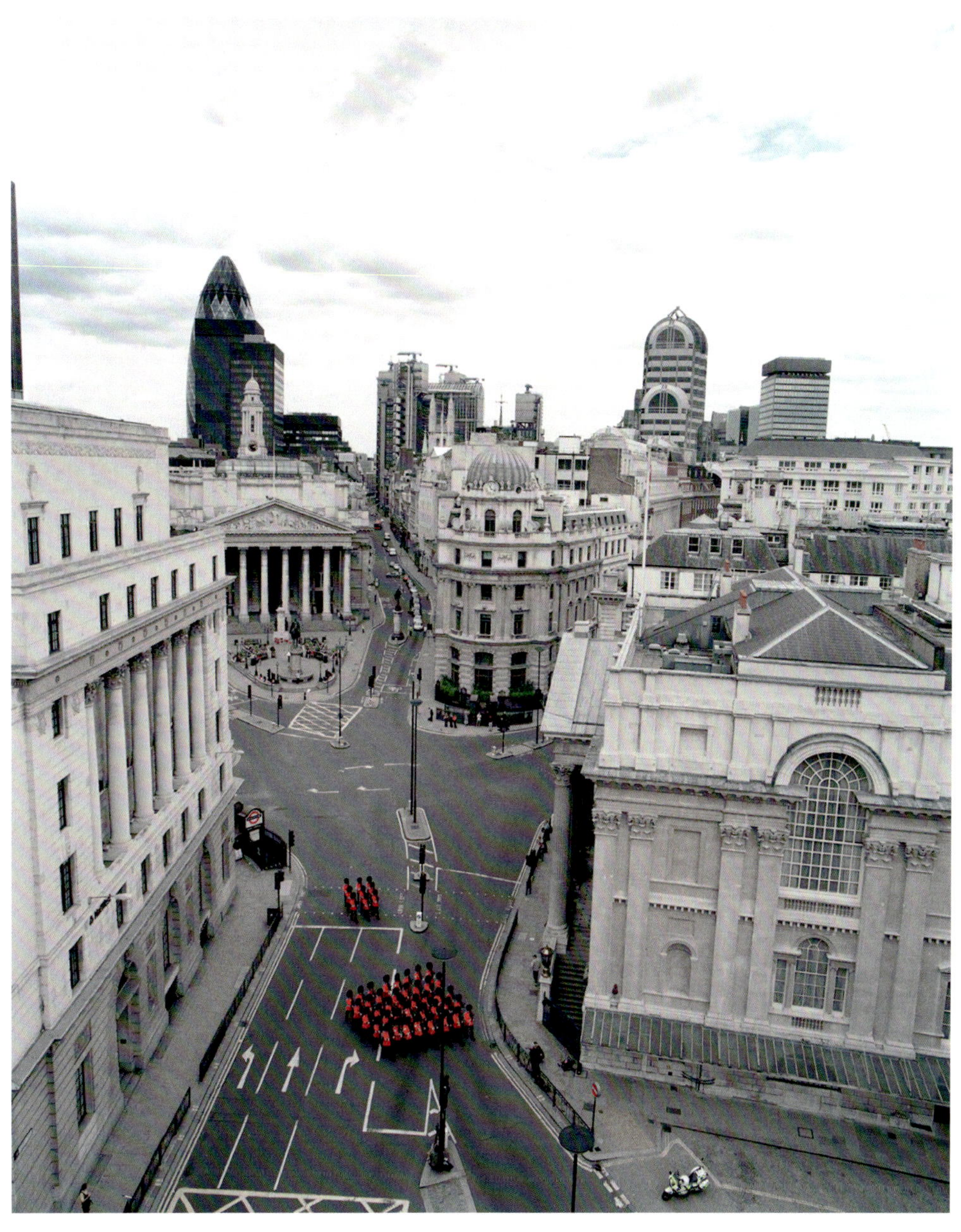

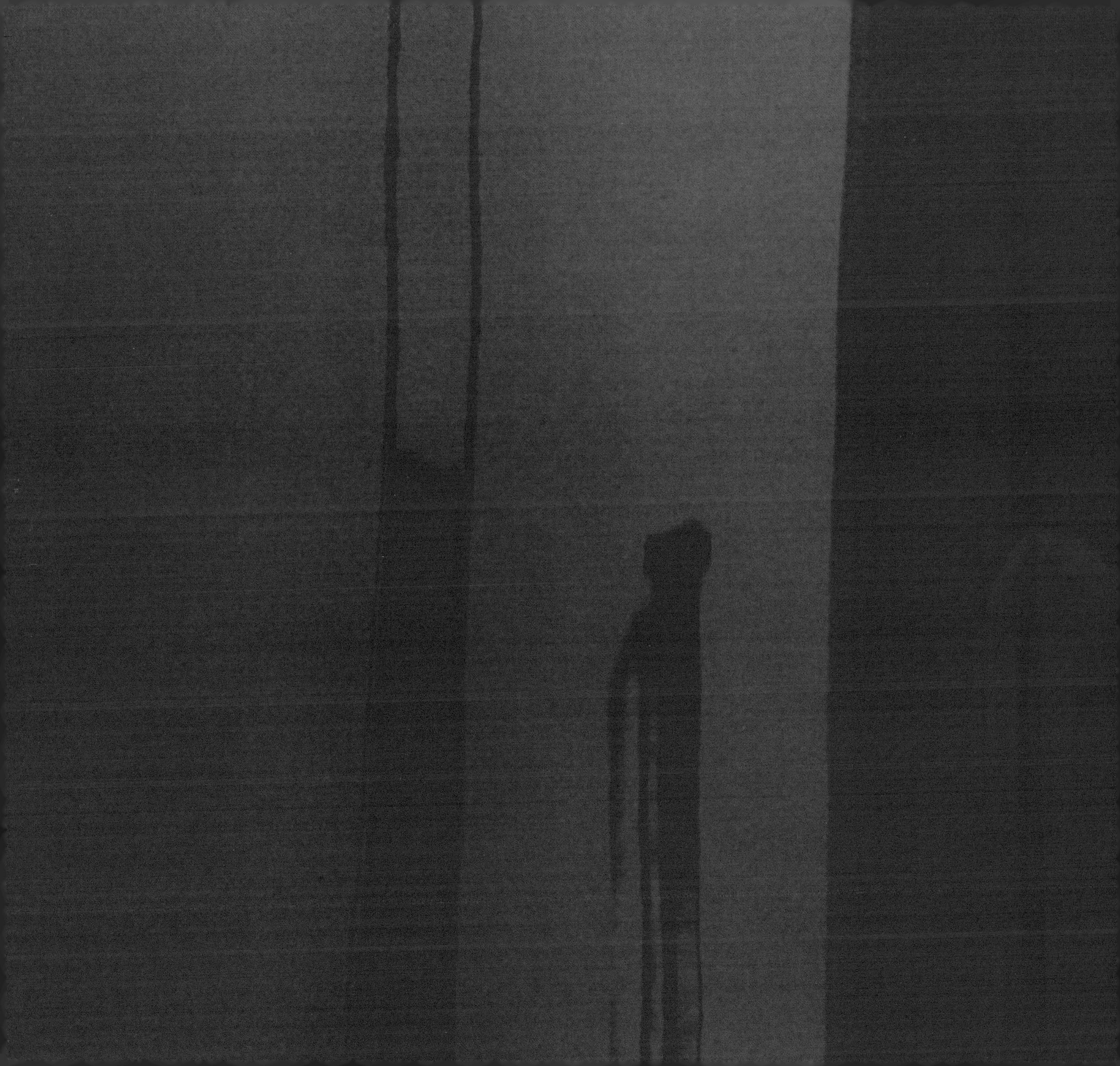

Visitors to the
exhibition can strike one of Davina Semo's bells, should they choose to issue a call,
at any time, for any reason,

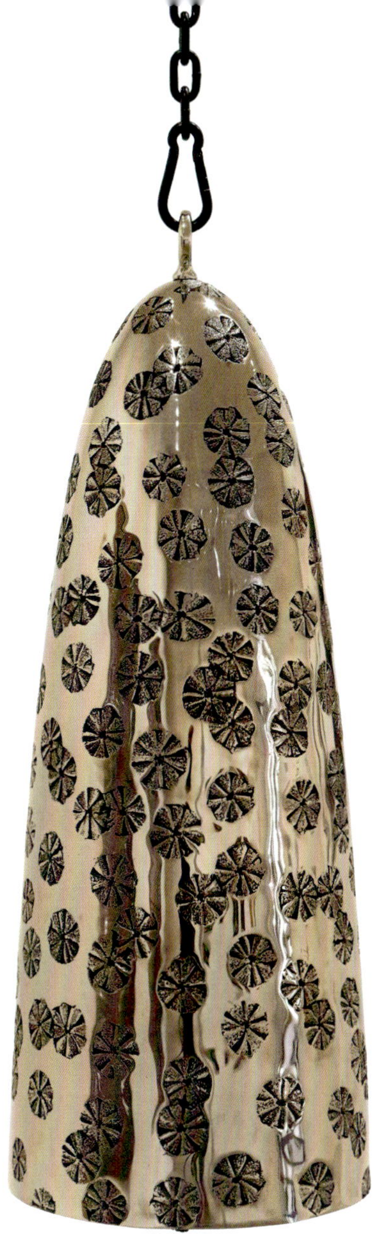

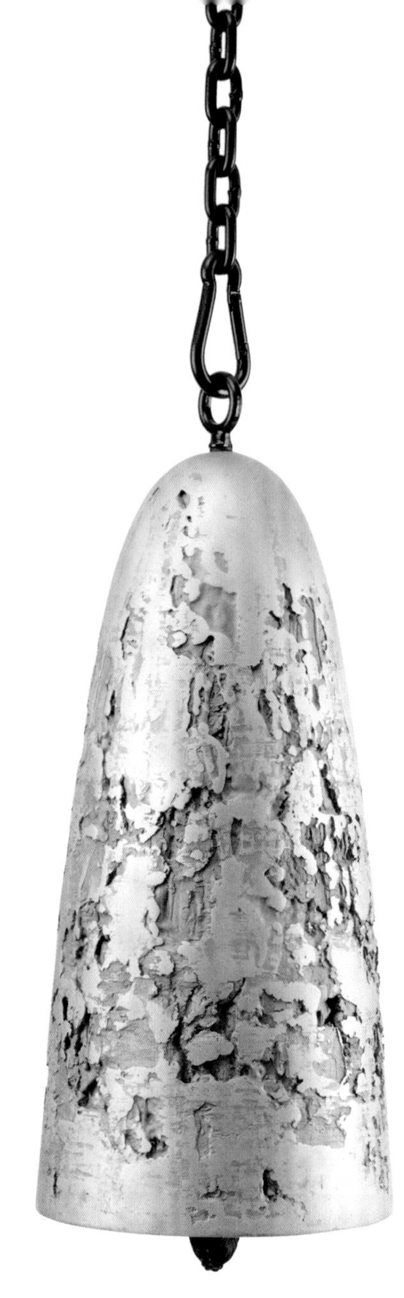

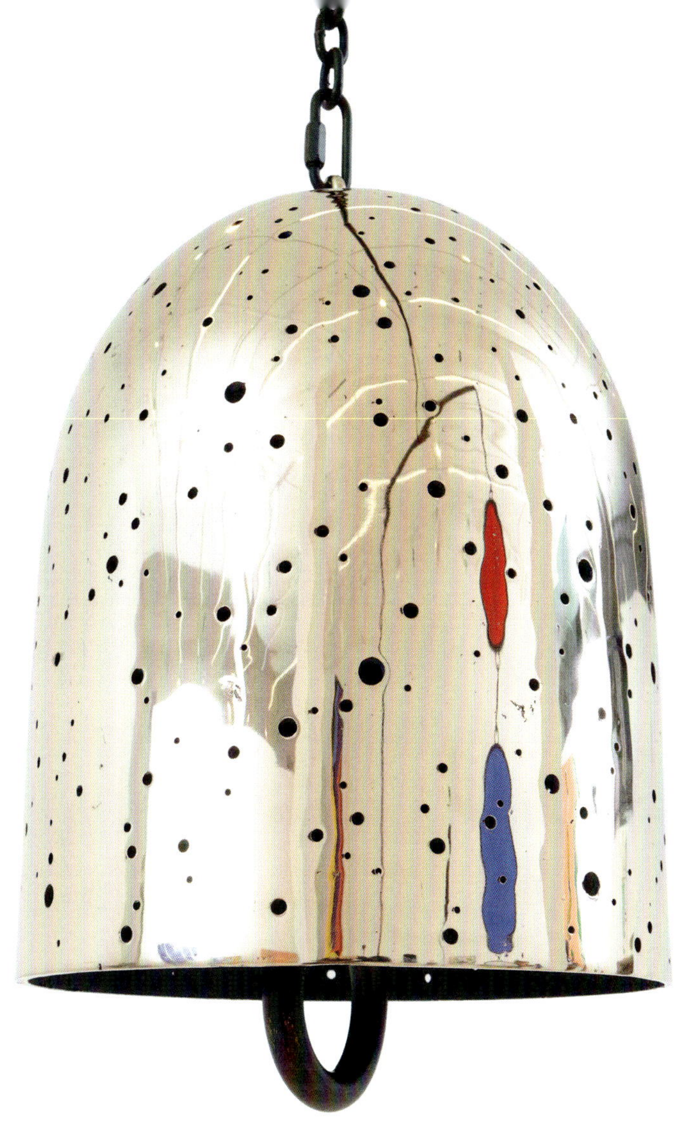

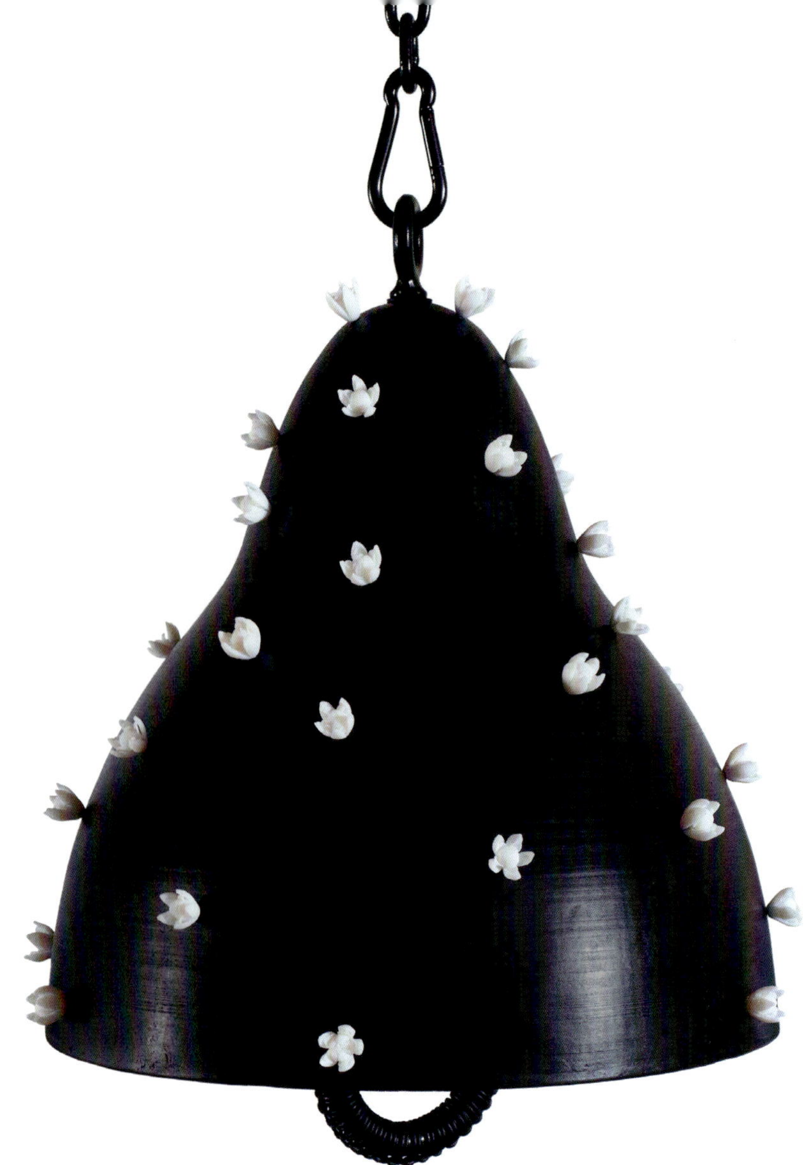

190

191

and anyone can wear Haegue Yang's scarves and bracelets made of brass- and nickel-plated bells.

and anyone can wear Haegue Yang's scarves and bracelets made of brass- and nickel-plated bells.

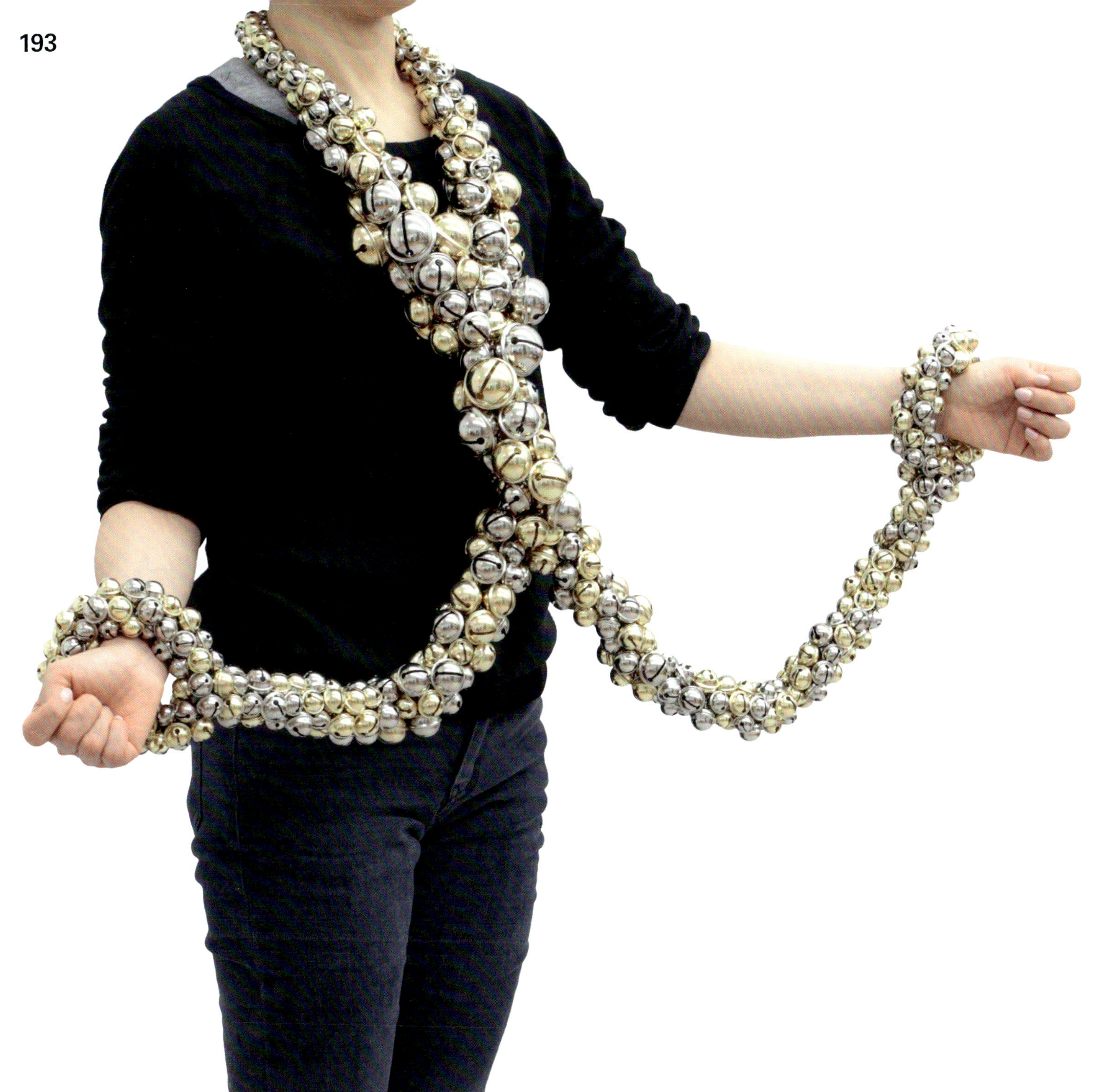

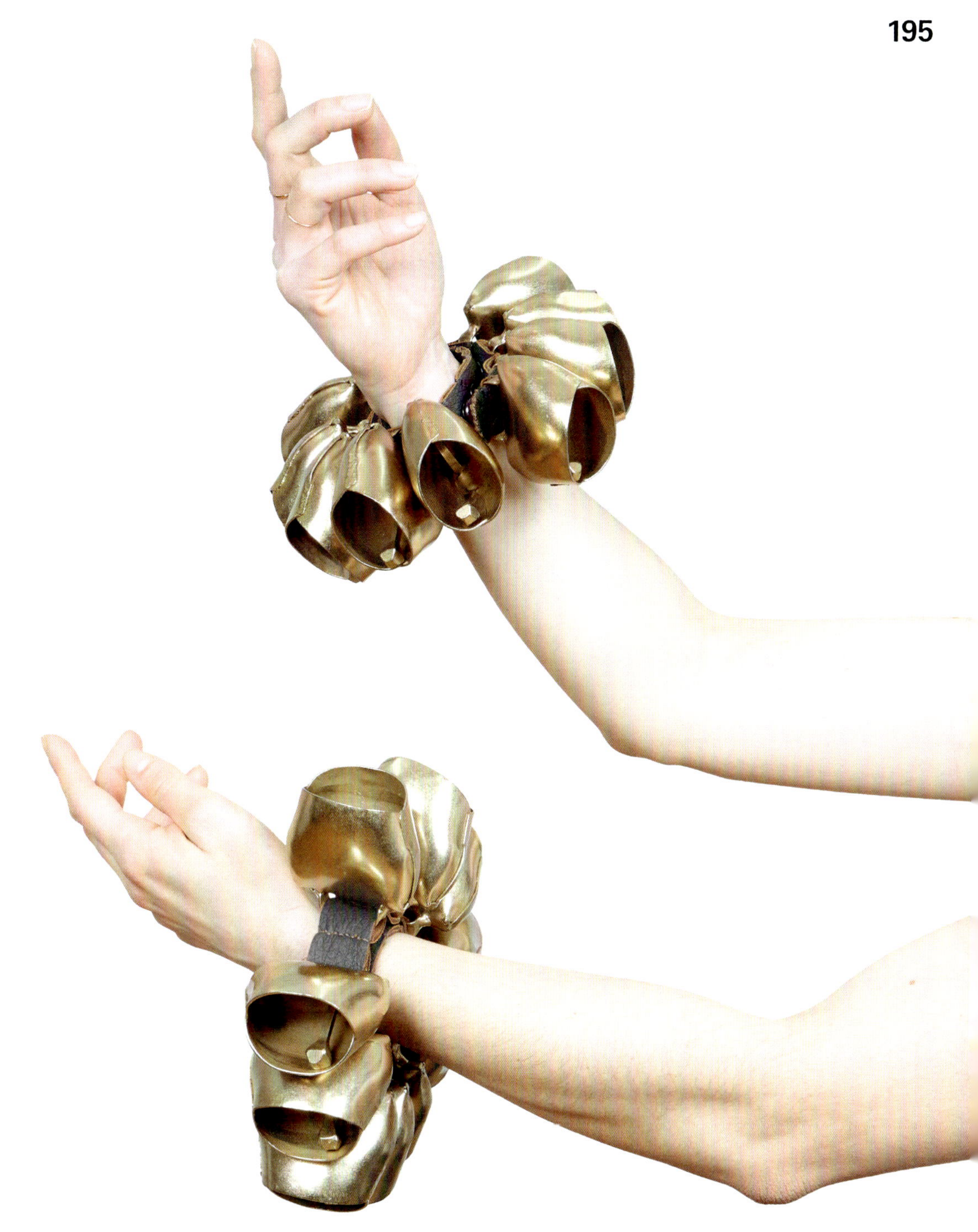

Our metronome, short one-minute tracks that occur every fifteen minutes, is the voice of poet Susan Howe, accompanied by David Grubbs on keyboard, reading her collages where words and bits of words are cut up and spliced into each other to create a language that starts, stops, sputters, and erupts again, in percussive rhythm.

EN WITHOUT

ALL BUT THE LOUD BE   a;
ALL THINGS BUT THE   tis
E END: •   •   •   •   lla
E END: •   •   •   •   lla
HE END: •   •   •   •   lla
AND LONGS FOR THE E   lla
are azure spreads   lla

E.

ME WAS BURU
ITE HUSH END
ITE HUSH END
IN LOVE IN TH
IN LOVE IN TI

:e is to start a passage with a few pencill

ontinue it on the typewriter, so that I sho

pt of any poem of any length, and I nev

s/u/a/v/i
a/b/c/d/

A beat cuts in different ways—it's the part of a song that inspires the body to come alive, but it's also an act of physical violence that forces another body to collapse. To some, the drum is the peaceful and restorative heartbeat of Mother Earth, while to others, it signals an urgent call to war.

Drum Listens to Heart weaves all of these different forms of percussion together—physical and sociopolitical, literal and metaphorical—and juxtaposes instances of physical impact and vibration with forms of control, emancipation, and community building. It offers a framework and a vocabulary that binds art and politics to each other in percussive ways.

—ANTHONY HUBERMAN

LISTENS

HEART

LIVE
PERFORMANCE
SERIES

DRUM

TO

KAREN STACKPOLE & GINO ROBAIR

OCT. 29, 2022

LIVE AT THE WATTIS INSTITUTE

360 KANSAS STREET, SAN FRANCISCO
WATTIS.ORG

4:00 PM | FREE

RAVEN CHACON

PERFORMANCE CONDUCTED BY ANDY MEYERSON

OCT. 29, 2022

LIVE AT THE WATTIS INSTITUTE

360 KANSAS STREET, SAN FRANCISCO
WATTIS.ORG

3:00 PM | FREE

NKISI

NOV. 26, 2022

LIVE AT THE LAB

2948 16TH STREET, SAN FRANCISCO
THELAB.ORG

9:00 PM | $15

MOOR MOTHER ENSEMBLE

DEC. 17, 2022

LIVE AT THE LAB

2948 16TH STREET, SAN FRANCISCO
THELAB.ORG

7:30 PM | $15

VALENTINA MAGALETTI

NOMON

WILLIAM WINANT & IKUE MORI

JAN. 21, 2023
LIVE AT THE LAB

2948 16TH STREET, SAN FRANCISCO
THELAB.ORG

7:30 PM | $15

MUSIC RESEARCH STRATEGIES

RAVEN CHACON
PERFORMANCE CONDUCTED BY ANDY MEYERSON

FEB. 25, 2023
LIVE AT THE LAB

2948 16TH STREET, SAN FRANCISCO
THELAB.ORG

7:30 PM | $15

RINGING IN A HAUNTED ROOM

RINGING IN A HAUNTED ROOM

RINGING IN A HAUNTED ROOM

RINGING IN A HAUNTED ROOM

RINGING IN A HAUNTED ROOM

RINGING IN A HAUNTED ROOM

RINGING IN A HAUNTED ROOM

RINGING IN A HAUNTED ROOM

RINGING IN A HAUNTED ROOM

RINGING IN A HAUNTED ROOM

RINGING IN A HAUNTED ROOM

RINGING IN A HAUNTED ROOM

RINGING IN A HAUNTED ROOM

RINGING IN A HAUNTED ROOM

RINGING IN A HAUNTED ROOM

RINGING IN A HAUNTED ROOM

RINGING IN A HAUNTED ROOM

DIEGO
VILLALOBOS

DIEGO
VILLALOBOS

DIEGO
VILLALOBOS

DIEGO
VILLALOBOS

DIEGO
VILLALOBOS

DIEGO
VILLALOBOS

We live in a time that's out of joint. The philosopher Jacques Derrida gave us this diagnosis through a term disguised as a pun: *hauntology*. Merging *haunted* with the *ontological*, this term first appeared in *Specters of Marx: The State of the Debt, the Work of Mourning and the New International*, which he wrote after the collapse of the Soviet Union and the presumed "end of history." In this work, Derrida thinks of the present as a temporality that's always haunted by the ghosts of unrealized futures, where paths not taken have real consequences for the ways things are.

Repurposing the term in order to write about music, the late cultural theorist Mark Fisher claimed that the West is haunted by the lost futures that never arrived and that it is trapped in between two ontological (and hauntological) states of being——the *no longer* and the *not yet*.[1] The first refers to that which *is no longer* but that continues to resonate as a traumatic compulsion by way of repeating the same fatalistic patterns from the past; the second refers to that which has *not yet* happened but that generates an anticipation that is already influencing certain forms of behavior.[2] For Fisher, nostalgia and

trauma are keynotes in this hauntological soundtrack, and he recognizes its lost futures in the crackling music of electronic musicians like The Caretaker and Burial. Many of these musicians are interested in the fragile nature of memory and the sounds of it breaking down through the wear and tear of vinyl records and cassette tapes, as heard on The Caretaker's *Selected Memories from the Haunted Ballroom* (1999), for example, in which he re-records melancholic British ballroom music from the 1930s and brings it back to life through crackling noise and choppy editing.

For the Congolese musician Nkisi, rhythms have the potentiality of accessing precolonial forms of knowledge and technology. And yet this information isn't audible to everyone. Tapping into these ghost frequencies requires tuning oneself to a different key, listening beyond one's ears and with the senses. For Nkisi, the repetitive beats of techno music allow her to enter a state of trance and unlock this ancestral code, as the dance floor becomes a site for epiphany and rhythm a tool for world building. Brought together, this can conjure a diverse range of possible futures, some of them intersecting through resonance and others leading toward Fisher's "lost futures," caught between the *no longer* and the *not yet*.

In a parallel gesture, the Diné artist Raven Chacon's 2003 album *Meet The Beatless*

reimagines the most iconic rock and roll band of all time as a Frankenstein monster. Consisting of ten songs assembled by 140 shards of Beatles tracks, the album is a collection of catchy pop tunes that have been transformed into a frenetic poltergeist of sound. Chacon released the album (or counter-album) under the moniker The Kleptones, a play on the words *kleptomaniac* and *tone*. The name references the fact that, just as Frankenstein's monster was assembled from stolen body parts, The Beatles— and rock and roll more generally—came to be by taking from and abstracting the blues music that came before them. While Fisher's hauntological musicians reflect on the disappearing white working class and rave culture in the UK, Chacon's *Meet The Beatless* creates a sonic palimpsest that makes audible a musical history suppressed by the practice of appropriation. Simultaneously, it fills in the gaps with noise and unrecognizable musical passages, crafting a sonic camouflage that keeps hidden what once was colonized.

By reclaiming the past, Chacon also reclaims the future. In his book *Hungry Listening: Resonant Theory for Indigenous Sound Studies*, the Stó:lō scholar Dylan Robinson refers to what he calls a critical listening positionality, which "involves a self-reflexive questioning of how race, class, gender, sexuality, ability, and cultural background intersect and influence the way we are able to

1   Mark Fisher, *Ghosts of My Life: Writings on Depression, Hauntology and Lost Futures* (Winchester, UK: Zero Books, 2014), 107.

2   Ibid., 19.

hear sound, music, and the world around us."[3] To listen outward, we must first actively listen inward. Robinson continues by referencing the music theorist J. Martin Daughtry, who draws on the structure of the palimpsest to ask "that we engage with the 'scriptio inferior' of music that can be considered a haunting of the manuscript by its earlier layers."[4] This form of haunting amplifies the seemingly inaudible histories and contexts embedded within a song or soundscape, and while certain sounds are meant to resonate with a few, others are audible and recognizable by many more.

So where does this leave us?

In line with Nkisi's and Chacon's musical practices, communing with ghost frequencies requires a decolonial way of listening. As Robinson notes throughout his book, this is an intersectional practice where listening is a form of relation, of respecting boundaries (histories and contexts), and of finding common intersections—of calling-and-responding. Sound does not exist in a vacuum but comes already encoded with information. In the words of drummer Chris Corsano, to play music in an ensemble means

"to seamlessly incorporate your sound into the group's, while letting the group's sound dictate what you do."[5]

In preparing a performance, sound technicians need to establish the acoustic resonance of a room by testing its limits. To do that, they push the sound system until it feeds back—what they call *ringing out the room*—which provides them with the parameters for setting the mixing board levels to prevent unwanted feedback during the performance. However, Corsano also speaks of *resonant improvisation*—when an improvisational ensemble intentionally *rings itself in*, creating nothing but feedback. If we listen deeply into the feedback, what will its reverberations say? If we were to ring in a haunted room, will we hear Derrida's ghosts of speculative futures or listen to the dormant epistemologies inside our bodies? Will the room disappear in the reverberations between the audience and the space, leaving nothing but lingering resonance or time rejoined? Do ghosts have heartbeats?

3   Dylan Robinson. *Hungry Listening: Resonant Theory for Indigenous Sound Studies* (Minneapolis: University of Minnesota Press, 2020), 10.

4   Ibid., 58–59.

5   Chris Corsano, "Improvisation and Resonance," in François J. Bonnet and Bartolomé Sanson, *Spectres*, II, *Resonances* (Rennes, France: Shelter Press), 75.

Diego Villalobos curated the live performances that accompany the exhibition.

WORKS IN THE EXHIBITION

Images of the works appear on the corresponding page numbers. Captions that do not have corresponding page numbers are not pictured in the catalogue.

These texts are written by Katherine Hamilton (KH), Anthony Huberman (AH), and Meghan Smith (MS).

FRANCIS ALŸS

(b. 1959, Antwerp, Belgium)

Guards, 2004
(pp. **177–179**)
Single-channel projected video, color, sound
29 minutes 23 seconds
Courtesy of David Zwirner Gallery, New York

The lonely *tap tap tap* of a British Guard's boots on the cement ground opens Francis Alÿs's single-channel film *Guards*. The first soldier finds a second, and magnetically "snaps into formation" with him, attracting more as they march through London, ultimately uniting sixty-four individual soldiers into a cohesive whole. Bit by bit, the polyrhythms of free and independent bodies are transformed into the single coordinated meter of a military march. Their action subverts the idea of a *dérive* by imposing order on it: rather than an unplanned journey following spontaneous attractions, the soldiers focus their awareness to notice only each other. (KH)

LUKE ANGUHADLUQ (ᓗᒃ ᐊᖑᐊᓗᖅ)

(b. 1895, Tariunnuaq [Chantrey Inlet], Canada; d. 1982, Qamani'tuaq [Baker Lake], Canada)

Drum Dance, 1970
Stonecut on Japanese paper
16 × 22 inches
Collection of the Perlman Teaching Museum, Carleton College, Northfield, MN

A Time for Celebration, 1974
(p. **109**)
Stonecut and stencil on paper
25 × 35 inches
Collection of the Perlman Teaching Museum, Carleton College, Northfield, MN

The Drummer Stopped the Drum Beat, 1982 (p. **111**)
Lithograph
27 ¼ × 40 inches
Collection of the Perlman Teaching Museum, Carleton College, Northfield, MN

The late artist and printmaker Luke Anguhadluq began drawing at age seventy-three, focusing on scenes of hunting, community, and drum dancing in Qamani'tuaq, Nunavut. To move away from linear narratives, Anguhadluq composed multidirectional scenes of flattened figures spiraling around a central drum, as if seen simultaneously from above and from all sides. These rhythmic, circular compositions—coupled with the wide eyes of his mesmerized dancers under trance—communicate the social and spiritual significance of drumming in Qamani'tuaq. (MS)

MARCOS ÁVILA FORERO

(b. 1983, Paris, France)

Atrato, 2014
(pp. **113–116**, **121**)
Single-channel HD video, color, sound
13 minutes 52 seconds
Courtesy of the artist

If all bodies are drums, so too is a body of water. Marcos Ávila Forero's film *Atrato* shows a group of Afro-Colombians standing together in a river in northwestern Colombia, learning the *tambor de agua*. A main artery in the armed conflict between the guerrillas and the state, the Atrato river is a site of shared pain but also life and triumph. Working with anthropologists and ethnomusicologists, Ávila Forero introduced a group of local residents to the language of water drumming, a traditional practice that had once served as a coded form of communication but had disappeared in the years since European domination. As descendants of the enslaved Africans who brought this tradition to the Americas, members of this community recuperate and reactivate this ancestral technique in order to create a composition that reflects the bursting and explosive sounds of their contemporary environment, where gunshots are so often heard hitting the river's surface. (KH)

RAVEN CHACON

(b. 1977, Fort Defiance, Navajo Nation)

American Ledger no. 1, 2018
(p. **107**)
Performance score on Army blanket
79 ½ × 58 inches
Courtesy of the artist

American Ledger no. 1, 2018/2022
Performance score on flag
Dimensions variable
Courtesy of the artist

Artist and composer Raven Chacon knows that a musical score is more than notations toward future action, interpretation, or performance, but can be a prompt for collective narrative. In *American Ledger no. 1*, which visually mimics the layout of the American flag, musicians interpret the score through the story of the founding of the United States, including moments of contact, violence, building, erasure, destruction, and rebirth. Displayed as an army blanket and a flag—forms that usually represent a state's authority, militancy, and hostility towards others—Chacon's score suggests that stories, like music, do not have to be told in the same way forever: within notation there is room to reconsider, reinterpret, and revolutionize. (KH)

TRISHA DONNELLY
(b. 1974, San Francisco, CA)

Untitled, 2009
Sound
Courtesy of the artist

EM'KAL EYONGAKPA
(b. 1981, Manyu, Cameroons)

*batu kɛnɔŋ XII-rh; babhi-
bɛrat XII-r [babhi-manyɛp/
babhi-bawɛt, (mbaŋ)]*, 2022

Mixed media installation:
8-channel sound installation,
8 transducers, 4 hydroponic
microphones, oil drum,
ammunition boxes, myceli-
um-based sound baffles, wood
floor, wood chips, water
pumps, plastic tubes, yarn
Dimensions variable
Courtesy of the artist

Em'kal Eyongakpa's multime-
dia environment pulsates with
polyrhythmic beats. Drawing on
his background in botany and
applied mycology, Eyongakpa
fuses organic matter and human
debris into an alternate world. Yarn
drips from the ceiling; repurposed
ammunition boxes vibrate with
recorded beats; *pleurotus ostrea-
tus* mycelium blooms from the
walls; the sound of flowing water
fills the gallery. Visitors move on
paths through the installation—
babhi meaning routes in Kɛnyaŋ,
a language widely spoken in the
Cross River basin of Cameroon—
and experience his work through
the senses. (MS)

THEASTER GATES
(b. 1973, Chicago, IL)

*Gone are the Days of Shelter
and Martyr*, 2014 (pp. **90–95**)

Single-channel video,
color, sound
6 minutes 31 seconds
Courtesy of the artist and
White Cube, London

Theaster Gates's background in
urban planning and religious studies imbues *Gone Are the Days of
Shelter and Martyr* with a solemn
power. The Black Monks, Gates's
musical ensemble, move through
the debris-filled St. Laurence
Catholic Church that once stood on
the South Side of Chicago, filling it
with their voices and mournful cello
as they flip heavy broken doors,
crashing them to the ground with
resounding thuds. Their gravity—
literal and spiritual—reanimates
the abandoned church with raw
percussive force. (MS)

MILFORD GRAVES
(b. 1941, Queens, NY;
d. 2021, Queens, NY)

*Pathways of Infinite Poss-
ibilities: Heartbeat*, 2017
Wood, display spinal column,
scientific models, acupuncture model, printed diagrams
and labels, old circuitry,
wooden construction, video
monitor, lights, amplifier,
wires, metal brackets,
glue, casters
76 ½ × 40 × 29 inches
Courtesy of the Estate of
Milford Graves

*Pathways of Infinite
Possibilities: Skeleton*, 2017
(p. **21**, detail)
Human skeleton, steel pipe,
wires, stickers, medical
ear model, dundun (talking
drum), preserved heart,
stethoscope, video monitor,
transducer, amplifier,
wood, metal, printed
labels, marker, casters
68 ½ × 27 ½ × 25 inches
Courtesy of the Estate of
Milford Graves

*Pathways of Infinite
Possibilities: Yara*, 2017
Wood, metal brackets,
copper wire, plastic
medical figures, artifacts,
medical heart specimen,
wooden model hand,
religious figurine, water
element, printed labels,
lights, stones, glue,
amplifier, speaker, metal
brackets, casters
88 ½ × 38 ¼ × 33 ½ inches
Courtesy of the Estate of
Milford Graves

*Bikongo-Ifá: Spirit of
the Being*, 2020
(pp. **22–23**, detail)
Wood, tabla, acupuncture
model, bata drum, Nkondi
figure, George Washington
Carver bust, compass, glass,
peanuts, LabVIEW animation,
computer monitors, bells,
plasma lamp, globe, eagle
figurine, alarm clock,
collaged paper printouts,
copper wire, paint marker,
metal fasteners, casters
69 × 38 ½ × 36 inches
Courtesy of the Estate of
Milford Graves

The late percussionist Milford
Graves tried to understand the
drum by studying the heart. To
do so, he would hook people up
to a homemade EKG machine,
process the recording through a
self-produced algorithm, and chart
the data in a complex system of
measurements. In his later years,
he made sculptures that brought
together this sense of the scientific with his interest in spirituality,
ritual, and a deep knowledge of
percussive traditions. (AH)

DAVID HAMMONS
(b. 1943, Springfield, IL)

Basketball Installation, 1995
(pp. **46–51**, details)
Tree trunk, basketball
hoop, African vessel,
dirt, basket
Dimensions variable
Collection of Eleanor
Heyman Propp

Gong, n.d. (pp. **144–151**)
Single-channel video,
color, sound
5 minutes 15 seconds
Courtesy of the artist and
Hauser & Wirth, Los Angeles

David Hammons's installation
is made by bouncing a dirt-
covered basketball onto a gallery
wall. The impact of the "Harlem
earth" becomes a playful form of
mark-making and transforms a
casual (and often racialized) game
into an empowered act of claiming
space. His video *Gong* shows
the artist observing a construction
site on a city street, clamoring
with the sound of power tools.
Instead of avoiding the noise, he
joins the workers, adding his own

instrument (a gong) to the mix and transforming the construction crew into members of an improvised orchestra. (AH)

SUSAN HOWE
(b. 1937, Boston MA)

Pages from *Concordance*, 2020
(pp. **197–199**)
Letterpress prints
6 × ½ × 8 ¾ inches each
Courtesy of the artist

SUSAN HOWE AND DAVID GRUBBS
(b. 1937, Boston, MA);
(b. 1967, Louisville, KY)

Six Pages from
Concordance, 2022
Audio recording
60 minutes
Courtesy of the artists

Susan Howe works to unearth ghost voices on the field of the printed page. Her recent book *Concordance* includes short poems composed of paste-ups cut and reassembled from concordances of various canonical authors, as well as wildlife field guides. Read aloud, the poems start, stop, sputter, echo, and erupt in percussive rhythms. The musician David Grubbs recomposes these recordings with instrumentation to create a series of short duo performances, one of which is played every fifteen minutes throughout the duration of the exhibition. They serve as the exhibition's steady, yet polyrhythmic, metronome. (MS)

NIC KAY
(b. 1989, Bronx, NY)

Name the playlist, Deep down inside, deep deep inside, or Table thumping with Uncle djembe, 2022 (pp. **166–175**)
Video installation
Courtesy of the artist

Interdisciplinary artist, performer, and conceptual choreographer NIC Kay explores ways that Black online communities have engaged in the transcultural exchange of dance, movement, and music, claiming and maneuvering the internet as a space for visible, culturally coded play, political organization, and innovation. In their series #blackpeopledancingontheinternet, NIC Kay tailors content to the specific "digital architecture" of various social media platforms, like TikTok, Instagram, and Pinterest. In this new work, NIC Kay layers footage of people *thump-thump-thumping* their hands to a beat, enacting bodily force on the surfaces of tables and desks in a complex ensemble. Shared rhythms, music, references, and memes become the connective tissue between African diasporic communities. (MS)

BARRY LE VA
(b. 1941, Long Beach, California; d. 2021, New York, NY).

1 Edge/2 Corners; 2 Edges/ 1 Corner, 1968–71/2019
(pp. **43–45**)
Shattered glass
Dimensions variable
Courtesy of David Nolan Gallery, New York

This sculpture by Barry Le Va consists of a stack of glass sheets and the simple instruction to deliver multiple blows to them with a sledgehammer, causing them to shatter. The broken glass brings together the beauty and formal precision of a line drawing within a square, the violence of destructive force, the embrace of chance-based operations, and an engagement with minimal and process-based work popular in the late 1960s. Intersecting on the fractured layers of glass, these incompatible yet parallel forces create a polyrhythmic composition. (AH)

ROSE LOWDER
(b. 1941, Lima, Peru)

Les Tournesols + Les Tournesols Colorés, 1982–1983
(pp. **71–75**)
Digital transfer of 16mm film, color, silent. 6 minutes
Courtesy of Light Cone, Paris

Rose Lowder "undoes" a film by applying the logic of stop-motion animation. In *Les Tournesols*, she filmed a field of flowers by moving the focal point of her camera from front to back to front again. This technique transforms the flowers' natural swaying movement into a jittery or electrified one, creating a vibrating pastoral landscape. Lowder unlocks the omnipresent pulsations of the earth, making them visible to the eye. (AH)

LEE LOZANO
(b. 1930, Newark, NJ; d. 1999, Dallas, TX).

Untitled, 1963
(pp. **52**, **61–63**, details, p. **65**)
Oil on canvas
65 × 80 inches
Private collection
Courtesy of Hauser & Wirth Collection Services

A large "triple hammer" painting by Lee Lozano is not merely a strike, but a polyrhythmic strike, with many moments of impact occurring at once. In this series of paintings, Lozano made grandiose that which society sees as every day: hammers, wrenches, screws, and other tools, all depicted in huge, sweeping strokes. This painting also works against the gendered dynamics of many white women's public and private lives by approaching them head-on with a *bang*. (KH)

GUADALUPE MARAVILLA
(b. 1976, San Salvador, El Salvador)

Disease Thrower #4, 2019
(pp. **124–125**)
Gong, steel, wood, cotton, glue mixture, plastic, loofah, and objects collected from a ritual of retracing the artist's original migration route
96 × 57 × 63 inches
Courtesy of P.P.O.W Gallery, New York, and Robert S. Wennett and Mario Cader-Frech Foundation, Miami

Disease Thrower #16, 2020
(pp. **127**)
Gong, glass, steel, wood,
glue mixture, cotton, wood,
plastic, loofah, paint,
straw, Florida Water cologne,
and objects collected from a
ritual retracing the artist's
original migration route
91 × 55 × 45 inches.
Courtesy of Guadalupe
Maravilla; The Museum of
Modern Art, New York; and
P·P·O·W, New York

Guadalupe Maravilla's *Disease Thrower* series considers the role of illness and disease as a tactic of colonization, encouraging viewers to consider how they could reach a path to healing through spirituality and non-Western medicines. The large gongs in the sculptures refer to the practice of sound baths, where sonic vibrations align with the vibrations of a body. The wide range of mixed materials and found objects, including toy snakes, plastic anatomical models, baskets, and conch shells, were collected by the artist as he retraced the long journey he had taken as a young migrant from Central America to the United States. In their multiplicity, these sculptures evoke mythical beasts, magnetic shrines, or what he calls "healing instruments." (KH)

HAROLD MENDEZ
(b. 1977, Chicago, IL)

but I sound better since you cut my throat, 2016
(pp. **32**, **37–41**, details)
Reclaimed galvanized steel,
wood, chain-link fence
Approx. 180 inches
Courtesy of the artist and
Patron Gallery, Chicago

Titled after a poem by Fred Moten, Harold Mendez's *but I sound better since you cut my throat*, creates a skeletal body with everything stripped away except its spine and its heart. Propped up against a gallery wall and unable to stand without it, the sculpture is made of parts of a fence and a tree, and while both are dismembered fragments from a larger whole, worn down by precarious conditions or the slow transformations of time, they contain the transient presence of the bodies and borders they once belonged to. The sculpture feels ossified, frozen in time, its former beat lingering in the air. (MS)

RIE NAKAJIMA
(b. 1976, Yokohama, Japan)

*Kaeru Oto
(Sound, returning)*, 2022
Motor, timer, wire, objects
Dimensions variable
Courtesy of the artist

Rie Nakajima brings everyday objects to life via simple mechanical triggers: a small motorized stick taps a can, making it hit a wall over and over; another handmade device forces a small cardboard box to turn in circles, causing the tiny ball inside to roll from corner to corner in a series of small thuds; another device repeatedly strikes a sheet of plastic, making it bounce and vibrate. These miniature ecosystems of material, machine, and percussive sounds embody the playfulness of toys as well as the meditative spirituality of sacred objects. Spread throughout a gallery, her mechanisms form a polyrhythmic landscape of cricket-like sounds playing together but separately. (AH)

THE OTOLITH GROUP
Kodwo Eshun (b. 1967, London,
UK), Anjalika Sagar (b. 1968,
London, UK)

The Third Part of the Third Measure, 2017
(pp. **96**, **101–105**)
Two-channel HD video,
color, stereo
43 minutes 43 seconds
Director: The Otolith Group
Editor: Simon Arazi
Pianists: Zubin Kanga,
Siwan Rhys, Rolf Hind,
Eliza McCarthy
Courtesy of The Otolith
Group and LUX, London

The Otolith Group's *The Third Part of the Third Measure* opens with Dante Micheaux reading a speech that composer and musician Julius Eastman gave at Northwestern University about why he gave the musical compositions he would perform that night such controversial titles— *Crazy N******, *Evil N******, and *Gay Guerrilla*. Rolf Hind, Zubin Kanga, Eliza McCarthy, and Siwan Rhys then begin playing Eastman's works, sitting at shiny black baby grand pianos as though they are behind the control board of a spaceship. Echoing content from the composer's speech, the four pianists are the "Gay Guerrillas": queer fighters from the future who have come to give us courage and fortitude in the face of fear, as felt through the continued horrors of disease, police violence, and other necropolitics of the past few years. (KH)

LUCY RAVEN
(b. 1977, Tucson, AZ)

Shape Notes, 2016
(pp. **76**, **81**, details, pp. **82–89**)
Photographic animation,
color, sound
3 minutes 9 seconds
Courtesy of the artist and
Lisson Gallery, New York

Lucy Raven's stop-motion animation *Shape Notes* records (but also obscures) a performance of avant-garde musician Earle Brown's 1963 composition "Calder Piece," meant to be performed using one of Calder's famous mobiles as an instrument. Since the hanging sculpture moves and rotates each time one of the percussionists strikes it, Brown conceived of the object not only as an instrument but also as a conductor, its movements indicating to the performers what to play next. Made with hundreds of still photographs, Raven's animation amplifies the jerky, jostling score: the performers seem to move from one spot to another in many short, stilted motions, embodying none of the grace or lightness of a Calder mobile. The animation presents the musicians as the machine, forging their movements to the mechanism of the mobile that directs the tempo and structure of the score. (KH)

DAVINA SEMO
(b. 1981, Washington, D.C.)

Receiver, 2019 (p. **191**)
Patinated cast bronze bell, whipped nylon line, wooden clapper, powder-coated chain, hardware
20 x 11 inches
Courtesy of the artist and Jessica Silverman Gallery, San Francisco

Admirer, 2020 (pp. **180**, **185**, details)
Cast bronze bell, UV protected 2-stage catalyzed urethane, stainless steel chain, polyurethane clapper, hardware
32 x 13 inches
Courtesy of Renu Agrawal and David Weber, San Francisco

Drop, 2020
Patinated cast bronze bells, UV protected 2-stage catalyzed urethane, stainless steel chain and hardware, polyurethane clapper
Each bell: 7 ¾ x 5 ¾ inches
Courtesy of the artist and Jessica Silverman Gallery, San Francisco

Erode, 2021 (p. **188**)
Cast aluminum, patinated solid bronze clapper, hemp shibari rope, leather cord, powder-coated galvanized steel chain, powder coated stainless steel hardware
20 x 9 ½ inches
Overall dimensions variable
Courtesy of the artist and Jessica Silverman Gallery, San Francisco

Hot Sun, 2021 (p. **189**)
Polished cast bronze bell, solid bronze clapper, hemp shibari rope, powder coated stainless steel hardware, etched steel chain
21 x 17 ¼ inches
Courtesy of the artist and Jessica Silverman Gallery, San Francisco

Bloom (bronze), 2022 (p. **187**)
Polished cast bronze bell, polished bronze and powder coated stainless steel hardware, leather wrapped solid bronze clapper, hemp shibari rope, and powder coated galvanized steel chain
32 x 13 inches
Courtesy of the artist and Jessica Silverman Gallery, San Francisco

Fetish, 2022 (p. **190**)
Patinated cast bronze bell, PolyJet 3D-printed opaque VeroWhite resin, leather wrapped solid bronze clapper, hemp shibari rope, powder coated stainless steel hardware, and powder coated galvanized steel chain
18 x 19 inches
Courtesy of the artist and Jessica Silverman Gallery, San Francisco

Ringing bells can announce anything from the mundane to the monumental: the simple passage of time, the joy of celebration, the mourning of lost lives, even the urgency of an alarm that calls us to action. Davina Semo's bronze bells bring together the possibility of bells being objects or instruments for personal reflection, as well as tools for gathering a community and calling attention to societal concerns. While bells are usually kept out of reach to maintain a sense of reliability and purpose, the artist places them at arm's length, inviting visitors to ring them at any time, for any reason, giving them the agency to determine what, why, how, and when a call is to be issued. Their overlapping tones reverberate throughout the room and strengthen each other, forming a symphony in space. (MS)

MICHAEL E. SMITH
(b. 1977, Detroit, MI)

Untitled, 2018 (pp. **27–31**)
Sweatshirt, laser
Dimensions variable
Courtesy of Andrew Kreps Gallery, New York

Michael E. Smith's untitled sculpture involves a black sweater hanging gingerly on the wall as a red laser beam bounces up and down between its crew neck and torso. The metronome-like laser beam seems to provide an artificial heartbeat that gives life to an inanimate object but equally evokes the deadly precision of a predator targeting its prey. (KH)

CONSUELO TUPPER HERNÁNDEZ
(b. 1992, Los Ángeles, Chile)

Applause Dictionary, 2020/2022 (p. **69**)
Inkjet on paper
Dimensions variable
Courtesy of the artist

Consuelo Tupper Hernández's *Applause Dictionary* defines the many forms of applause we perform or encounter throughout our lives. Applause is confident, uncomfortable, professional, sad, self-sufficient, even silent. Tupper Hernández's work expresses the communal and open nature of this simple act—slapping two hands together—that carries countless meanings, depending on social context. (KH)

DAVID ZINK YI
(b. 1973, Lima, Peru)

Angel, bist du es? 2010 (pp. **66–67**)
Three C-Prints
24 ½ x 34 ¼ inches each
Courtesy of the artist and Hauser and Wirth, New York

In David Zink Yi's trio of photographs *Angel, bist du es?* the camera captures two pairs of feet, one standing firmly on the ground, the other suspended mysteriously in the air. Anticipating their eventual thud, we are left wondering if they are levitating, jumping, or ascending, instead of falling. Music informs much of Zink Yi's work, and these six pairs of feet form a fluctuating rhythm, with each photograph a slight variation on the others, where the beat is left in suspension. (MS)

HAEGUE YANG

Sonicwear – Scarf with Mitten Ends, Brass and Nickel Plated #1, 2013
Brass and nickel plated bells, metal rings, elastic cord
6 ¼ × 99 inches
Courtesy of the artist

Sonicwear – Scarf with Mitten Ends Connected in the Front, Brass and Nickel Plated #1, 2013 (p. **193**)
Brass and nickel plated bells, metal rings, elastic cord
6 ¼ × 40 ½ inches
Courtesy of the artist

Sonicwear – Scarf with Mitten Ends Crossed in the Back, Brass and Nickel Plated #1, 2013
Brass and nickel plated bells, metal rings, elastic cord
6 × 42 ⅛ inches
Courtesy of the artist

Sonicwear – Quasi-Pagan Bracelets, 2019 (p. **195**)
Synthetic leather, thread, press fasteners, cowbells
7 ⅞ × 7 ⅞ × 2 ¾ inches each
Courtesy of the artist

Since 2013, Haegue Yang has worked with bells to create diverse sculptural works. Yang's *Sonicwear* sculptures are informed in part by ritual uses of bells: in Korean shamanism as well as in European pagan customs, their sound has served to intercede between the human and spirit realms. Both traditions are somewhat marginal (not being the dominant religion of their time and place), yet have flourished and persisted over centuries and across civilizations. Yang is also inspired by artists of the European avant-garde, in particular Sophie Taeuber-Arp and Oskar Schlemmer, whose multidisciplinary work—combining architecture, costume design, theater, and choreography—opened a door to Western culture for Yang, whose seemingly disparate influences share an inclination toward movement and performance. Visitors are invited to wear the *Sonicwears* around their wrists or draped over their shoulders, and allow their movements to activate the artworks' latent audible properties. (AH)

IMAGE CREDITS

Full captions for each work included in the exhibition are listed in the Works in the Exhibition section. For images of works not included in the exhibition, a full caption and image credit is included below.

pp. 21-25: Courtesy of the Estate of Milford Graves. Photo: Constance Mensch

pp. 27-31: Courtesy of the artist and Andrew Kreps Gallery, New York

pp. 32, 37-41: Courtesy of the artist and Patron Gallery Chicago

p. 43: Courtesy of David Nolan Gallery, New York

pp. 44-45: Courtesy of David Nolan Gallery, New York. Photo: Nicholas Lea Bruno

pp. 46-51: Courtesy of Nahmad Contemporary, New York. Photo: Tom Powell Imaging. © David Hammons

pp. 52, 61-63: Private collection, courtesy of Hauser and Wirth Collection Services. Photos: Nicholas Lea Bruno

p. 65: Private collection, courtesy of Hauser and Wirth Collection Services

pp. 66-67: Courtesy of the artist and Hauser and Wirth, New York

p. 69: Courtesy of the artist

pp. 71-75: Film stills courtesy of Light Cone, Paris

pp. 76, 81-89: Video stills courtesy of the artist and Lisson Gallery

pp. 90-95: Video stills courtesy of the artist and White Cube, London. © the artist

pp. 96, 101-105: Video stills courtesy of The Otolith Group and LUX, London

p. 107: Courtesy of the artist

pp. 109-111: Photos courtesy of the Estate of Luke Anguhadluq

pp. 113-116, 121: Video stills courtesy of the artist

pp. 122-123: Trisha Donnelly, *Untitled*, 2022. Courtesy of the artist

pp. 124-125: Courtesy of the artist and the Mario Cader-Frech Collection

p. 127: Courtesy of the artist; Museum of Modern Art, New York; and PPOW, New York

pp. 126, 128-129: Guadalupe Maravilla, *Disease Thrower #15*, 2021; gong, steel, wood, cotton, glue mixture, plastic, loofah, and objects collected from a ritual of retracing the artist's original migration route; 98 × 96 × 52 inches. Courtesy of the artist; Museum of Modern Art, New York; and P·P·O·W, New York

pp. 131, 136-141: Em'kal Eyongakpa, *ɛfáp baka #3, study. (mbaŋ)*, 2021; video stills. Courtesy of the artist and Bɔɔ Bɛtɔk © Eyongakpa

pp. 132-135: Em'kal Eyongakpa, *babhi-bɛrat XXI-r [babhi-manyɛp/ babhi-bawɛt, (mbaŋ)*, 2021; installation view, Oudekerk Museum, Amsterdam. Courtesy of the artist and Bɔɔ Bɛtɔk © Eyongakpa

pp. 144-151: Video stills courtesy of the artist and Hauser & Wirth, Los Angeles

pp. 152-153: Rie Nakajima, *See-Saw*, 2020 (detail); installation view of solo exhibition at Labor Neunzehn, Berlin; metal, wood, bottles, timers. Courtesy of the artist. Photo: Serena Salvadori

pp. 154-155: Rie Nakajima, *Stepping*, 2019 (detail); installation view of solo exhibition at STUK, Leuven; motors, timers, polystyrene, paper boxes, seeds, bottle, batteries, plastic. Courtesy of the artist. Photo: Kain Walgrave

pp. 156, 165: Rie Nakajima, *Cyclic*, 2018 (detail); installation view of solo exhibition at IKON Gallery, Birmingham; tinfoil, motors, concrete, metal, whistles, plastic, cans, buckets, plastic bags, tubes, batteries, brushes, tape, seeds, timer, wire, sponges, stones. Courtesy of the artist. Photo: Stuart Whipps

pp. 166-175: Video stills courtesy of the artist

pp. 177-179: Video stills courtesy of Francis Alÿs and David Zwirner Gallery, New York

pp. 180, 185: Courtesy of Renu Agrawal and David Weber, San Francisco

p. 187: Courtesy of the artist and Jessica Silverman Gallery, San Francisco

pp. 188-189: Courtesy of the artist and Jessica Silverman Gallery, San Francisco. Photos: John Wilson White

p. 191: Courtesy of Ribordy Thetaz, Geneva. Photo: Annika Wetter

pp. 193-195: Courtesy of the artist. Photo: Studio Haegue Yang

pp. 197-199: Susan Howe, *Concordance*, copyright © 2019, 2020 by Susan Howe. Used by permission of New Directions Publishing Corp.

Cover: Details of Milford Graves, *Pathways of Infinite Possibilities: Skeleton*, 2017, and *Pathways of Infinite Possibilities: Heartbeat*, 2017. Courtesy of the Estate of Milford Graves. Photos: Constance Mensch

ACKNOWLEDGMENTS

First and foremost, we thank the artists in the exhibition for their collaboration and guidance.

We thank the many who provided invaluable help and assistance: Miguel Armas; Laura Bechter, Ronja Primke, and Johanna Schultheiss; Mark Christman; Sara Cluggish and Teresa Lenzen; Eleanor Cayre, Jacob King and Scott Roben; Alice Conconi; Joel Draper; Rebecca Holmberg and Elizabeth Calzado Michel; Hannah Liley; David Nolan; Wendy Olsoff and Ella Blanchon; Soraya Rodriguez, Robert Owen, and Emma German; Katharina Schwerendt, Liene Harms, and Taylor Walsh; and Jessica Silverman and Kathryn Wade; as well as the lenders to the exhibition.

The curator would also like to thank many friends and colleagues for their advice and support over the past several years, as the exhibition took shape: 2 Bridges Music & Arts, Steve Beal, Dena Beard, Jose Berrío, Juana Berrío, Jenni Crain, Naz Cuguoğlu Cacekli, Larissa Harris, Carmen Hammons, Peter Eleey, Anthony Elms, Vincent Fecteau, Milford Graves, Lawrence Kumpf, Illaria Marotta and Andrea Baccin, Trinh T. Minh-ha, Fred Moten, Debbie Rachleff, Tyler Rowland, Judy and Wylie Sheldon, Jo-ey Tang, Hamza Walker, and Mary Zlot. A special thanks to the incredible staff at the Wattis, especially Robin Beard, Diego Villalobos, Meghan Smith, and Katherine Hamilton, as well as the installation team: Christopher Paddock, Anthony Russell, Cole Solinger, and Agnes Widbom.

This exhibition is made possible thanks to generous support from Teiger Foundation, Phyllis C. Wattis Foundation, VIA Art Fund, National Endowment for the Arts, Westridge Foundation, Etant donnés*, Mondriaan Fund, Michael Asher Foundation, Emily Hall Tremaine Foundation (EHTF); and from Kaitlyn and Mike Krieger, Diana Nelson and John Atwater, Katie and Matt Paige, Lauren and Jamie Ford, and Robin Wright.

*Etant donnés Contemporary Art is a program of Villa Albertine and FACE Foundation, in partnership with the French Embassy in the United States, with support from the French Ministry of Culture, Institut français, Ford Foundation, Helen Frankenthaler Foundation, CHANEL, and ADAGP.

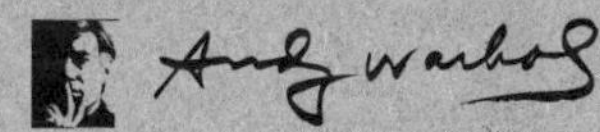
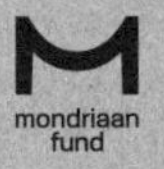
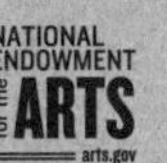
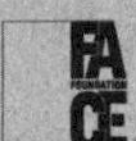
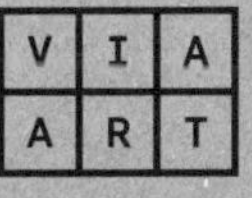
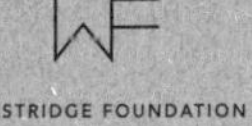
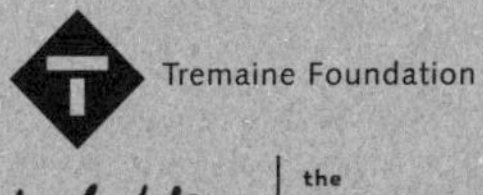
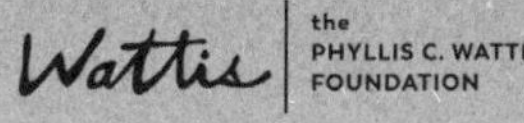

This catalogue accompanies the exhibition *Drum Listens to Heart* organized by CCA Wattis Institute, on view from September 1, 2022 through March 4, 2023.

PUBLISHED BY

Inventory Press
2305 Hyperion Ave
Los Angeles, CA 90027
inventorypress.com
&
CCA Wattis Institute for
Contemporary Arts
360 Kansas St
San Francisco, CA 94103
wattis.org

ISBN: 978-1-941753-52-1
LCCN: 2022935284

All rights reserved. No part of this publication may be reproduced or transmitted, in any form or by any means, electronic or mechanical, including photocopy, recording, or any other information storage or retrieval system, without prior permission in writing from the publisher.

© 2022 the authors, CCA Wattis Institute for Contemporary Arts, Inventory Press

Distributed by:
ARTBOOK | D.A.P.
75 Broad St
Suite 630
New York, NY 10004
artbook.com

CATALOGUE

Editor: Anthony Huberman

Managing Editor:
Jeanne Gerrity

Editorial assistant:
Katherine Jemima Hamilton

Copyeditor:
Victoria Gannon

Proofreader: Eugenia Bell

Design: IN-FO.CO (Adam Michaels, Dani Grossman)

Printed and bound in Belgium by die Keure

Typeset in Fluxisch Else (OSP), Korinna (ITC), and Manifold Sans (HEX)

EXHIBITION

Curator: Anthony Huberman

Assistant Curator:
Diego Villalobos

Head of Installation and Exhibition Design:
Robin Beard

Assistants:
Katherine Jemima Hamilton, Meghan Smith

WATTIS STAFF

Robin Beard
Head of Installation and Exhibition Design

Niko Bellott
Senior Director, Grants, Partnerships, and Engagement, CCA

Jeanne Gerrity
Deputy Director and Head of Publications

Anthony Huberman
Director and Chief Curator

Christina Linden
Head of Academic Engagement

Carleigh McDonald
Head of Membership and Senior Director, Advancement, CCA

Diego Villalobos
Assistant Curator

Addy Rabinovitch
Operations Coordinator

Meghan Smith
Curatorial Fellow

Justine Xi
Visitor Engagement Coordinator

The Wattis Institute is part of California College of the Arts.

FOUNDING PATRON

Phyllis C. Wattis

LEAD GIFTS AND LEADERSHIP CIRCLE

The Andy Warhol Foundation for the Visual Arts

San Francisco Grants for the Arts

Westridge Foundation

Katie and Matt Paige

Lauren and James Ford

Mary and Harold Zlot

Jonathan Gans and Abigail Turin

CURATOR'S FORUM

John Atwater and Diana Nelson, Johanna and Tom Baruch, Joachim Bechtle, Frish Brandt and Jeffrey Fraenkel, Nina and Chris Buchbinder, Sabrina Buell and Yves Béhar, Wayee Chu and Ethan Beard, Carla Emil and Rich Silverstein, Randi and Bob Fisher, Stanlee Gatti, Lizelle and Martin Green, Pamela and David Hornik, Kaitlyn and Mike Krieger, Nion McEvoy and Leslie Berriman, Anthony and Celeste Meier, Lorna Meyer Calas and Dennis Calas, Brittany and Justin Pattner, Amnon and Katie Rodan, Helen and Charles Schwab, Jessica Silverman and Sarah Thornton, Susan Swig, Phyllis and John Walker, John Wendler, Robin Wright and Ian Reeves, and Sonya Yu